Ultimate Air Fryer Cookbook 2022-2023 UK

800+ delicious recipes for the best experience for beginners and advanced users

Chloe Miles

All Rights Reserved.

The contents of this book may not be reproduced, copied or transmitted without the direct written permission of the author or publisher. Under no circumstances will the publisher or the author be held responsible or liable for any damage, compensation or pecuniary loss arising directly or indirectly from the information contained in this book.

Legal notice. This book is protected by copyright. It is intended for personal use only. You may not modify, distribute, sell, use, quote or paraphrase any part or content of this book without the consent of the author or publisher.

Notice Of Disclaimer.

Please note that the information in this document is intended for educational and entertainment purposes only. Every effort has been made to provide accurate, up-to-date, reliable and complete information. No warranty of any kind is declared or implied. The reader acknowledges that the author does not engage in the provision of legal, financial, medical or professional advice. The content in this book has been obtained from a variety of sources. Please consult a licensed professional before attempting any of the techniques described in this book. By reading this document, the reader agrees that in no event shall the author be liable for any direct or indirect damages, including but not limited to errors, omissions or inaccuracies, resulting from the use of the information in this document.

CONTENTS

Introduction 12
- What Is an Air Fryer? 14
- Features and Functions of Air Fryers 15
- How to Use It 16
- Benefits of Air Fryer 17
- Caring for Your Air Fryer 18
- Cleaning your air fryer 18

Breakfast 19
- Hot Italian-style Sub 19
- Baked Eggs And Bacon 19
- French Toast 19
- Egg-loaded Potato Skins 19
- Savory Breakfast Bread Pudding 20
- Berry Crisp 20
- Almond Granola With Dried Fruit 20
- Lemon Blueberry Scones 21
- Bagel Melt 21
- Crispy Bacon 21
- Hole In One 21
- Morning Glory Muffins 22
- Garlic-cheese Biscuits 22
- Tuscan Toast 22
- Strawberry Shortcake With Buttermilk Biscuits 22
- Portable Omelet 23
- Sheet Pan French Toast 23
- Mushroom-spinach Frittata With Feta 23
- Buttered Poppy Seed Bread 24
- Green Onion Pancakes 24
- Ham And Swiss Melts 24
- Banana Baked Oatmeal 25
- Not-so-english Muffins 25
- Bread Boat Eggs 25
- Hashbrown Potatoes Lyonnaise 25
- Roasted Vegetable Frittata 26
- Cheddar Cheese Biscuits 26
- Salmon Burgers 27
- Savory Salsa Cheese Rounds 27
- Good Stuff Bread 27

Creamy Bacon + Almond Crostini..27
Soft Pretzels..28
Blueberry Lemon Muffins..28
Mediterranean Egg Sandwich...29
Breakfast Banana Bread...29
Chocolate Chip Banana Muffins...29
Cherries Jubilee..29
Zucchini Bread..30
Honey Ham And Swiss Broiler..30
Cinnamon Rolls...30

Snacks Appetizers And Sides 31

Smoked Gouda Bacon Macaroni And Cheese...31
Sage Butter Roasted Butternut Squash With Pepitas..31
Sweet Potato Casserole...31
Creamy Parmesan Polenta...32
Garlic Breadsticks...32
Grilled Ham & Muenster Cheese On Raisin Bread..32
Crispy Chili Kale Chips...33
Sweet Potato Fries With Sweet And Spicy Dipping Sauce..33
Bacon Corn Muffins..33
Wonton Cups...33
Potato Samosas..33
Creamy Scalloped Potatoes...34
Asparagus With Pistachio Dukkah..34
Caramelized Onion Dip...35
Garden Fresh Bruschetta..35
Cherry Chipotle Bbq Chicken Wings..36
Sheet Pan Chicken Nachos..36
Pork Pot Stickers With Yum Yum Sauce..36
Smoked Salmon Puffs...37
Savory Sausage Balls...37
Buffalo Cauliflower..37
Rumaki...38
Thick-crust Pepperoni Pizza...38
Fried Wontons...38
Roasted Brussels Sprouts Au Gratin..39
Simple Holiday Stuffing...39
Garlic Parmesan Kale Chips..40
Creamy Crab Dip..40
Classic Potato Chips...40
Brazilian Cheese Bread (pão De Queijo)...40

Barbecue Chicken Nachos...41
Cinnamon Apple Chips...41
Hot Mexican Bean Dip..41
Stuffed Baby Bella Caps...41
Crab Rangoon Dip With Wonton Chips..42
Warm And Salty Edamame..42
Sweet Or Savory Baked Sweet Potatoes..42
Cinnamon Pita Chips..43
Turkey Burger Sliders...43
Ham And Cheese Palmiers..43

Beef Pork And Lamb..44

Pretzel-coated Pork Tenderloin...44
Pork Cutlets With Almond-lemon Crust..44
Spicy Flank Steak With Fresh Tomato-corn Salsa..44
Beer-baked Pork Tenderloin..45
Skirt Steak Fajitas...45
Spanish Pork Skewers...45
Albóndigas...46
Calf's Liver...46
Indian Fry Bread Tacos..47
Pork Taco Gorditas...47
Sloppy Joes...48
Vietnamese Beef Lettuce Wraps..48
Lamb Burger With Feta And Olives..49
Steak With Herbed Butter..49
Glazed Meatloaf..49
Lamb Koftas Meatballs..50
Slow Cooked Carnitas...50
Chipotle-glazed Meat Loaf..50
Italian Meatballs..51
Chicken Fried Steak...51
Red Curry Flank Steak...51
Minted Lamb Chops..52
Almond And Sun-dried Tomato Crusted Pork Chops...52
Italian Sausage & Peppers..52
Better-than-chinese-take-out Pork Ribs...53
Steak Pinwheels With Pepper Slaw And Minneapolis Potato Salad..........................53
Lamb Curry..53
Crispy Smoked Pork Chops..53
Easy Tex-mex Chimichangas..54
Cilantro-crusted Flank Steak...54

Lime-ginger Pork Tenderloin	54
Barbecued Broiled Pork Chops	55
Seasoned Boneless Pork Sirloin Chops	55
Spicy Little Beef Birds	55
Beef-stuffed Bell Peppers	55
Barbeque Ribs	56
Beef And Spinach Braciole	56
Kielbasa Sausage With Pierogies And Caramelized Onions	57
Mustard-herb Lamb Chops	57
Crunchy Fried Pork Loin Chops	57

Poultry 58

Pecan Turkey Cutlets	58
Roasted Game Hens With Vegetable Stuffing	58
Italian Roasted Chicken Thighs	58
Chicken Fajitas	59
Chicken Breast With Chermoula Sauce	59
Orange-glazed Roast Chicken	59
Sweet-and-sour Chicken	60
Hot Thighs	60
I Forgot To Thaw—garlic Capered Chicken Thighs	60
Chicken Hand Pies	61
Buffalo Egg Rolls	61
Spice-rubbed Split Game Hen	61
Light And Lovely Loaf	62
Pickle Brined Fried Chicken	62
Foiled Rosemary Chicken Breasts	62
Pesto-crusted Chicken	63
Chicken Potpie	63
Chicken Cutlets With Broccoli Rabe And Roasted Peppers	63
Jerk Turkey Meatballs	64
Coconut Chicken With Apricot-ginger Sauce	64
Rotisserie-style Chicken	65
Quick Chicken For Filling	65
Tandoori Chicken	65
Gluten-free Nutty Chicken Fingers	65
Parmesan Crusted Chicken Cordon Bleu	66
Harissa Lemon Whole Chicken	66
Sesame Chicken Breasts	66
Crispy Curry Chicken Tenders	67
Oven-crisped Chicken	67
Chicken Wellington	67

Sesame Orange Chicken 68
Poblano Bake 68
Sticky Soy Chicken Thighs 69
Chicken In Mango Sauce 69
Guiltless Bacon 69
Chicken Souvlaki Gyros 69
Teriyaki Chicken Drumsticks 70
Philly Chicken Cheesesteak Stromboli 70
Fiesta Chicken Plate 71
Chicken-fried Steak With Gravy 71

Lunch And Dinner 72

Favorite Baked Ziti 72
Quick Pan Pizza 72
Sage, Chicken + Mushroom Pasta Casserole 72
Kashaburgers 73
Pea Soup 73
French Onion Soup 73
Italian Stuffed Zucchini Boats 74
Crunchy Baked Chicken Tenders 74
Herbal Summer Casserole 74
Gardener's Rice 75
Inspirational Personal Pizza 75
Parmesan Crusted Tilapia 75
Moroccan Couscous 75
Healthy Southwest Stuffed Peppers 76
Chicken Noodle Soup 76
Pesto Pizza 76
Parmesan Artichoke Pizza 77
Family Favorite Pizza 77
Honey Bourbon–glazed Pork Chops With Sweet Potatoes + Apples 77
Crab Chowder 78
Chicken Thighs With Roasted Rosemary Root Vegetables 78
Connecticut Garden Chowder 79
Oven-baked Couscous 79
Oven-baked Rice 79
Spanish Rice 79
Cheesy Chicken–stuffed Shells 80
Lentil And Carrot Soup 80
Scalloped Corn Casserole 80
Maple Bacon 80
Homemade Pizza Sauce 81

Classic Beef Stew	81
Salad Lentils	81
Roasted Vegetable Gazpacho	82
Very Quick Pizza	82
Middle Eastern Roasted Chicken	82
Baked Tomato Casserole	82
Dijon Salmon With Green Beans Sheet Pan Supper	83
One-step Classic Goulash	83
Classic Tuna Casserole	83
Yeast Dough For Two Pizzas	84

Fish And Seafood 85

Tuna Nuggets In Hoisin Sauce	85
Maple-crusted Salmon	85
Broiled Scallops	85
Classic Crab Cakes	85
Ginger Miso Calamari	86
Miso-rubbed Salmon Fillets	86
Shrimp, Chorizo And Fingerling Potatoes	86
Crunchy And Buttery Cod With Ritz® Cracker Crust	87
Pecan-crusted Tilapia	87
Almond Crab Cakes	87
Fish Sticks For Kids	88
Fish Tacos With Jalapeño-lime Sauce	88
Tex-mex Fish Tacos	88
Sweet Chili Shrimp	89
Crab Cakes	89
Shrimp	89
Coconut-shrimp Po' Boys	90
Halibut Tacos	90
Crab-stuffed Peppers	90
Blackened Catfish	91
Beer-battered Cod	91
Capered Crab Cakes	91
Light Trout Amandine	92
Crispy Smelts	92
Better Fish Sticks	92
Spicy Fish Street Tacos With Sriracha Slaw	92
Sesame-crusted Tuna Steaks	93
Skewered Salsa Verde Shrimp	93
Romaine Wraps With Shrimp Filling	94
Flounder Fillets	94

Best-dressed Trout 94
Stuffed Baked Red Snapper 94
Crispy Sweet-and-sour Cod Fillets 95
Sea Bass With Potato Scales And Caper Aïoli 95
Sea Scallops 95
Tortilla-crusted Tilapia 96
Almond-crusted Fish 96
Crunchy Clam Strips 96
Fried Scallops 97
Snapper With Capers And Olives 97

Vegetables And Vegetarian 98

Air-fried Potato Salad 98
Asparagus Ronald 98
Fried Okra 98
Balsamic Sweet Potatoes 99
Fried Corn On The Cob 99
Cheesy Potato Skins 99
Empty-the-refrigerator Roasted Vegetables 100
Fried Eggplant Slices 100
Rosemary Roasted Potatoes With Lemon 100
Moroccan Cauliflower 101
Pecan Parmesan Cauliflower 101
Home Fries 101
Blistered Green Beans 101
Lemon-glazed Baby Carrots 101
Baked Stuffed Acorn Squash 102
Buttery Rolls 102
Hasty Home Fries 102
Grits Casserole 103
Ranch Potatoes 103
Crispy Herbed Potatoes 103
Blistered Tomatoes 103
Green Beans 104
Crispy Noodle Salad 104
Perfect Asparagus 104
Florentine Stuffed Tomatoes 105
Tandoori Cauliflower 105
Fried Cauliflowerwith Parmesan Lemon Dressing 105
Roasted Brussels Sprouts With Bacon 105
Onions 106
Salt And Pepper Baked Potatoes 106

Fingerling Potatoes ... 106
Asparagus And Cherry Tomato Quiche ... 106
Mushrooms ... 107
Rolled Chinese (napa) Cabbage With Chickpea Filling ... 107
Stuffed Onions ... 107
Panzanella Salad With Crispy Croutons ... 108
Cauliflower ... 108
Parmesan Asparagus ... 108
Sesame Carrots And Sugar Snap Peas ... 109
Zucchini Boats With Ham And Cheese ... 109

Desserts ... 110

Coconut Cake ... 110
Cheesecake Wontons ... 110
Buttermilk Confetti Cake ... 110
Lemon Torte ... 111
Bourbon Bread Pudding ... 111
Almond-roasted Pears ... 111
Goat Cheese–stuffed Nectarines ... 112
Individual Peach Crisps ... 112
Coconut Rice Cake ... 112
Chewy Coconut Cake ... 113
Midnight Nutella® Banana Sandwich ... 113
Blueberry Clafoutis ... 113
Keto Cheesecake Cups ... 114
Glazed Apple Crostata ... 114
Peanut Butter Cup Doughnut Holes ... 114
Chocolate Caramel Pecan Cupcakes ... 115
Fried Snickers Bars ... 115
Baked Apple ... 116
Coconut Drop Cookies ... 116
Make-ahead Chocolate Chip Cookies ... 116
Mississippi Mud Brownies ... 116
Raspberry Hand Pies ... 117
Easy Churros ... 117
Heritage Chocolate Chip Cookies ... 118
Carrot Cake ... 118
Baked Custard ... 118
Donut Holes ... 119
Chocolate And Vanilla Swirled Pudding ... 119
Peanut Butter S'mores ... 119
Orange Strawberry Flan ... 120

Strawberry Blueberry Cobbler 120
Vegan Swedish Cinnamon Rolls (kanelbullar) 120
Blueberry Cookies 121
Black And Blue Clafoutis 121
Heavenly Chocolate Cupcakes 121
Cinnamon Sugar Rolls 122
Cheese Blintzes 122
Orange Almond Ricotta Cookies 122
Sweet Potato Donut Holes 123
Sour Cream Pound Cake 123

INDEX 124

Introduction

The air fryer was inspired by the need to make a healthier alternative to fried food. It was first introduced in the 1990s and had been growing ever since.

The air fryer works by circulating hot air thanks to its rotating fan. It's also equipped with a temperature sensor that controls the cooking operation to guarantee perfect results every time.

Air fryers are a great way to prepare food at home without the need for any oil or fat, and it's easy to use too. You can get a great homemade taste with a lot less fat and fewer calories.

There are so many recipes that you can make using your air fryer, and these recipes will help you utilize your appliance to the fullest.

We hope that this book will be an excellent resource for you to use at home by making delicious dishes with your air fryer.

Results from air frying are healthy if done correctly. But, it would be best if you were careful when cooking with your oven, stovetop, or microwave.

The most significant benefit of air frying is that oils and fat are eliminated. Air-fried recipes are also much safer than traditional oil-based cooking methods.

You don't need any special equipment or kitchen tools to cook a delicious meal in minutes with your air fryer. The only things you need are your air fryer, your favorite recipe, and the right ingredients for the dish.

Air-fried recipes are also very fast when compared to traditional oil-based cooking methods. Some recipes take a mere 10 minutes or less to cook in your air fryer!

Seasoning is significant for air-fried recipes. Different types of food require different types of herbs. The key to coming up with a delicious dish is to season it properly. You can follow your favorite recipe or modify it as you please. It's a great way to explore the tastiest seasoning combinations and create new recipes from scratch.

Air fryer cooking works well for so many different types of food, so you'll have plenty of recipes to choose from that you can make in your own home. Some of the best recipes are meatless, which is a great way to eat healthier.

There are so many different cooking styles that you can try with your air fryer that you won't choose just one. You will enjoy experimenting with new flavors and creating new dishes every time.

Some of the best cooking methods you can try with your air fryer include sous-vide, pressure frying, popcorn popping, deep-frying, and baking.

Using your air fryer frequently will help you to ensure that it lasts a long time. This is because an air fryer is made to last a long time when properly cared for. Air fryers are designed to perform at an optimal level for many years with proper maintenance.

Air frying is also healthier than cooking with oils and fat because it doesn't require a lot of oil or grease. You just need to use a small amount of oil when air frying, making it a much healthier cooking method than traditional cooking methods.

Baking Setting in an air fryer comes down to the temperature of your device. Some ovens have preset temperatures while others don't.

If your device doesn't have preset temperatures, then you must use the temperature knob to control the heat being output by the air fryer.

Most baking recipes are done at a lower temperature at around 200 degrees Fahrenheit for an hour or more, depending on what you want to cook. This method is ideal because it allows for even cooking throughout the entire food product.

Air fryer cooking temperature Air frying is all about the cooking temperature. High temperatures cook quickly, but they also burn food easily.

Low temperatures can help you simmer food over a longer time frame, but higher temperatures allow for faster cooking times.

The key to cooking well in an air fryer is to understand that both high and low settings are necessary for great results. This means using both a low and high set every once in a while, depending on your recipe.

What Is an Air Fryer?

It's a hot air convection cooker that uses oscillating currents of heat and cold to cook your food. It can be used to prepare delectable, crispy-on-the-outside french fries or golden brown, moist chicken in minutes! Perfect for organizing all your favorite pizza, fish, chicken, and more at home. Air fryers are the best for preparing your food without oil or grease and extra delicious flavor. Having an air fryer can be an excellent choice for anyone trying to cut down on their high fat and calorie intake. Whatever you cook in an air fryer comes out not only tastier but also healthier and fat-free. Our Air Fryer Recipes section features recipes on making Fish and Chips, Pizza, French fries, and many other mouthwatering dishes.

It is excellent for any meal of the day. It is specially designed to conserve energy while cooking food. We have collected some basic information on the Air fryer, which will help get started with it easier than ever before.

Newer models can be used to simulate the cooking effects of deep-frying while using much less oil, or none at all. Air fryers are often marketed as healthier cooking tools since they use significantly less fat than regular deep fryers. These cookers can be used to prepare a variety of foods, including but not limited to: Salmon, Chicken, Fish, Veggies, and Poultry.

An air fryer is essentially a convection oven that circulates hot air by circulating hot air every few minutes.

It cooks food very fast and keeps its natural taste while preventing it from getting oil-covered or burnt.

An air fryer is preferable over a deep fryer, which submerges food in hot oil. With an air fryer, you have to put the food in the basket, and it will start rotating on its own.

Air Fryers are convection ovens used to cook healthy foods without waiting much longer than they would take in a normal range.

The new addition to the kitchen has gained tremendous popularity among people who want their meals quick and tasty.

The air fryer is a new cooking appliance that has gained tremendous popularity amongst people who want their meals quick and tasty!

Air fryers use infrared heat technology to cook food selectively.

The space inside the machine is filled with hot air, which circulates around the food 360 degrees. Since air fryers don't have any open flame or heating coils like the conventional ovens, they are considered more energy efficient and safe to use.

Tips and tricks

Air Fryer cooking is 2-3 times faster than deep frying. Cooking time in an air fryer is normally about half of what it would take to cook in a conventional oven.

The heating element temperature should be at about 200-250 degrees Celsius (392-482 Fahrenheit). Use correct and adequate oil for cooking, as the food can stick easily if you do not use the right oil. The recommended oil is peanut, sunflower or canola oil. Keep all the vents open while cooking to get crispier food. Always use a timer to ensure even heat distribution. It helps to avoid over browning, which leads to burnt food.

Air fryers are "dry" cookers, so you can cook frozen foods in them as well. They also do not create any steam while cooking, which is great for people who want their food crispy and dry.

Air fryers are energy efficient. They produce heat very fast and spread it evenly throughout the food. By keeping the vents open, you can use less oil in cooking. If you have your air-fryer running, make sure to keep an eye on the temperature.

Be sure not to overload your basket since it will cause uneven heating inside the machine and will also overflow with oil in case the opening is larger than what is needed for cooking. Make sure to read the instructions and recipe carefully, since it is important to adjust cooking time for each type of food.

Features and Functions of Air Fryers

Depending on the brand of air fryers that you have, most air fryers come with general features and functions. Below is the general feature of air fryers that allow you to cook foods healthy and delicious meals.

Temperature Control Dial: The temperature control dial allows you to select frying temperatures from 1750F to 4000F. The control dial can be adjusted during the entire cooking period.

Power Indicators: Power indicators are located on the Control Panel of the air fryer. The control power indicates power indicators. The red power light indicates that the machine is turned on.

Automatic Timer Button: Air fryers also come with an automatic timer button that will immediately turn off the machine once the cooking time is over. The machine usually gives off a beep sound to set off the timer.

Pre-Cooked Buttons: Pre-cooked buttons are shortcut functions that are specifically designed to cook certain kinds of foods including fish and poultry. Other air fryers come with baking functions that allow you to cook baked goods.

How to Use It

Air fryers are not created equally thus the features can vary from model or brand to the other. For instance, parts of some air fryers may be dishwasher safe while others are not. It is for this reason that it is crucial to read your appliance manual before using it. That way, you will get to know more about what your air fryer can and cannot do. Reading the safety information ensures that you do not misuse your air fryer in any way.

Reading the user manual also provides you instructions on how to use your air fryer properly. This also includes the type of accessories that you need to use in order to successfully make different dishes using this unconventional kitchen appliance. Now when it comes to general tips on using your air fryer, there are certain tips that you need to know. Below are some tips on how to use your air fryer. These tips are applicable for most models of air fryer that are available in the market:

Cook your food between 1450F to 1600F: Cook food using this temperature range to ensure that your food is cooked through and that you avoid the risk for contracting food-borne diseases.

Check your device's wattage: The higher the wattage often means the shorter the cooking time. For most recipes, the total cooking time can vary by a minute or two so it is crucial to follow the recipe book to avoid overcooking your food.

Start with the shortest cooking time: Opt for the shortest cooking time as indicated in your recipe book. Constantly check for doneness and increase the cooking time as needed. This may be challenging but you will eventually learn how to adjust the cooking time on your air fryer to get your food done.

Constantly check your food if you are new to air frying: This is especially true if you are new to cooking with an air fryer.

Benefits of Air Fryer

Cooking with an air fryer is touted to be good for your health. The reason for this is that you can use less oil but still get the same effects similar when cooking with a deep fryer. But more than being able to cook delicious fried foods with less oil, below are the benefits of cooking with an air fryer.

May aid to weight loss: Because you can use less oil with the air fryer, it is a great kitchen appliance for people who want to lose weight or maintain a healthy weight without the need for you to sacrifice your favorite "fried" comfort foods.

Fewer mess: Unlike cooking in a deep fryer, there is too little mess involved when cooking with the air fryer. Gone are the days when you have to suffer from oil splattering all over your kitchen. But more than anything else, you don't need to use too many pots, pans, baking sheets, and others as you only need the air fryer basket to cook your food. And because you save yourself from being splattered with hot oil, air fryers are very safe.

Portable and practical: The air fryer is a great kitchen device for people who have a small kitchen or living in an RV as it does not take too much space, unlike conventional convection ovens.

Easy to operate: Air fryers are very easy to use. It does not come with complicated buttons so anyone can operate the device even kitchen neophytes. It also comes with automatic cooking functions so there is no guesswork when it comes to choosing the right cooking setting for a particular food that you are making.

Faster cooking time: People who are always on the go can also benefit from air fryers. The convection cooking mechanism of air fryers allows you to cook food faster than conventional ovens. Moreover, cooking with air fryers does not only require you to preheat the air fryer prior to cooking your food so you can save more time spending in the kitchen and more time doing other equally important things.

Caring for Your Air Fryer

You don't have to invest in any specific detergent or cleanser to keep your air fryer smelling like new. Use this section as your guide to keep your new kitchen appliance in tip-top shape so you can use it for years to come.

Cleaning your air fryer

Cleaning your air fryer is actually a really simple task. With a little elbow grease, some regular dish detergent, and hot water, your air fryer will come back to life, even with the toughest of buildup.

We've experimented with various makes and models and had our fair share of epic disasters in our air fryers (think: cream cheese melted with panko all over the baking tray), but guess what? After letting the basket and/or tray cool, we were easily able to get the buildup off with a regular kitchen sponge and hot soapy water.

Plus, even when switching between seafood and a decadent dessert, the air fryer doesn't require a deep clean.

Wipe down the outside of your fryer after each use. A hot, soapy towel is all that's necessary. This helps get off any grease or food particles that may have latched on during cooking.

Storing your air fryer

You can purchase a snazzy air fryer cover online, but this isn't necessary. We store our air fryers on the countertop because, well, we're writing a cookbook and we use them more frequently! Unfortunately, many models are too bulky for under-the-counter storage. Wherever you choose to store your air fryer, just be sure to put it in an area of your kitchen that isn't near your stovetop or oven so you don't get the residual grease from your day-to-day cooking building up on the outside of it.

Breakfast

Hot Italian-style Sub

Servings: 3
Cooking Time: 15 Minutes
Ingredients:
- 3 Italian-style hoagie rolls
- 3 tablespoons unsalted butter, softened
- 1 teaspoon Italian seasoning
- ½ teaspoon garlic powder
- 9 slices salami
- 12 slices pepperoni
- 3 thin slices ham
- 3 tablespoons giardiniera mix, chopped
- 6 tablespoons shredded mozzarella cheese

Directions:
1. Preheat the toaster oven to 350°F. Split the rolls lengthwise, cutting almost but not quite though the roll. Place the sandwiches in a 12 x 12-inch baking pan, side by side with the open side face up.
2. Combine the butter, Italian seasoning, and garlic powder in a small bowl. Spread evenly on the inside of the hoagie rolls.
3. Layer a third of the salami, pepperoni, and ham on each sandwich. Sprinkle with the giardiniera mix and mozzarella cheese.
4. Bake for 10 to 15 minutes or until heated through and the cheese is melted.

Baked Eggs And Bacon

Servings: 2
Cooking Time: 25 Minutes
Ingredients:
- 8 slices bacon
- 4 large eggs
- 2 teaspoons fresh chives or scallion greens, chopped
- Sea salt, for seasoning
- Freshly ground black pepper, for seasoning

Directions:
1. Place the baking tray on position 1 and preheat the toaster oven on BAKE to 400°F for 5 minutes.
2. Arrange the bacon slices in four (4-ounce) ramekins, 2 per cup. Overlap the slices over the bottom and sides so that as much of the cup is covered as possible.
3. Bake for 10 to 15 minutes. The fat will start to render, and the bacon will start to crisp and brown on the edges. Take the ramekins out of the oven and lightly blot any excess oil in the bottom of each one.
4. Crack 1 egg into each cup, sprinkle with chives, and season lightly with salt and pepper.
5. Bake for 10 minutes, or until the egg yolks reach the desired consistency.
6. Take them out of the oven and run a knife around the edge of each cup to loosen and remove from the ramekin. Serve.

French Toast

Servings: 4
Cooking Time: 40 Minutes
Ingredients:
- 2 eggs
- 1 cup skim milk or low-fat soy milk
- 1 tablespoon honey
- Salt
- 4 slices multigrain bread
- Vegetable oil

Directions:
1. Whisk together the eggs, milk, honey, and salt to taste in a shallow bowl. Add a bread slice to the mixture and let it soak for one minute. Carefully turn it over and let the liquid saturate the other side. With a spatula, place the bread slice in an oiled 6½ × 6½ × 2-inch square (cake) pan.
2. BROIL for 5 minutes, then turn carefully with a spatula and broil for another 5 minutes, or until golden brown. Repeat the soaking and broiling procedure for the remaining slices.

Egg-loaded Potato Skins

Servings: 4
Cooking Time: 55 Minutes
Ingredients:
- 2 large russet potatoes
- ½ teaspoon olive oil
- ½ cup Gruyère cheese, shredded and divided
- 4 large eggs
- ¼ cup heavy (whipping) cream, divided
- 1 scallion, both white and green parts, finely chopped
- Sea salt, for seasoning
- Freshly ground black pepper, for seasoning

Directions:

1. Preheat the toaster oven to 400°F on BAKE.
2. Prick the potatoes all over with a fork and rub with the olive oil.
3. Place the potatoes directly on the rack and bake for 40 minutes. The potatoes should be soft and tender, and the skin lightly browned. If not done, set the timer for 5 minutes more.
4. Take the potatoes out and set aside until cool enough to handle, about 10 minutes.
5. Cut the potatoes in half lengthwise and scoop out the flesh so that you have about ½-inch flesh and the intact skin. Place the potato halves in the air-fryer basket (placed on the baking tray) and sprinkle 2 tablespoons of cheese in each skin. Crack an egg into each potato half and spoon 1 tablespoon of cream over each egg. Sprinkle with scallion and lightly season with salt and pepper.
6. In position 1, bake for 15 minutes until the egg whites are set, and the yolks are still runny. If the eggs need more time, set the timer for 3 to 5 minutes more. Serve.

Savory Breakfast Bread Pudding

Servings: 4
Cooking Time: 30 Minutes
Ingredients:
- Oil spray (hand-pumped)
- 4 slices whole-wheat bread, cubed
- 1 cup frozen potato hash browns, thawed
- 5 large eggs
- 1 cup whole milk
- ½ cup diced ham
- ½ cup shredded cheddar cheese
- 1 teaspoon fresh parsley, chopped
- ⅛ teaspoon sea salt
- ⅛ teaspoon freshly ground black pepper

Directions:
1. Place the baking tray on position 1 and preheat the toaster oven on BAKE to 350°F for 5 minutes.
2. Lightly oil an 8-inch-square baking dish with spray.
3. Spread the bread cubes and potatoes in the baking dish evenly.
4. In a medium bowl, combine the eggs, milk, ham, cheese, parsley, salt, and pepper.
5. Pour the egg mixture over the bread and potatoes in the dish.
6. Bake for 30 minutes. The bread pudding should be lightly golden, the eggs set, and a knife inserted in the center should come out clean.
7. Cool the pudding for 5 minutes and serve.

Berry Crisp

Servings: 4
Cooking Time: 25 Minutes
Ingredients:
- 2 16-ounce packages frozen berries or 4 cups fresh berries
- 2 tablespoons lemon juice
- ½ cup rolled oats
- 1 tablespoon margarine, at room temperature
- 3 tablespoons wheat germ
- 4 ¼ cup honey
- 5 1 teaspoon vanilla extract
- Salt to taste

Directions:
1. Preheat the toaster oven to 400° F.
2. Combine the berries or fruit and lemon juice in a 1-quart-size 8½ × 8½ × 4-inch ovenproof baking dish, tossing well to mix. Set aside.
3. Combine the rolled oats, margarine, wheat germ, honey, vanilla, and salt in a small bowl and stir with a fork until the mixture is crumbly. Sprinkle evenly on top of the berries.
4. BAKE, covered, for 20 minutes, or until the berries are bubbling. Remove from the oven and uncover.
5. BROIL for 5 minutes, or until the topping is lightly browned.

Almond Granola With Dried Fruit

Servings: 5
Cooking Time: 45 Minutes
Ingredients:
- 2½ tablespoons maple syrup
- 2½ tablespoons packed light brown sugar
- 2 teaspoons vanilla extract
- ¼ teaspoon table salt
- ¼ cup vegetable oil
- 2½ cups (7½ ounces) old-fashioned rolled oats
- 1 cup whole almonds, chopped
- 1 cup raisins, currants, dried cranberries, and/or chopped dried cherries

Directions:
1. Adjust toaster oven rack to middle position and preheat the toaster oven to 325 degrees. Line small rimmed baking sheet with parchment paper.
2. Whisk maple syrup, sugar, vanilla, and salt together in large bowl, then whisk in oil until fully combined. Fold in oats and almonds until thoroughly coated. Transfer oat mixture to prepared sheet and spread into even layer. Using stiff metal spatula, compress oat mixture until very compact.

Bake until lightly browned, 35 to 45 minutes, rotating sheet halfway through baking.

3. Remove granola from oven and let cool on wire rack to room temperature, about 1 hour. Break cooled granola into pieces of desired size and transfer to large clean bowl. Add dried fruit and gently toss to combine. (Granola can be stored in airtight container for up to 2 weeks.)

Lemon Blueberry Scones

Servings: 6
Cooking Time: 25 Minutes
Ingredients:
- 1 ½ cups all-purpose flour
- 2 tablespoons granulated sugar
- 2 ¼ teaspoons baking powder
- 1 teaspoon grated lemon zest
- ¼ teaspoon table salt
- ¼ cup unsalted butter, cut into 1-tablespoon pieces
- ¾ cup fresh or frozen blueberries
- ¾ cup plus 1 tablespoon heavy cream, plus more for brushing
- Coarse white sugar
- LEMON GLAZE
- 1 cup confectioners' sugar
- 2 to 3 tablespoons fresh lemon juice

Directions:
1. Line a 12 x 12-inch baking pan with parchment paper.
2. Whisk the flour, granulated sugar, baking powder, lemon zest, and salt in a large bowl. Cut in the butter using a pastry cutter or two knives until the mixture is crumbly throughout. Gently stir in the blueberries, taking care not to mash them. Add ¾ cup cream and gently stir until a soft dough forms. If needed, stir in an additional tablespoon of cream so all of the flour is moistened.
3. Turn the dough onto a lightly floured board. Pat the dough into a circle about ¾ inch thick and 6 inches in diameter. Cut into 6 triangles. Arrange the triangles on the prepared pan. Freeze for 15 minutes.
4. Preheat the toaster oven to 400°F. Brush the scones lightly with cream and sprinkle with coarse sugar. Bake for 20 to 25 minutes or until golden brown. Let cool for 5 minutes.
5. Meanwhile, make the glaze: Stir the confectioners' sugar and lemon juice in a small bowl, blending until smooth. Drizzle the glaze over the scones. Let stand for about 5 minutes. These taste best served freshly made and slightly warm.

Bagel Melt

Servings: 1
Cooking Time: 3 Minutes
Ingredients:
- 1 bagel, split
- 4 slices Swiss cheese
- 4 strips lean turkey bacon, cut in half

Directions:
1. Layer the bagel halves with 2 slices of Swiss cheese and 4 half strips of turkey bacon each.
2. TOAST once on the oven rack.

Crispy Bacon

Servings: 6
Cooking Time: 20 Minutes
Ingredients:
- 12 ounces bacon

Directions:
1. Preheat the toaster oven to 350°F for 3 minutes.
2. Lay out the bacon in a single layer, slightly overlapping the strips of bacon.
3. Air fry for 10 minutes or until desired crispness.
4. Repeat until all the bacon has been cooked.

Hole In One

Servings: 1
Cooking Time: 7 Minutes
Ingredients:
- 1 slice bread
- 1 teaspoon soft butter
- 1 egg
- salt and pepper
- 1 tablespoon shredded Cheddar cheese
- 2 teaspoons diced ham

Directions:
1. Place a 6 x 6-inch baking dish inside air fryer oven and preheat fryer to 330°F.
2. Using a 2½-inch-diameter biscuit cutter, cut a hole in center of bread slice.
3. Spread softened butter on both sides of bread.
4. Lay bread slice in baking dish and crack egg into the hole. Sprinkle egg with salt and pepper to taste.
5. Air-fry for 5 minutes.
6. Turn toast over and top it with shredded cheese and diced ham.
7. Air-fry for 2 more minutes or until yolk is done to your liking.

Morning Glory Muffins

Servings: 6
Cooking Time: 25 Minutes
Ingredients:
- Oil spray (hand-pumped)
- ¼ cup raisins
- 1 cup whole-wheat flour
- ½ cup packed dark brown sugar
- 1 teaspoon baking soda
- 1¼ teaspoons pumpkin pie spice
- ¼ teaspoon sea salt
- 1 cup carrot, finely shredded
- 1 small apple, peeled, cored, and shredded
- ⅓ cup shredded, sweetened coconut
- 2 large eggs
- ¼ cup canola oil
- Juice and zest of ½ orange

Directions:
1. Place the rack on position 1 and preheat the toaster oven on BAKE to 350°F for 5 minutes. Lightly spray 6 muffin cups with the oil or line them with paper liners.
2. In a small bowl, cover the raisins with hot water and set aside.
3. In a large bowl, whisk the flour, brown sugar, baking soda, pumpkin pie spice, and salt. Add the carrot, apple, and coconut, and toss to mix.
4. In a small bowl, beat the eggs, oil, orange juice, and orange zest.
5. Drain the raisins, squeezing out as much water as possible.
6. Add the wet ingredients and raisins to the dry ingredients and mix until the batter is just combined.
7. Spoon the batter into the muffin cups.
8. Bake for 25 minutes or until a knife inserted in the center comes out clean.
9. Remove from the oven and let cool before serving.

Garlic-cheese Biscuits

Servings: 8
Cooking Time: 8 Minutes
Ingredients:
- 1 cup self-rising flour
- 1 teaspoon garlic powder
- 2 tablespoons butter, diced
- 2 ounces sharp Cheddar cheese, grated
- ½ cup milk
- cooking spray

Directions:
1. Preheat the toaster oven to 330°F.
2. Combine flour and garlic in a medium bowl and stir together.
3. Using a pastry blender or knives, cut butter into dry ingredients.
4. Stir in cheese.
5. Add milk and stir until stiff dough forms.
6. If dough is too sticky to handle, stir in 1 or 2 more tablespoons of self-rising flour before shaping. Biscuits should be firm enough to hold their shape. Otherwise, they'll stick to the air fryer oven.
7. Divide dough into 8 portions and shape into 2-inch biscuits about ¾-inch thick.
8. Spray air fryer oven with nonstick cooking spray.
9. Place all 8 biscuits in air fryer oven and air-fry at 330°F for 8 minutes.

Tuscan Toast

Servings: 4
Cooking Time: 5 Minutes
Ingredients:
- ¼ cup butter
- ½ teaspoon lemon juice
- ½ clove garlic
- ½ teaspoon dried parsley flakes
- 4 slices Italian bread, 1-inch thick

Directions:
1. Place butter, lemon juice, garlic, and parsley in a food processor. Process about 1 minute, or until garlic is pulverized and ingredients are well blended.
2. Spread garlic butter on both sides of bread slices.
3. Place bread slices upright in air fryer oven. (They can lie flat but cook better standing on end.)
4. Air-fry at 390°F for 5 minutes or until toasty brown.

Strawberry Shortcake With Buttermilk Biscuits

Servings: 8
Cooking Time: 15 Minutes
Ingredients:
- 1 quart fresh strawberries, rinsed and sliced
- 2 tablespoons sugar
- 1 tablespoon lemon juice
- Buttermilk biscuit mix:
- 2 cups unbleached flour
- 2 teaspoons baking powder
- ½ teaspoon baking soda
- Salt to taste

- ¼ cup margarine
- 1 cup low-fat buttermilk
- Vegetable oil
- Nonfat whipped topping

Directions:
1. Preheat the toaster oven to 400° F.
2. Combine the strawberries, sugar, and lemon juice in a large bowl, mixing well to blend. Set aside.
3. Combine the flour, baking powder, baking soda, and salt in a large bowl. Add the margarine, cutting it into the flour with a knife or pastry cutter. Add just enough buttermilk so that the dough will hold together when pinched.
4. Turn the dough out onto a lightly floured surface and knead 5 or 6 times. Drop the dough from a tablespoon onto an oiled or nonstick 6½ × 10-inch baking sheet. Make 8 mounds 1½ inches across and flatten the tops with a spoon.
5. BAKE for 15 minutes, or until the biscuits are lightly browned. Cool. Spoon on the fresh strawberries. Top with nonfat whipped topping and serve.

Portable Omelet

Servings: 1
Cooking Time: 4 Minutes
Ingredients:
- 2 slices multigrain bread
- 2 eggs
- 1 tablespoon plain nonfat yogurt
- Salt and freshly ground black pepper
- 2 strips turkey bacon
- 2 tablespoons shredded low-moisture, part-skim mozzarella cheese

Directions:
1. TOAST the bread slices and set aside.
2. Whisk together the eggs and yogurt in a small bowl and season with salt and pepper to taste.
3. Layer bacon strips in a small 4 × 8 × 2¼-inch loaf pan. Pour the egg mixture on top and sprinkle with the cheese.
4. TOAST once, or until the egg is done to your preference. Cut the omelet into toast-size squares and place between the 2 slices of toast to make a sandwich. (TOAST takes 2 to 3 minutes.)

Sheet Pan French Toast

Servings: 2
Cooking Time: 15 Minutes
Ingredients:
- Oil spray (hand-pumped)
- 2 large eggs
- ¼ cup milk
- 1 teaspoon vanilla extract
- ¼ teaspoon ground cinnamon
- 4 slices whole-grain bread
- ¾ cup maple syrup, or to taste

Directions:
1. Preheat the toaster oven on BAKE to 350°F for 5 minutes.
2. Line the baking tray with parchment paper and generously spray the paper with oil.
3. In a medium bowl, whisk the eggs, milk, vanilla, and cinnamon until well blended.
4. Dredge a slice of bread in the egg mixture until submerged, turn, and take it out. Gently shake the bread to remove any excess egg mixture and place the bread on the baking sheet. Repeat with the remaining bread.
5. Bake for 10 minutes.
6. Flip the bread and bake for 5 minutes longer until both sides are golden brown and crispy.
7. Serve with maple syrup.

Mushroom-spinach Frittata With Feta

Servings: 4
Cooking Time: 35 Minutes
Ingredients:
- 1 tablespoon olive oil
- 1 cup white mushrooms, chopped
- 1 shallot, finely chopped
- 1 teaspoon minced garlic
- 4 large eggs
- ½ cup milk
- ½ cup fresh baby spinach, shredded
- 1 tablespoon fresh basil, chopped
- ⅛ teaspoon sea salt
- ⅛ teaspoon freshly ground black pepper
- ¾ cup feta cheese, crumbled

Directions:
1. Place the baking tray on position 1 and preheat the toaster oven on BAKE to 350°F for 5 minutes.
2. Add the oil to an 8-inch-square baking dish, tilting the dish to coat the bottom.
3. Combine the mushrooms, shallot, and garlic in the baking dish. Bake the vegetables for 5 minutes or until softened, stirring halfway through.
4. While the vegetables are cooking, in a large bowl, whisk the eggs, milk, spinach, basil, salt, and pepper.

5. Take the baking dish out of the oven and pour in the egg mixture, stirring slightly to evenly disperse the vegetables.
6. Top the frittata with the feta cheese and bake for 30 minutes. The frittata should be puffy and golden, and a knife inserted in the center should come out clean.
7. Cool for 5 minutes and serve.

Buttered Poppy Seed Bread

Servings: 6
Cooking Time: 25 Minutes
Ingredients:
- 3 tablespoons unsalted butter, melted
- 1 (1-pound) loaf frozen white bread dough
- 1 teaspoon poppy seeds
- ¼ teaspoon onion powder
- ¼ teaspoon garlic powder
- ¼ teaspoon freshly ground black pepper

Directions:
1. Pour about half of the melted butter into a 9 x 5-inch loaf pan. Brush the butter to cover the sides and bottom of the pan. Place the frozen bread loaf in the pan. Brush the top of the loaf with the remaining butter, covering completely. Stir the poppy seeds, onion powder, garlic powder, and pepper in a small bowl. Sprinkle the seasonings over the top of the bread. Cover with plastic wrap and refrigerate overnight.
2. Remove the bread from the refrigerator and loosen the plastic wrap so it is loosely covered. Let it rise at room temperature until the top of the bread is just over the top edge of the pan, about 2 to 4 hours.
3. Preheat the toaster oven to 350°F.
4. Bake for 20 to 25 minutes or until the bread is golden brown.
5. Let cool for 5 minutes, then remove the loaf from the pan and place on a wire rack to cool for a few minutes. Slice and serve warm.

Green Onion Pancakes

Servings: 4
Cooking Time: 8 Minutes
Ingredients:
- 2 cup all-purpose flour
- ½ teaspoon salt
- ¾ cup hot water
- 1 tablespoon vegetable oil
- 1 tablespoon butter, melted
- 2 cups finely chopped green onions
- 1 tablespoon black sesame seeds, for garnish

Directions:
1. In a large bowl, whisk together the flour and salt. Make a well in the center and pour in the hot water. Quickly stir the flour mixture together until a dough forms. Knead the dough for 5 minutes; then cover with a warm, wet towel and set aside for 30 minutes to rest.
2. In a small bowl, mix together the vegetable oil and melted butter.
3. On a floured surface, place the dough and cut it into 8 pieces. Working with 1 piece of dough at a time, use a rolling pin to roll out the dough until it's ¼ inch thick; then brush the surface with the oil and butter mixture and sprinkle with green onions. Next, fold the dough in half and then in half again. Roll out the dough again until it's ¼ inch thick and brush with the oil and butter mixture and green onions. Fold the dough in half and then in half again and roll out one last time until it's ¼ inch thick. Repeat this technique with all 8 pieces.
4. Meanwhile, preheat the toaster oven to 400°F.
5. Place 1 or 2 pancakes into the air fryer oven (or as many as will fit in your fryer), and air-fry for 2 minutes or until crispy and golden brown. Repeat until all the pancakes are cooked. Top with black sesame seeds for garnish, if desired.

Ham And Swiss Melts

Servings: 2
Cooking Time: 8 Minutes
Ingredients:
- Spread:
- 2 scallions, finely chopped
- 2 tablespoons finely chopped radishes
- 2 tablespoons brown mustard
- 1 teaspoon Worcestershire sauce
- 2 tablespoons low-fat mayonnaise
- 4 slices low-fat Swiss cheese
- 4 slices lean baked ham
- 2 6-inch submarine rolls, cut in half lengthwise

Directions:
1. Combine the spread ingredients in a small bowl and spread in equal portions on the flat side of the bread halves. Add 2 slices of cheese and ham per each, folding to fit, if necessary. Place on an oiled or nonstick 6½ × 10-inch baking sheet.
2. BROIL for 8 minutes, or until the cheese is melted and browned lightly.

Banana Baked Oatmeal

Servings: 4
Cooking Time: 35 Minutes
Ingredients:
- Oil spray (hand-pumped)
- 1 cup rolled gluten-free oats
- ¾ teaspoon baking powder
- ¾ teaspoon ground cinnamon
- ¼ teaspoon sea salt
- ¾ cup whole milk
- ¼ cup maple syrup
- 1 large egg
- 2 tablespoons unsalted butter, melted
- 1 teaspoon vanilla extract
- 1 banana, chopped

Directions:
1. Place the rack on position 1 and preheat the toaster oven on BAKE to 375°F for 5 minutes.
2. Lightly spray an 8-inch-square baking dish with oil and set aside.
3. In a large bowl, stir the oats, baking powder, cinnamon, and salt until well combined.
4. In a small bowl, whisk the milk, maple syrup, egg, butter, and vanilla until blended.
5. Add the wet ingredients to the dry and stir until well mixed. Stir in the banana.
6. Spoon the batter into the baking dish and place the wire rack on position 1.
7. Place the baking dish on the rack and bake for 35 minutes. The oatmeal should look just set in the middle; if not, add 5 minutes more.
8. Cool the baked oatmeal for 5 minutes and serve with desired toppings.

Not-so-english Muffins

Servings: 4
Cooking Time: 10 Minutes
Ingredients:
- 2 strips turkey bacon, cut in half crosswise
- 2 whole-grain English muffins, split
- 1 cup fresh baby spinach, long stems removed
- ¼ ripe pear, peeled and thinly sliced
- 4 slices Provolone cheese

Directions:
1. Place bacon strips in air fryer oven and air-fry for 2minutes. Check and separate strips if necessary so they cook evenly. Air-fry for 4 more minutes, until crispy. Remove and drain on paper towels.
2. Place split muffin halves in air fryer oven and air-fry at 390°F for 2minutes, just until lightly browned.
3. Open air fryer oven and top each muffin with a quarter of the baby spinach, several pear slices, a strip of bacon, and a slice of cheese.
4. Air-fry at 360°F for 2minutes, until cheese completely melts.

Bread Boat Eggs

Servings: 4
Cooking Time: 10 Minutes
Ingredients:
- 4 pistolette rolls
- 1 teaspoon butter
- ¼ cup diced fresh mushrooms
- ½ teaspoon dried onion flakes
- 4 eggs
- ½ teaspoon salt
- ¼ teaspoon dried dill weed
- ¼ teaspoon dried parsley
- 1 tablespoon milk

Directions:
1. Cut a rectangle in the top of each roll and scoop out center, leaving ½-inch shell on the sides and bottom.
2. Place butter, mushrooms, and dried onion in air fryer oven baking pan and air-fry for 1 minute. Stir and cook 3 more minutes.
3. In a medium bowl, beat together the eggs, salt, dill, parsley, and milk. Pour mixture into pan with mushrooms.
4. Air-fry at 390°F for 2 minutes. Stir. Continue cooking for 3 or 4 minutes, stirring every minute, until eggs are scrambled to your liking.
5. Remove baking pan from air fryer oven and fill rolls with scrambled egg mixture.
6. Place filled rolls in air fryer oven and air-fry at 390°F for 2 to 3 minutes or until rolls are lightly browned.

Hashbrown Potatoes Lyonnaise

Servings: 4
Cooking Time: 33 Minutes
Ingredients:
- 1 Vidalia (or other sweet) onion, sliced
- 1 teaspoon butter, melted
- 1 teaspoon brown sugar
- 2 large russet potatoes (about 1 pound), sliced ½-inch thick
- 1 tablespoon vegetable oil
- salt and freshly ground black pepper

Directions:
1. Preheat the toaster oven to 370°F.
2. Toss the sliced onions, melted butter and brown sugar together in the air fryer oven. Air-fry for 8 minutes, help the onions cook evenly.
3. While the onions are cooking, bring a 3-quart saucepan of salted water to a boil on the stovetop. Par-cook the potatoes in boiling water for 3 minutes. Drain the potatoes and pat them dry with a clean kitchen towel.
4. Add the potatoes to the onions in the air fryer oven and drizzle with vegetable oil. Toss to coat the potatoes with the oil and season with salt and freshly ground black pepper.
5. Increase the air fryer oven temperature to 400°F and air-fry for 22 minutes tossing the vegetables a few times during the cooking time to help the potatoes brown evenly. Season to taste again with salt and freshly ground black pepper and serve warm.

Roasted Vegetable Frittata

Servings: 1
Cooking Time: 19 Minutes
Ingredients:
- ½ red or green bell pepper, cut into ½-inch chunks
- 4 button mushrooms, sliced
- ½ cup diced zucchini
- ½ teaspoon chopped fresh oregano or thyme
- 1 teaspoon olive oil
- 3 eggs, beaten
- ½ cup grated Cheddar cheese
- salt and freshly ground black pepper, to taste
- 1 teaspoon butter
- 1 teaspoon chopped fresh parsley

Directions:
1. Preheat the toaster oven to 400°F.
2. Toss the peppers, mushrooms, zucchini and oregano with the olive oil and air-fry for 6 minutes, redistribute the ingredients once or twice during the cooking process.
3. While the vegetables are cooking, beat the eggs well in a bowl, stir in the Cheddar cheese and season with salt and freshly ground black pepper. Add the air-fried vegetables to this bowl when they have finished cooking.
4. Place a 6- or 7-inch non-stick metal cake pan into the air fryer oven with the butter using an aluminum sling to lower the pan into the air fryer oven. (Fold a piece of aluminum foil into a strip about 2-inches wide by 24-inches long.) Air-fry for 1 minute at 380°F to melt the butter. Remove the cake pan and rotate the pan to distribute the butter and grease the pan. Pour the egg mixture into the cake pan and return the pan to the air fryer oven, using the aluminum sling.
5. Air-fry at 380°F for 12 minutes, or until the frittata has puffed up and is lightly browned. Let the frittata sit in the air fryer oven for 5 minutes to cool to an edible temperature and set up. Remove the cake pan from the air fryer oven, sprinkle with parsley and serve immediately.

Cheddar Cheese Biscuits

Servings: 8
Cooking Time: 22 Minutes
Ingredients:
- 2⅓ cups self-rising flour
- 2 tablespoons sugar
- ½ cup butter (1 stick), frozen for 15 minutes
- ½ cup grated Cheddar cheese, plus more to melt on top
- 1⅓ cups buttermilk
- 1 cup all-purpose flour, for shaping
- 1 tablespoon butter, melted

Directions:
1. Line a buttered 7-inch metal cake pan with parchment paper or a silicone liner.
2. Combine the flour and sugar in a large mixing bowl. Grate the butter into the flour. Add the grated cheese and stir to coat the cheese and butter with flour. Then add the buttermilk and stir just until you can no longer see streaks of flour. The dough should be quite wet.
3. Spread the all-purpose (not self-rising) flour out on a small cookie sheet. With a spoon, scoop 8 evenly sized balls of dough into the flour, making sure they don't touch each other. With floured hands, coat each dough ball with flour and toss them gently from hand to hand to stir any excess flour. Place each floured dough ball into the prepared pan, right up next to the other. This will help the biscuits rise up, rather than spreading out.
4. Preheat the toaster oven to 380°F.
5. Transfer the cake pan to the air fryer oven, lowering it into the air fryer oven using a sling made of aluminum foil (fold a piece of aluminum foil into a strip about 2-inches wide by 24-inches long). Let the ends of the aluminum foil sling hang across the cake pan before returning to the air fryer oven.
6. Air-fry for 20 minutes. Check the biscuits a couple of times to make sure they are not getting too brown on top. If they are, re-arrange the aluminum foil strips to cover any brown parts. After 20 minutes, check the biscuits by inserting a toothpick into the center of the biscuits. It should come out clean. If it needs a little more time, continue to air-fry for a couple of extra minutes. Brush the tops of the biscuits with some melted butter and sprinkle a little more grated cheese on top if desired. Air-fry for another 2 minutes.

Remove the cake pan from the air fryer oven using the aluminum sling. Let the biscuits cool for just a minute or two and then turn them out onto a plate and pull apart. Serve immediately.

Salmon Burgers

Servings: 4
Cooking Time: 25 Minutes
Ingredients:
- ¾ cup Homemade Bread Crumbs
- 1 15-ounce can salmon, drained
- 1 small zucchini, finely chopped
- 2 tablespoons finely chopped onions
- 1 egg
- 1 teaspoon dried rosemary
- 1 teaspoon lemon juice
- 1 teaspoon garlic powder
- Salt and freshly ground black pepper to taste
- 1 teaspoon vegetable oil

Directions:
1. Preheat the toaster oven to 400° F.
2. Blend all ingredients except the oil and form patties 1½ inches thick. Place on an oiled or nonstick 8½ × 8½ × 2-inch square baking (cake) pan.
3. BAKE for 25 minutes, or until the patties are lightly browned.

Savory Salsa Cheese Rounds

Servings: 6
Cooking Time: 6 Minutes
Ingredients:
- 1 French baguette, cut to make 12
- 1-inch slices (rounds)
- ¼ cup olive oil
- 1 cup Tomato Salsa (recipe follows)
- ½ cup shredded low-fat mozzarella
- 2 tablespoons finely chopped fresh cilantro

Directions:
1. Brush both sides of each round with olive oil.
2. Spread one side of each slice with salsa and sprinkle each with mozzarella. Place the rounds in an oiled or nonstick 8½ × 8½ × 2-inch square baking (cake) pan.
3. BROIL for 6 minutes, or until the cheese is melted and the rounds are lightly browned. Garnish with the chopped cilantro and serve.

Good Stuff Bread

Servings: 2
Cooking Time: 40 Minutes
Ingredients:
- First mixture:
- 1 apple, peeled and grated
- 1 carrot, peeled and grated
- 1 cup unbleached flour
- 2 teaspoons baking powder
- ⅓ cup chopped walnuts
- ⅓ cup raisins
- ⅓ cup rolled oats
- ⅓ cup shredded sweetened coconut
- Blending mixture:
- 1 banana
- 1 egg
- 1 cup low-fat buttermilk
- 2 tablespoons dark brown sugar
- 2 tablespoons vegetable oil
- Salt to taste

Directions:
1. Preheat the toaster oven to 375° F.
2. Combine all the first mixture ingredients in a medium bowl and stir to mix well. Set aside.
3. Process all the blending mixture ingredients in a blender or food processor until the mixture is smooth. Add to the first mixture ingredients and stir to mix thoroughly. Transfer to an oiled or nonstick 8½ × 4½ × 2¼-inch regular size loaf pan.
4. BAKE for 40 minutes, or until a toothpick inserted in the center comes out clean and the top is well browned.

Creamy Bacon + Almond Crostini

Servings: 20
Cooking Time: 10 Minutes
Ingredients:
- 1 baguette loaf, cut into ½-inch-thick slices
- 2 tablespoons olive oil
- 4 ounces cream cheese, cut into cubes, softened
- ½ cup mayonnaise
- 1 cup shredded fontina cheese or Monterey Jack cheese
- 4 slices bacon, cooked until crisp and crumbled
- 1 green onion, white and green portions, finely chopped
- ¼ teaspoon Sriracha or hot sauce
- Dash kosher salt
- ¼ cup sliced almonds, toasted
- Minced fresh flat-leaf (Italian) parsley

Directions:
1. Toast the slices of the baguette in the toaster oven.
2. Arrange the toasted baguette slices on a 12-inch pizza pan or a 12 x 12-inch baking pan. Lightly brush the slices with the olive oil.
3. Preheat the toaster oven to 375°F.
4. Beat the cream cheese and mayonnaise in a medium bowl with an electric mixer at medium speed until creamy and smooth. Stir in the fontina, bacon, green onion, Sriracha, and salt and blend until combined.
5. Distribute the cheese mixture evenly over the toasted bread. Top with the sliced almonds. Bake for 6 to 8 minutes or until the cheese is hot and beginning to melt. Allow to cool for 1 to 2 minutes, then garnish with minced parsley. Serve warm.

Soft Pretzels

Servings: 12
Cooking Time: 6 Minutes
Ingredients:
- 2 teaspoons yeast
- 1 cup water, warm
- 1 teaspoon sugar
- 1 teaspoon salt
- 2½ cups all-purpose flour
- 2 tablespoons butter, melted
- 1 cup boiling water
- 1 tablespoon baking soda
- coarse sea salt
- melted butter

Directions:
1. Combine the yeast and water in a small bowl. Combine the sugar, salt and flour in the bowl of a stand mixer. With the mixer running and using the dough hook, drizzle in the yeast mixture and melted butter and knead dough until smooth and elastic – about 10 minutes. Shape into a ball and let the dough rise for 1 hour.
2. Punch the dough down to release any air and decide what size pretzels you want to make.
3. a. To make large pretzels, divide the dough into 12 portions.
4. b. To make medium sized pretzels, divide the dough into 24 portions.
5. c. To make mini pretzel knots, divide the dough into 48 portions.
6. Roll each portion into a skinny rope using both hands on the counter and rolling from the center to the ends of the rope. Spin the rope into a pretzel shape (or tie the rope into a knot) and place the tied pretzels on a parchment lined baking sheet.
7. Preheat the toaster oven to 350°F.
8. Combine the boiling water and baking soda in a shallow bowl and whisk to dissolve (this mixture will bubble, but it will settle down). Let the water cool so that you can put your hands in it. Working in batches, dip the pretzels (top side down) into the baking soda-water mixture and let them soak for 30 seconds to a minute. (This step is what gives pretzels their texture and helps them to brown faster.) Then, remove the pretzels carefully and return them (top side up) to the baking sheet. Sprinkle the coarse salt on the top.
9. Air-fry in batches for 3 minutes per side. When the pretzels are finished, brush them generously with the melted butter and enjoy them warm with some spicy mustard.

Blueberry Lemon Muffins

Servings: 12
Cooking Time: 23 Minutes
Ingredients:
- 2 ¼ cups all-purpose flour
- 1 ½ cups fresh blueberries
- 3/4 cup granulated sugar
- 2 teaspoons baking powder
- ½ teaspoon lemon zest
- ½ teaspoon salt
- ¾ cup milk
- ¼ cup butter, melted
- 1 tablespoon lemon juice
- 1 large egg

Directions:
1. Preheat the toaster oven to 375°F. Grease or line a 12-cup muffin pan with paper baking cups. Set aside.
2. In a large bowl, stir together flour, blueberries, granulated sugar, baking powder and salt.
3. In a small bowl, using an electric mixer or whisk, beat milk, butter, lemon juice and egg until blended.
4. Gradually add milk mixture to flour mixture. Stir until just blended.
5. Spoon into prepared muffin pan.
6. Bake 20 to 23 minutes or until toothpick inserted in center comes out clean.

Mediterranean Egg Sandwich

Servings: 1
Cooking Time: 8 Minutes
Ingredients:
- 1 large egg
- 5 baby spinach leaves, chopped
- 1 tablespoon roasted bell pepper, chopped
- 1 English muffin
- 1 thin slice prosciutto or Canadian bacon

Directions:
1. Spray a ramekin with cooking spray or brush the inside with extra-virgin olive oil.
2. In a small bowl, whisk together the egg, baby spinach, and bell pepper.
3. Split the English muffin in half and spray the inside lightly with cooking spray or brush with extra-virgin olive oil.
4. Preheat the toaster oven to 350°F for 2 minutes. Place the egg ramekin and open English muffin into the air fryer oven, and air-fry at 350°F for 5 minutes. Open the air fryer oven and add the prosciutto or bacon; air-fry for an additional 1 minute.
5. To assemble the sandwich, place the egg on one half of the English muffin, top with prosciutto or bacon, and place the remaining piece of English muffin on top.

Breakfast Banana Bread

Servings: 6
Cooking Time: 40 Minutes
Ingredients:
- 2 ripe bananas
- 1 egg
- ½ cup skim milk
- 2 tablespoons honey
- 1 tablespoon vegetable oil
- 1 cup unbleached flour
- ¾ cup chopped trail mix
- 1 teaspoon baking powder
- Salt

Directions:
1. Preheat the toaster oven to 400° F.
2. Process the bananas, egg, milk, honey, and oil in a blender or food processor until smooth and transfer to a mixing bowl.
3. Add the flour and trail mix, stirring to mix well. Add the baking powder and stir just enough to blend it into the batter. Add salt to taste. Pour the mixture into an oiled or nonstick 4½ × 8½ × 2¼-inch loaf pan.
4. BAKE for 40 minutes, or until a toothpick inserted in the center comes out clean.

Chocolate Chip Banana Muffins

Servings: 12
Cooking Time: 14 Minutes
Ingredients:
- 2 medium bananas, mashed
- ¼ cup brown sugar
- 1½ teaspoons vanilla extract
- ⅔ cup milk
- 2 tablespoons butter
- 1 large egg
- 1 cup white whole-wheat flour
- ½ cup old-fashioned oats
- 1 teaspoon baking soda
- ½ teaspoon baking powder
- ⅛ teaspoon sea salt
- ¼ cup mini chocolate chips

Directions:
1. Preheat the toaster oven to 330°F.
2. In a large bowl, combine the bananas, brown sugar, vanilla extract, milk, butter, and egg; set aside.
3. In a separate bowl, combine the flour, oats, baking soda, baking powder, and salt.
4. Slowly add the dry ingredients into the wet ingredients, folding in the flour mixture ⅓ cup at a time.
5. Mix in the chocolate chips and set aside.
6. Using silicone muffin liners, fill 6 muffin liners two-thirds full. Carefully place the muffin liners in the air fryer oven and bake for 20 minutes (or until the tops are browned and a toothpick inserted in the center comes out clean). Carefully remove the muffins from the air fryer oven and repeat with the remaining batter.
7. Serve warm.

Cherries Jubilee

Servings: 4
Cooking Time: 10 Minutes
Ingredients:
- 1 15-ounce can cherries, pitted and drained, with 2 tablespoons juice reserved
- 1 tablespoon orange juice
- 1 tablespoon sugar
- 1 tablespoon cornstarch
- ¼ cup warmed Kirsch or Cognac
- Vanilla yogurt or fat-free half-and-half

Directions:

1. Combine the reserved juice, orange juice, sugar, and cornstarch in a shallow baking pan, blending well.
2. BROIL for 5 minutes, or until the juice clarifies and thickens slightly. Add the cherries and heat, broiling for 5 minutes more and stirring to blend. Remove from the oven and transfer to a flameproof serving dish.
3. Spoon the Kirsch over the cherries and ignite. Top with vanilla yogurt or drizzle with warm fat-free half-and-half and serve.

Zucchini Bread

Servings: 6
Cooking Time: 30 Minutes
Ingredients:
- 1 cup grated zucchini
- 2 tablespoons grated onion
- 2 tablespoons grated Parmesan Cheese
- ½ cup skim milk
- 1 egg
- 2 tablespoons vegetable oil
- 1½ cups unbleached flour
- 1 tablespoon baking powder
- Salt to taste

Directions:
1. Preheat the toaster oven to 375° F.
2. Stir together all the ingredients in a medium bowl until smooth. Pour the batter into an oiled or nonstick regular-size 8½ × 4½ × 2¼-inch loaf pan.
3. BAKE for 30 minutes, or until a toothpick inserted in the center comes out clean.

Honey Ham And Swiss Broiler

Servings: 2
Cooking Time: 5 Minutes
Ingredients:
- 4 slices pumpernickel bread
- 1 tablespoon olive oil
- 1 tablespoon spicy brown mustard
- 1 tablespoon horseradish
- 4 slices reduced-fat honey ham
- 4 slices reduced-fat Swiss cheese
- 2 tablespoons finely chopped fresh parsley

Directions:
1. Brush one side of the 4 bread slices with oil and lay, oil side down, in an oiled or nonstick 8½ × 8½ × 2-inch square baking (cake) pan.
2. Spread 2 slices with mustard and 2 slices with horseradish.
3. Layer each with 1 slice honey ham and 1 slice Swiss cheese.
4. BROIL for 5 minutes, or until the cheese is melted. Sprinkle with equal portions of parsley and serve.

Cinnamon Rolls

Servings: 12
Cooking Time: 10 Minutes
Ingredients:
- Buttermilk Biscuit dough
- Cinnamon mixture:
- 3 tablespoons dark brown sugar
- 3 tablespoons chopped pecans
- 2 tablespoons margarine
- 1 teaspoon ground cinnamon
- Salt to taste
- Icing:
- 1 cup confectioners' sugar, sifted
- 1 tablespoon fat-free half-and-half
- ½ teaspoon vanilla extract
- Salt to taste

Directions:
1. Preheat the toaster oven to 400° F.
2. Make the buttermilk biscuit dough.
3. Roll out or pat the dough to ½ inch thick. In a small bowl, combine the cinnamon mixture ingredients. Spread the dough evenly with the cinnamon mixture and roll up like a jelly roll. With a sharp knife, cut the roll into 1-inch slices. Place on an oiled or nonstick 6½ × 10-inch baking sheet.
4. BAKE for 15 minutes, or until lightly browned. Let cool before frosting.
5. Combine the icing ingredients in a small bowl, adding more half-and-half or confectioners' sugar until the consistency is like thick cream. Drizzle over the tops of the cinnamon rolls and serve

Snacks Appetizers And Sides

Smoked Gouda Bacon Macaroni And Cheese

Servings: 10-12
Cooking Time: 30 Minutes
Ingredients:
- 1 (4 oz.) French baguette, torn
- 6 slices cooked bacon, chopped
- 1/4 cup loosely packed parsley
- 2 Tablespoons butter, melted
- 1 package (16 oz.) corkscrew or elbow pasta
- 1/3 cup butter
- 1/4 cup flour
- 4 cups milk
- 1 package (8 oz.) extra sharp Cheddar cheese, shredded
- 1 package (8 oz.) smoked Gouda cheese, shredded
- 2 1/2 teaspoons Creole seasoning

Directions:
1. Preheat the toaster oven to 400°F.
2. Using S-blade with food processor running, drop bread, 1/2 of the bacon and parsley into food chute. Process until finely chopped. Gradually add melted butter; process until crumbs form. Set aside.
3. Cook pasta according to package directions for al dente. Drain and rinse with cold water. Set aside.
4. Melt 1/3 cup butter in Dutch oven over medium-high heat. Gradually add flour, whisking until smooth, about 1 minute. Slowly add milk, stirring 8 to 10 minutes until mixture is thickened and smooth. Remove from heat.
5. Stir in cheeses, remaining bacon and Creole seasoning until cheese is melted. Fold in pasta.
6. Pour mixture into 11x7-inch baking dish sprayed with nonstick cooking spray. Sprinkle with breadcrumb mixture.
7. Bake 25 to 30 minutes or until crumbs are browned and mixture is heated through.

Sage Butter Roasted Butternut Squash With Pepitas

Servings: 4
Cooking Time: 20 Minutes
Ingredients:
- Nonstick cooking spray
- 1 medium butternut squash, peeled
- 2 tablespoons unsalted butter, melted
- 2 tablespoons minced fresh sage, plus more leaves for garnish (optional)
- 1 teaspoon honey
- ¼ cup shelled pumpkin seeds, or pepitas
- Kosher salt and freshly ground black pepper

Directions:
1. Preheat the toaster oven to 375°F. Spray a 12 x 12-inch baking pan with nonstick cooking spray.
2. Cut the squash crosswise into ¾-inch slices. Use a teaspoon to remove the seeds, as needed, from the center of the slices. Arrange the slices in a single layer on the baking sheet.
3. Stir the butter, sage, honey, and pumpkin seeds in a small bowl. Season with salt and pepper. Spoon the butter mixture over the squash slices, then brush to coat each slice of squash evenly.
4. Roast for 20 minutes or until the squash is tender. Transfer to a serving platter and spoon the seeds and any drippings over the squash. Garnish with extra sage leaves, if desired.

Sweet Potato Casserole

Servings: 4
Cooking Time: 90 Minutes
Ingredients:
- 2 tablespoons packed brown sugar, divided
- ½ teaspoon grated orange zest, divided, plus 1 tablespoon juice
- 1½ pounds sweet potatoes, peeled and cut into 1½-inch pieces
- 2 tablespoons unsalted butter, cut into 4 pieces
- 2 tablespoons heavy cream
- ½ teaspoon table salt
- ¼ teaspoon ground cinnamon
- ⅛ teaspoon pepper
- Pinch cayenne pepper

Directions:
1. Adjust toaster oven rack to middle position and preheat the toaster oven to 400 degrees. Mix 4 teaspoons sugar and ¼ teaspoon orange zest in small bowl until thoroughly combined; set aside.
2. Toss sweet potatoes and remaining 2 teaspoons sugar together in bowl, then spread into even layer on aluminum foil–lined small rimmed baking sheet. Cover sheet tightly with foil and roast until sweet potatoes are tender, 45 to 60

minutes, rotating sheet halfway through roasting. Remove sheet from oven, select broiler function, and heat broiler.

3. Transfer potatoes and any accumulated liquid to food processor. Add butter, cream, salt, cinnamon, pepper, cayenne, remaining ¼ teaspoon orange zest, and orange juice and process until completely smooth, 30 to 60 seconds, scraping down sides of bowl as needed.

4. Transfer potato puree to 8-inch square broiler-safe baking dish or pan and sprinkle evenly with reserved sugar-zest mixture. Broil sweet potatoes until topping is melted and beginning to caramelize, 10 to 12 minutes. Transfer dish to wire rack and let cool for 10 minutes. Serve.

Creamy Parmesan Polenta

Servings: 4
Cooking Time: 60 Minutes
Ingredients:
- 2½ cups boiling water, divided, plus extra as needed
- ½ cup coarse-ground cornmeal
- ½ teaspoon table salt
- Pinch baking soda
- 1 ounce Parmesan cheese, grated (½ cup)
- 1 tablespoon unsalted butter

Directions:
1. Adjust toaster oven rack to middle position and preheat the toaster oven to 325 degrees. Combine 2 cups boiling water, cornmeal, salt, and baking soda in greased 8-inch square baking dish or pan. Transfer dish to oven and bake until water is absorbed and polenta is thickened, 35 to 40 minutes, rotating dish halfway through baking.

2. Remove baking dish from oven. Stir in remaining ½ cup boiling water, then stir in Parmesan and butter until polenta is smooth and creamy. Adjust consistency with extra boiling water as needed. Serve.

Garlic Breadsticks

Servings: 12
Cooking Time: 7 Minutes
Ingredients:
- 1½ tablespoons Olive oil
- 1½ teaspoons Minced garlic
- ¼ teaspoon Table salt
- ¼ teaspoon Ground black pepper
- 6 ounces Purchased pizza dough (vegan dough, if that's a concern)

Directions:
1. Preheat the toaster oven to 400°F. Mix the oil, garlic, salt, and pepper in a small bowl.

2. Divide the pizza dough into 4 balls for a small air fryer oven, 6 for a medium machine, or 8 for a large, each ball about the size of a walnut in its shell. (Each should weigh 1 ounce, if you want to drag out a scale and get obsessive.) Roll each ball into a 5-inch-long stick under your clean palms on a clean, dry work surface. Brush the sticks with the oil mixture.

3. When the machine is at temperature, place the prepared dough sticks in the air fryer oven, leaving a 1-inch space between them. Air-fry undisturbed for 7 minutes, or until puffed, golden, and set to the touch.

4. Use kitchen tongs to gently transfer the breadsticks to a wire rack and repeat step 3 with the remaining dough sticks.

Grilled Ham & Muenster Cheese On Raisin Bread

Servings: 1
Cooking Time: 10 Minutes
Ingredients:
- 2 slices raisin bread
- 2 tablespoons butter, softened
- 2 teaspoons honey mustard
- 3 slices thinly sliced honey ham (about 3 ounces)
- 4 slices Muenster cheese (about 3 ounces)
- 2 toothpicks

Directions:
1. Preheat the toaster oven to 370°F.

2. Spread the softened butter on one side of both slices of raisin bread and place the bread, buttered side down on the counter. Spread the honey mustard on the other side of each slice of bread. Layer 2 slices of cheese, the ham and the remaining 2 slices of cheese on one slice of bread and top with the other slice of bread. Remember to leave the buttered side of the bread on the outside.

3. Transfer the sandwich to the air fryer oven and secure the sandwich with toothpicks.

4. Air-fry at 370°F for 5 minutes. Flip the sandwich over, remove the toothpicks and air-fry for another 5 minutes. Cut the sandwich in half and enjoy!!

Crispy Chili Kale Chips

Servings: 4
Cooking Time: 10 Minutes
Ingredients:
- 2 cups kale, stemmed and torn into 2-inch pieces
- 1 tablespoon extra-virgin olive oil
- ½ teaspoon chipotle chili powder
- Sea salt, for seasoning

Directions:
1. Preheat the toaster oven to 350°F on AIR FRY for 5 minutes.
2. Dry the kale with paper towels. Transfer the kale to a medium bowl and add the olive oil and chili powder. Toss the kale using your hands to evenly coat the leaves with the oil.
3. Place the air-fryer basket in the baking sheet and spread the kale in a single layer in the basket. You might have to cook two batches.
4. Air fry in position 2 for 5 minutes, until the leaves are crispy.
5. Transfer the kale chips to a large bowl and repeat with the remaining kale. Season the chips with salt and serve immediately.

Sweet Potato Fries With Sweet And Spicy Dipping Sauce

Servings: 2
Cooking Time: 20 Minutes
Ingredients:
- 1 large sweet potato (about 1 pound)
- 1 teaspoon vegetable or canola oil
- salt
- Sweet & Spicy Dipping Sauce
- ¼ cup light mayonnaise
- 1 tablespoon spicy brown mustard
- 1 tablespoon sweet Thai chili sauce
- ½ teaspoon sriracha sauce

Directions:
1. Scrub the sweet potato well and then cut it into ¼-inch French fries. (A mandolin slicer can really help with this.)
2. Preheat the toaster oven to 200°F.
3. Toss the sweet potato sticks with the oil and transfer them to the air fryer oven. Air-fry at 200°F for 10 minutes. Toss the fries with salt, increase the air fryer oven temperature to 400°F and air-fry for another 10 minutes.
4. To make the dipping sauce, combine all the ingredients in a small bowl and stir until combined.
5. Serve the sweet potato fries warm with the dipping sauce on the side.

Bacon Corn Muffins

Servings: 6
Cooking Time: 17 Minutes
Ingredients:
- 1 1/4 cups self rising cornmeal mix
- 3/4 cup buttermilk
- 1/3 cup chopped cooked bacon
- 1/4 cup butter, melted
- 1 large egg, slightly beaten

Directions:
1. Preheat toaster oven to 425°F on CONVECTION setting.
2. Stir cornmeal mix, buttermilk, bacon, butter and egg until blended.
3. Spoon batter into lightly greased muffin pan, filling 3/4 full.
4. Bake 15 to 17 minutes until toothpick inserted in center comes out clean.
5. Cool 10 minutes on wire rack; remove.

Wonton Cups

Servings: 6
Cooking Time: 10 Minutes
Ingredients:
- 6 wonton wrappers (3-inch squares)
- 2 Tablespoons melted butter
- Filling of choice

Directions:
1. Preheat toaster oven to 350°F.
2. Carefully press and fold one wonton wrapper in each cup of a 6-cup muffin pan.
3. Very lightly brush edges of wrappers with butter.
4. Bake 8 to 10 minutes or until golden brown.

Potato Samosas

Servings: 12
Cooking Time: 10 Minutes
Ingredients:
- ¾ cup Instant mashed potato flakes
- ¾ cup Boiling water
- ⅓ cup Plain full-fat or low-fat yogurt (not Greek yogurt or fat-free yogurt)
- 1 teaspoon Yellow curry powder, purchased or homemade

- ½ teaspoon Table salt
- 1½ Purchased refrigerated pie crust(s), from a minimum 14.1-ounce box
- All-purpose flour
- Vegetable oil spray

Directions:

1. Put the potato flakes in a medium bowl and pour the boiling water over them. Stir well to form a mixture like thick mashed potatoes. Cool for 15 minutes.
2. Preheat the toaster oven to 400°F.
3. Stir the yogurt, curry powder, and salt into the potato mixture until smooth and uniform.
4. Unwrap and unroll the sheet(s) of pie crust dough onto a clean, dry work surface. Cut out as many 4-inch circles as you can with a big cookie cutter or a giant sturdy water glass, or even by tracing the circle with the rim of a 4-inch plate. Gather up the scraps of dough. Lightly flour your work surface and set the scraps on top. Roll them together into a sheet that matches the thickness of the original crusts and cut more circles until you have the number you need—8 circles for the small batch, 12 for the medium batch, or 16 for the large.
5. Pick up one of the circles and create something like an ice cream cone by folding and sealing the circle together so that it is closed at the bottom and flared open at the top, in a conical shape. Put 1 tablespoon of the potato filling into the open cone, then push the filling into the cone toward the point. Fold the top over the filling and press to seal the dough into a triangular shape with corners, taking care to seal those corners all around. Set aside and continue forming and filling the remainder of the dough circles as directed.
6. Lightly coat the filled dough pockets with vegetable oil spray on all sides. Set them in the air fryer oven in one layer and air-fry undisturbed for 10 minutes, or until lightly browned and crisp.
7. Gently turn the contents of the air fryer oven out onto a wire rack. Use kitchen tongs to gently set all the samosas seam side up. Cool for 10 minutes before serving.

Creamy Scalloped Potatoes

Servings: 4
Cooking Time: 58 Minutes
Ingredients:

- Oil spray (hand-pumped)
- 2 tablespoons salted butter
- 1 small onion, finely chopped
- 1 teaspoon minced garlic
- 2 tablespoons all-purpose flour
- 1 cup whole milk
- ½ cup low-sodium chicken broth
- ¼ teaspoon ground nutmeg
- ⅛ teaspoon sea salt
- ⅛ teaspoon freshly ground black pepper
- 1½ pounds russet potatoes, cut into ⅛-inch-thick slices

Directions:

1. Place the rack on position 1 and preheat the toaster oven on BAKE to 350°F for 5 minutes.
2. Lightly spray an 8-inch-square baking dish with oil and set aside.
3. Melt the butter in a medium saucepan over medium-high heat. Sauté the onion and garlic in the butter until softened, about 4 minutes. Add the flour and cook, whisking, for 1 minute.
4. Whisk in the milk and chicken broth until well blended and cook, whisking constantly, until thickened, about 3 minutes. Remove the sauce from the heat and whisk in the nutmeg, salt, and pepper. Set aside.
5. Layer one-third of the potato slices in the baking dish and top with one-third of the sauce. Repeat the layering in thirds, ending with the cream sauce.
6. Cover the dish with aluminum foil and bake for 25 minutes. Remove the foil and bake for an additional 25 minutes until golden brown and the potatoes are tender. Serve.

Asparagus With Pistachio Dukkah

Servings: 3
Cooking Time: 8 Minutes
Ingredients:

- Pistachio Dukkah Ingredients
- 3 tablespoons coriander seeds
- 1 tablespoon cumin seeds
- ½ cup shelled pistachios
- ¼ cup sesame seeds
- 1 teaspoon salt
- ½ teaspoon pepper
- Asparagus Ingredients
- 1 bundle asparagus spears
- 1 tablespoon olive oil
- Salt & pepper, to taste

Directions:

1. Make the pistachio dukkah by placing the coriander and cumin seeds in a skillet over medium heat. Toast for 2 minutes, or until fragrant. Transfer spices to a spice grinder or mortar and pestle. Allow spices to cool completely, then grind.
2. Toast the pistachios in a skillet for 5 minutes, or until golden brown and fragrant. Transfer to a cutting board and

chop finely. Add the sesame seeds to the same skillet and toast for 2 minutes, or until golden brown and
3. fragrant. Transfer the pistachios, sesame seeds, coriander, and cumin seeds to a bowl. Add salt and pepper, then stir to combine.
4. Select the Preheat function on the Cosori Smart Air Fryer Toaster Oven, adjust temperature to 430°F, and press Start/Pause.
5. Line the food tray with foil, then place the asparagus on the tray. Drizzle with olive oil and season with salt and pepper.
6. Insert food tray at top position in the preheated oven.
7. Select the Air Fry function, adjust time to 8 minutes, and press Start/Pause.
8. Remove when asparagus is tender. Place asparagus on a serving dish and sprinkle with pistachio dukkah.
9. Pistachio dukkah can be stored at room temperature in a sealed jar or container for up to 4 weeks.

Caramelized Onion Dip

Servings: 2
Cooking Time: 20 Minutes
Ingredients:
- 1 tablespoon unsalted butter
- 1 tablespoon olive oil
- 1 large sweet onion, quartered and very thinly sliced crosswise
- Kosher salt
- 1 clove garlic, minced
- 3 tablespoons dry white wine
- ½ teaspoon dried thyme leaves
- ½ teaspoon freshly ground black pepper
- 1 baguette, thinly sliced
- Nonstick cooking spray
- 1 cup shredded Gruyère or Swiss cheese
- ½ cup sour cream
- ½ cup mayonnaise
- ¼ cup shredded Parmesan cheese
- 3 strips bacon, cooked until crisp and crumbled

Directions:
1. Melt the butter and olive oil in a large skillet over medium heat. Add the onion and season with salt. Cook, stirring frequently, for 3 minutes. Reduce the heat to low and cook, stirring occasionally, for 20 to 25 minutes, or until the onions are a deep golden brown color.
2. Increase the heat to medium. Stir in the garlic, wine, thyme, and pepper. Cook, stirring frequently, for 3 minutes or until the wine has mostly evaporated. Remove from the heat.
3. Meanwhile, toast the baguette slices in the toaster oven until golden brown and crisp; set aside.
4. Preheat the toaster oven to 350°F. Spray a 1-quart casserole with nonstick cooking spray.
5. Stir the Gruyère, sour cream, mayonnaise, Parmesan, and bacon into the onions. Spoon the mixture into the prepared casserole dish. Cover and bake for 20 minutes or until hot and the cheese is melted. Allow to stand for 5 to 10 minutes before serving. To serve, spoon the warm onion-cheese mixture onto the toast.

Garden Fresh Bruschetta

Servings: 6
Cooking Time: 5 Minutes
Ingredients:
- 1/2 cup Parmigiano-Reggiano cheese
- 2 cloves garlic (or to taste)
- 2 tablespoons balsamic vinegar
- 1/3 cup pine nuts
- 1 loaf crusty Italian bread
- 1 or 2 fresh tomatoes, sliced or chopped
- Salt and pepper to taste
- 4 cups fresh basil leaves, stems removed

Directions:
1. With shredding disk inserted, shred cheese in food processor. Remove from food processor and set aside.
2. Insert S-blade in food processor and coarsely chop basil leaves and garlic. Add vinegar and pulse a few times. Add pine nuts to basil mixture and pulse until coarsely chopped. With food processor running, drizzle olive oil through feed chute until ingredients are coated and spreadable. Add half of the already grated Parmesan cheese and pulse until just blended.
3. To assemble: Slice crusty bread on diagonal, place on toaster oven size cookie sheet. On each piece of bread, spread basil mixture. Place tomatoes on top of basil, add salt and pepper to taste. Sprinkle some of the remaining cheese on top.
4. Place in preheated 350°F toaster oven for 5 minutes or until cheese melts and bread is warmed. Serve as an appetizer.

Cherry Chipotle Bbq Chicken Wings

Servings: 2
Cooking Time: 12 Minutes
Ingredients:
- 1 teaspoon smoked paprika
- ½ teaspoon dry mustard powder
- 1 teaspoon dried oregano
- 1 teaspoon dried thyme
- ½ teaspoon chili powder
- 1 teaspoon salt
- 2 pounds chicken wings
- vegetable oil or spray
- salt and freshly ground black pepper
- 1 to 2 tablespoons chopped chipotle peppers in adobo sauce
- ⅓ cup cherry preserves ¼ cup tomato ketchup

Directions:
1. Combine the first six ingredients in a large bowl. Prepare the chicken wings by cutting off the wing tips and discarding (or freezing for chicken stock). Divide the drumettes from the win-gettes by cutting through the joint. Place the chicken wing pieces in the bowl with the spice mix. Toss or shake well to coat.
2. Preheat the toaster oven to 400°F.
3. Spray the wings lightly with the vegetable oil and air-fry the wings in two batches for 10 minutes per batch. When both batches are done, toss all the wings back into the air fryer oven for another 2 minutes to heat through and finish cooking.
4. While the wings are air-frying, combine the chopped chipotle peppers, cherry preserves and ketchup in a bowl.
5. Remove the wings from the air fryer oven, toss them in the cherry chipotle BBQ sauce and serve with napkins!

Sheet Pan Chicken Nachos

Servings: 2
Cooking Time: 20 Minutes
Ingredients:
- Tortilla chips
- 2 cups shredded chicken
- 1 3/4 cup Fresh & Spicy Salsa, divided
- 1 cup drained black beans
- 1 package (2 cups) shredded colby and Monterey Jack cheese, divided
- 1 fresh jalapeno, sliced
- Guacamole

Directions:
1. Heat toaster oven to 350°F. Line a toaster oven pan with aluminum foil and spray foil with nonstick cooking spray.
2. Arrange tortilla chips in an even layer in pan.
3. In a small bowl, combine chicken, 3/4 cup salsa, black beans and 1 cup shredded cheese.
4. Spoon chicken mixture over chips. Top with remaining cheese and jalapeno slices.
5. Bake until cheese is melted and mixture is heated through, 18 to 20 minutes
6. Serve with remaining salsa and guacamole.

Pork Pot Stickers With Yum Yum Sauce

Servings: 48
Cooking Time: 8 Minutes
Ingredients:
- 1 pound ground pork
- 2 cups shredded green cabbage
- ¼ cup shredded carrot
- ½ cup finely chopped water chestnuts
- 2 teaspoons minced fresh ginger
- ¼ cup hoisin sauce
- 2 tablespoons soy sauce
- 1 tablespoon sesame oil
- freshly ground black pepper
- 3 scallions, minced
- 48 round dumpling wrappers (or wonton wrappers with the corners cut off to make them round)
- 1 tablespoon vegetable oil
- soy sauce, for serving
- Yum Yum Sauce:
- 1½ cups mayonnaise
- 2 tablespoons sugar
- 3 tablespoons rice vinegar
- 1 teaspoon soy sauce
- 2 tablespoons ketchup
- 1½ teaspoons paprika
- ¼ teaspoon ground cayenne pepper
- ¼ teaspoon garlic powder

Directions:
1. Preheat a large sauté pan over medium-high heat. Add the ground pork and brown for a few minutes. Remove the cooked pork to a bowl using a slotted spoon and discard the fat from the pan. Return the cooked pork to the sauté pan and add the cabbage, carrots and water chestnuts. Sauté for a minute and then add the fresh ginger, hoisin sauce, soy sauce, sesame oil, and freshly ground black pepper. Sauté for a few more minutes, just until cabbage and carrots are

soft. Then stir in the scallions and transfer the pork filling to a bowl to cool.

2. Make the pot stickers in batches of 1 Place 12 dumpling wrappers on a flat surface. Brush a little water around the perimeter of the wrappers. Place a rounded teaspoon of the filling into the center of each wrapper. Fold the wrapper over the filling, bringing the edges together to form a half moon, sealing the edges shut. Brush a little more water on the top surface of the sealed edge of the pot sticker. Make pleats in the dough around the sealed edge by pinching the dough and folding the edge over on itself. You should have about 5 to 6 pleats in the dough. Repeat this three times until you have 48 pot stickers. Freeze the pot stickers for 2 hours (or as long as 3 weeks in an airtight container).

3. Preheat the toaster oven to 400°F.

4. Air-fry the pot stickers in batches of 16. Brush or spray the pot stickers with vegetable oil just before putting them in the air fryer oven. Air-fry for 8 minutes, turning the pot stickers once or twice during the cooking process.

5. While the pot stickers are cooking, combine all the ingredients for the Yum Yum sauce in a bowl. Serve the pot stickers warm with the Yum Yum sauce and soy sauce for dipping.

Smoked Salmon Puffs

Servings: 2
Cooking Time: 8 Minutes
Ingredients:
- Two quarters of one thawed sheet (that is, a half of the sheet; wrap and refreeze the remainder) A 17.25-ounce box frozen puff pastry
- 4 ½-ounce smoked salmon slices
- 2 tablespoons Softened regular or low-fat cream cheese (not fat-free)
- Up to 2 teaspoons Drained and rinsed capers, minced
- Up to 2 teaspoons Minced red onion
- 1 Large egg white
- 1 tablespoon Water

Directions:
1. Preheat the toaster oven to 400°F.
2. For a small air fryer oven, roll the piece of puff pastry into a 6 x 6-inch square on a clean, dry work surface.
3. For a medium or larger air fryer oven, roll each piece of puff pastry into a 6 x 6-inch square.
4. Set 2 salmon slices on the diagonal, corner to corner, on each rolled-out sheet. Smear the salmon with cream cheese, then sprinkle with capers and red onion. Fold the sheet closed by picking up one corner that does not have an edge of salmon near it and folding the dough across the salmon to its opposite corner. Seal the edges closed by pressing the tines of a flatware fork into them.
5. Whisk the egg white and water in a small bowl until uniform. Brush this mixture over the top(s) of the packet(s).
6. Set the packet(s) in the air fryer oven (if you're working with more than one, they cannot touch). Air-fry undisturbed for 8 minutes, or until golden brown and flaky.
7. Use a nonstick-safe spatula to transfer the packet(s) to a wire rack. Cool for 5 minutes before serving.

Savory Sausage Balls

Servings: 10
Cooking Time: 8 Minutes
Ingredients:
- 2 cups all-purpose flour
- 1 tablespoon baking powder
- ½ teaspoon garlic powder
- ¼ teaspoon onion powder
- ½ teaspoon salt
- 3 tablespoons milk
- 2½ cups grated pepper jack cheese
- 1 pound fresh sausage, casing removed

Directions:
1. Preheat the toaster oven to 370°F.
2. In a large bowl, whisk together the flour, baking powder, garlic powder, onion powder, and salt. Add in the milk, grated cheese, and sausage.
3. Using a tablespoon, scoop out the sausage and roll it between your hands to form a rounded ball. You should end up with approximately 32 balls. Place them in the air fryer oven in a single layer and working in batches as necessary.
4. Air-fry for 8 minutes, or until the outer coating turns light brown.
5. Carefully remove, repeating with the remaining sausage balls.

Buffalo Cauliflower

Servings: 4
Cooking Time: 30 Minutes
Ingredients:
- 1 cup gluten free panko breadcrumbs
- 1 teaspoon ground paprika
- ½ teaspoon garlic powder
- ¼ teaspoon onion powder
- ½ teaspoon cayenne pepper
- 1 teaspoon kosher salt
- ½ teaspoon freshly ground black pepper
- 1 head cauliflower, cut into florets

- 2 tablespoons cornstarch
- 3 eggs, beaten
- Cooking spray
- ¾ cup buffalo wing sauce, warm
- Ranch or bleu cheese dressing, for serving

Directions:
1. Combine panko breadcrumbs, paprika, garlic powder, onion powder, cayenne pepper, kosher salt, and black pepper in a large bowl. Set aside.
2. Toss together cauliflower and cornstarch until the cauliflower is lightly coated.
3. Shake any excess cornstarch off the cauliflower, then dip into beaten eggs, then into seasoned breadcrumbs.
4. Spray the breaded cauliflower with cooking spray, place into the fry basket, and set aside. You may need to work in batches.
5. Preheat the toaster oven to 380°F.
6. Insert the fry basket with the cauliflower at top position in the preheated oven.
7. Select the Air Fry and Shake functions, adjust time to 30 minutes, and press Start/Pause.
8. Flip the cauliflower halfway through cooking. The Shake Reminder will let you know when.
9. Remove when done and place into a large bowl.
10. Toss the cauliflower in the buffalo wing sauce until they are well coated.
11. Serve with a side of ranch or blue cheese dressing.

Rumaki

Servings: 24
Cooking Time: 12 Minutes
Ingredients:
- 10 ounces raw chicken livers
- 1 can sliced water chestnuts, drained
- ¼ cup low-sodium teriyaki sauce
- 12 slices turkey bacon
- toothpicks

Directions:
1. Cut livers into 1½-inch pieces, trimming out tough veins as you slice.
2. Place livers, water chestnuts, and teriyaki sauce in small container with lid. If needed, add another tablespoon of teriyaki sauce to make sure livers are covered. Refrigerate for 1 hour.
3. When ready to cook, cut bacon slices in half crosswise.
4. Wrap 1 piece of liver and 1 slice of water chestnut in each bacon strip. Secure with toothpick.
5. When you have wrapped half of the livers, place them in the air fryer oven in a single layer.
6. Air-fry at 390°F for 12 minutes, until liver is done and bacon is crispy.
7. While first batch cooks, wrap the remaining livers. Repeat step 6 to cook your second batch.

Thick-crust Pepperoni Pizza

Servings: 2
Cooking Time: 10 Minutes
Ingredients:
- 10 ounces Purchased fresh pizza dough (not a prebaked crust)
- Olive oil spray
- ¼ cup Purchased pizza sauce
- 10 slices Sliced pepperoni
- ⅓ cup Purchased shredded Italian 3- or 4-cheese blend

Directions:
1. Preheat the toaster oven to 400°F.
2. Generously coat the inside of a 6-inch round cake pan for a small air fryer oven, a 7-inch round cake pan for a medium air fryer oven, or an 8-inch round cake pan for a large model with olive oil spray.
3. Set the dough in the pan and press it to fill the bottom in an even, thick layer. Spread the sauce over the dough, then top with the pepperoni and cheese.
4. When the machine is at temperature, set the pan in the air fryer oven and air-fry undisturbed for 10 minutes, or until puffed, brown, and bubbling.
5. Use kitchen tongs to transfer the cake pan to a wire rack. Cool for only a minute or so. Use a spatula to loosen the pizza from the pan and lift it out and onto the rack. Continue cooling for a few minutes before cutting into wedges to serve.

Fried Wontons

Servings: 24
Cooking Time: 6 Minutes
Ingredients:
- 6 ounces Lean ground beef, pork, or turkey
- 1 tablespoon Regular or reduced-sodium soy sauce or tamari sauce
- 1½ teaspoons Minced garlic
- ¾ teaspoon Ground dried ginger
- ½ teaspoon Ground white pepper
- 24 Wonton wrappers (thawed, if necessary)
- Vegetable oil spray

Directions:
1. Preheat the toaster oven to 350°F.

2. Stir the ground meat, soy or tamari sauce, garlic, ginger, and white pepper in a bowl until the spices are uniformly distributed in the mixture.

3. Set a small bowl of water on a clean, dry surface or next to a clean, dry cutting board. Set one wonton wrapper on the surface. Dip your clean finger in the water, then run it along the edges of the wrapper. Set 1 teaspoon of the ground meat mixture in the center of the wrapper. Fold it over, corner to corner, to create a filled triangle. Press to seal the edges, then pull the corners on the longest side up and together over the filling to create the classic wonton shape. Press the corners together to seal. Set aside and continue filling and making more filled wontons.

4. Generously coat the filled wontons on all sides with vegetable oil spray. Arrange them in the air fryer oven in one layer and air-fry for 6 minutes, at the 2- and 4-minute marks to rearrange the wontons (but always making sure they're still in one layer), until golden brown and crisp.

5. Pour the wontons in the pan onto a wire rack or even into a serving bowl. Cool for 2 or 3 minutes (but not much longer) and serve hot.

Roasted Brussels Sprouts Au Gratin

Servings: 6
Cooking Time: 36 Minutes
Ingredients:
- 1 pound fresh Brussels sprouts, trimmed and halved
- 2 tablespoons olive oil
- Kosher salt and freshly ground black pepper
- Nonstick cooking spray
- 2 slices bacon, cooked until crisp and crumbled
- 3 tablespoons unsalted butter
- 2 tablespoons all-purpose flour
- 1 cup whole milk
- 1 cup shredded Gruyère or Swiss cheese
- ½ teaspoon dried thyme leaves
- ¼ cup panko bread crumbs
- ¼ cup shredded Parmesan cheese

Directions:
1. Preheat the toaster oven to 450°F.
2. Toss the Brussels sprouts with the olive oil in a large bowl. Season with salt and pepper. Arrange the Brussels sprouts in a single layer in a 12 x 12-inch baking pan. Bake uncovered for 10 minutes. Stir and bake for an additional 8 to 10 minutes, or until the edges are beginning to char and the Brussels sprouts are just tender. Remove from the oven.
3. Reduce the toaster oven to 375°F. Spray a 1 ½-quart casserole dish or an 8 x 8-inch square baking pan with nonstick cooking spray. Place the Brussels sprouts in the casserole dish. Sprinkle with the crisp bacon.
4. Melt 2 tablespoons of the butter in a small saucepan over medium heat. Stir in the flour, blending until smooth and cook, stirring constantly, for 1 minute. Gradually add the milk and cook, stirring constantly, until the mixture is bubbly and thickened. Season with salt and pepper. Stir in the cheese and thyme and cook, stirring until melted. Pour the sauce over the Brussels sprouts.
5. Melt the remaining tablespoon of butter. Stir in the panko bread crumbs and Parmesan cheese. Sprinkle the bread crumb mixture over the casserole. Bake, uncovered, for 15 minutes or until golden brown and the edges are bubbling.

Simple Holiday Stuffing

Servings: 4
Cooking Time: 120 Minutes
Ingredients:
- 12 ounces hearty white sandwich bread, cut into ½-inch pieces (8 cups)
- 1 onion, chopped fine
- 1 celery rib, chopped fine
- 1 tablespoon unsalted butter, plus 5 tablespoons, melted
- 1 tablespoon minced fresh thyme or 1 teaspoon dried
- 2 teaspoons minced fresh sage or ½ teaspoon dried
- ¾ teaspoon table salt
- ¼ teaspoon pepper
- 1¼ cups chicken broth

Directions:
1. Adjust toaster oven rack to middle position and preheat the toaster oven to 300 degrees. Spread bread into even layer on small rimmed baking sheet and bake until light golden brown, 35 to 45 minutes, tossing halfway through baking. Let bread cool completely on sheet.
2. Increase oven temperature to 375 degrees. Microwave onion, celery, 1 tablespoon butter, thyme, sage, salt, and pepper in covered large bowl, stirring occasionally, until vegetables are softened, 2 to 4 minutes.
3. Stir in broth, then add bread and toss to combine. Let mixture sit for 10 minutes, then toss mixture again until broth is fully absorbed. Transfer bread mixture to 8-inch square baking dish or pan and distribute evenly but do not pack down. (Stuffing can be covered and refrigerated for up to 24 hours; increase covered baking time to 15 minutes.)
4. Drizzle melted butter evenly over top of stuffing. Cover dish tightly with aluminum foil and bake for 10 minutes. Uncover and continue to bake until top is golden brown and

crisp, 15 to 25 minutes. Transfer dish to wire rack and let cool for 10 minutes. Serve.

Garlic Parmesan Kale Chips

Servings: 2
Cooking Time: 6 Minutes
Ingredients:
- 16 large kale leaves, washed and thick stems removed
- 1 tablespoon avocado oil
- ½ teaspoon garlic powder
- 1 teaspoon soy sauce or tamari
- ¼ cup grated Parmesan cheese

Directions:
1. Preheat the toaster oven to 370°F.
2. Make a stack of kale leaves and cut them into 4 pieces.
3. Place the kale pieces into a large bowl. Drizzle the avocado oil onto the kale and rub to coat. Add the garlic powder, soy sauce or tamari, and cheese, tossing to coat.
4. Pour the chips into the air fryer oven and air-fry for 6 minutes, checking for crispness every minute. When done cooking, pour the kale chips onto paper towels and cool at least 5 minutes before serving.

Creamy Crab Dip

Servings: 4
Cooking Time: 20 Minutes
Ingredients:
- 6 ounces cream cheese, room temperature
- ½ cup sour cream
- ½ cup grated Parmesan cheese
- ½ cup shredded cheddar cheese
- Juice of ½ lemon
- ½ teaspoon garlic powder
- Dash hot sauce
- 1 (6-ounce) can crab meat, drained
- Sea salt, for seasoning
- Freshly ground black pepper, for seasoning
- Baguette, cut into ¼-inch-wide rounds, for serving

Directions:
1. Place the rack on position 1 and preheat the toaster oven on BAKE to 400°F for 5 minutes.
2. In a medium bowl, stir the cream cheese, sour cream, Parmesan, cheddar, lemon juice, garlic powder, and hot sauce until well blended.
3. Fold in the crab and season with salt and pepper.
4. Spoon the dip into a shallow heatproof 4-cup bowl.
5. Bake for 20 minutes until golden and bubbling.
6. Serve with baguette slices.

Classic Potato Chips

Servings: 4
Cooking Time: 8 Minutes
Ingredients:
- 2 medium russet potatoes, washed
- 2 cups filtered water
- 1 tablespoon avocado oil
- ½ teaspoon salt

Directions:
1. Using a mandolin, slice the potatoes into ⅛-inch-thick pieces.
2. Pour the water into a large bowl. Place the potatoes in the bowl and soak for at least 30 minutes.
3. Preheat the toaster oven to 350°F.
4. Drain the water and pat the potatoes dry with a paper towel or kitchen cloth. Toss with avocado oil and salt. Liberally spray the air fryer oven with olive oil mist.
5. Set the potatoes inside the air fryer oven, separating them so they're not on top of each other. Air-fry for 10 minutes, or until browned.
6. Remove and let cool a few minutes prior to serving. Repeat until all the chips are cooked.

Brazilian Cheese Bread (pão De Queijo)

Servings: 8
Cooking Time: 18 Minutes
Ingredients:
- 1 large egg, room temperature
- ⅓ cup olive oil
- ⅔ cups whole milk 1½ cups tapioca flour
- ½ cup feta cheese
- ¼ cup Parmesan cheese
- 1 teaspoon kosher salt
- ¼ teaspoon garlic powder
- Cooking spray

Directions:
1. Blend the egg, olive oil, milk, tapioca flour, feta, Parmesan, salt, and garlic powder in a stand mixer until smooth.
2. Spray the mini muffin pan with cooking spray.
3. Pour the batter into the muffin cups so they are ¾ full.
4. .Preheat the toaster oven to 380°F.
5. Place the muffin pan on the wire rack, then insert rack at mid position in the preheated oven.
6. Select the Bake function, adjust time to 18 minutes, and press Start/Pause.

7. Remove when done, then carefully pop the bread from the mini muffin tin and serve.

Barbecue Chicken Nachos

Servings: 3
Cooking Time: 5 Minutes
Ingredients:
- 3 heaping cups (a little more than 3 ounces) Corn tortilla chips (gluten-free, if a concern)
- ¾ cup Shredded deboned and skinned rotisserie chicken meat (gluten-free, if a concern)
- 3 tablespoons Canned black beans, drained and rinsed
- 9 rings Pickled jalapeño slices
- 4 Small pickled cocktail onions, halved
- 3 tablespoons Barbecue sauce (any sort)
- ¾ cup (about 3 ounces) Shredded Cheddar cheese

Directions:
1. Preheat the toaster oven to 400°F.
2. Cut a circle of parchment paper to line a 6-inch round cake pan for a small air fryer oven, a 7-inch round cake pan for a medium air fryer oven, or an 8-inch round cake pan for a large machine.
3. Fill the pan with an even layer of about two-thirds of the chips. Sprinkle the chicken evenly over the chips. Set the pan in the air fryer oven and air-fry undisturbed for 2 minutes.
4. Remove the pan from the machine. Scatter the beans, jalapeño rings, and pickled onion halves over the chicken. Drizzle the barbecue sauce over everything, then sprinkle the cheese on top.
5. Return the pan to the machine and air-fry undisturbed for 3 minutes, or until the cheese has melted and is bubbly. Remove the pan from the machine and cool for a couple of minutes before serving.

Cinnamon Apple Chips

Servings: 4
Cooking Time: 480 Minutes
Ingredients:
- 1 apple
- 1 tablespoon lemon juice
- ¼ teaspoon cinnamon

Directions:
1. Slice the apple into ⅛-inch-thick slices, preferably by using a mandoline slicer.
2. Place slices in a bowl of water mixed with the lemon juice to prevent browning. Remove after 2 minutes and dry thoroughly with paper towels.
3. Sprinkle the apple slices with cinnamon and place on the food tray.
4. Insert the food tray at mid position in the preheated oven.
5. Preheat the toaster oven to 130°F.
6. Remove when apple chips are crispy.

Hot Mexican Bean Dip

Servings: 8-10
Cooking Time: 15 Minutes
Ingredients:
- 2 cans (15 oz. each) black beans, well-drained
- 8 oz. Monterey Jack cheese or Cheddar cheese, shredded
- 1/2 cup sour cream
- 1/2 cup salsa
- 1 teaspoon hot pepper sauce

Directions:
1. Preheat the toaster oven to 350°F.
2. Place black beans, half of the cheese, sour cream, salsa and hot pepper sauce in food processor bowl. Process until slightly chunky.
3. Spoon into shallow 1-quart casserole dish.
4. Sprinkle remaining cheese on top.
5. Bake 15 minutes or until bubbly.
6. Top with additional cheese, salsa and sour cream, if desired. Serve with tortilla chips.

Stuffed Baby Bella Caps

Servings: 16
Cooking Time: 12 Minutes
Ingredients:
- 16 fresh, small Baby Bella mushrooms
- 2 green onions
- 4 ounces mozzarella cheese
- ½ cup diced ham
- 2 tablespoons breadcrumbs
- ½ teaspoon garlic powder
- ¼ teaspoon ground oregano
- ¼ teaspoon ground black pepper
- 1 to 2 teaspoons olive oil

Directions:
1. Remove stems and wash mushroom caps.
2. Cut green onions and cheese in small pieces and place in food processor.
3. Add ham, breadcrumbs, garlic powder, oregano, and pepper and mince ingredients.

4. With food processor running, dribble in just enough olive oil to make a thick paste.
5. Divide stuffing among mushroom caps and pack down lightly.
6. Place stuffed mushrooms in air fryer oven in single layer and air-fry at 390°F for 12 minutes or until tops are golden brown and mushrooms are tender.
7. Repeat step 6 to cook remaining mushrooms.

Crab Rangoon Dip With Wonton Chips

Servings: 6
Cooking Time: 18 Minutes
Ingredients:
- Wonton Chips:
- 1 (12-ounce) package wonton wrappers
- vegetable oil
- sea salt
- Crab Rangoon Dip:
- 8 ounces cream cheese, softened
- ¾ cup sour cream
- 1 teaspoon Worcestershire sauce
- 1½ teaspoons soy sauce
- 1 teaspoon sesame oil
- ⅛ teaspoon ground cayenne pepper
- ¼ teaspoon salt
- freshly ground black pepper
- 8 ounces cooked crabmeat
- 1 cup grated white Cheddar cheese
- ⅓ cup chopped scallions
- paprika (for garnish)

Directions:
1. Cut the wonton wrappers in half diagonally to form triangles. Working in batches, lay the wonton triangles on a flat surface and brush or spray both sides with vegetable oil.
2. Preheat the toaster oven to 370°F.
3. Place about 10 to 12 wonton triangles in the air fryer oven, letting them overlap slightly. Air-fry for just 2 minutes. Transfer the wonton chips to a large bowl and season immediately with sea salt. (You'll hear the chips start to spin around in the air fryer oven when they are almost done.) Repeat with the rest of wontons (keeping those fishing hands at bay!).
4. To make the dip, combine the cream cheese, sour cream, Worcestershire sauce, soy sauce, sesame oil, cayenne pepper, salt, and freshly ground black pepper in a bowl. Mix well and then fold in the crabmeat, Cheddar cheese, and scallions.
5. Transfer the dip to a 7-inch ceramic baking pan or shallow casserole dish. Sprinkle paprika on top and cover the dish with aluminum foil. Lower the dish into the air fryer oven using a sling made of aluminum foil (fold a piece of aluminum foil into a strip about 2-inches wide by 24-inches long). Air-fry for 11 minutes. Remove the aluminum foil and air-fry for another 5 minutes to finish cooking and brown the top. Serve hot with the wonton chips.

Warm And Salty Edamame

Servings: 4
Cooking Time: 10 Minutes
Ingredients:
- 1 pound Unshelled edamame
- Vegetable oil spray
- ¾ teaspoon Coarse sea salt or kosher salt

Directions:
1. Preheat the toaster oven to 400°F.
2. Place the edamame in a large bowl and lightly coat them with vegetable oil spray. Toss well, spray again, and toss until they are evenly coated.
3. When the machine is at temperature, pour the edamame into the air fryer oven and air-fry, tossing the pan quite often to rearrange the edamame, for 7 minutes, or until warm and aromatic. (Air-fry for 10 minutes if the edamame were frozen and not thawed.)
4. Pour the edamame into a bowl and sprinkle the salt on top. Toss well, then set aside for a couple of minutes before serving with an empty bowl on the side for the pods.

Sweet Or Savory Baked Sweet Potatoes

Servings: 6
Cooking Time: 60 Minutes
Ingredients:
- 6 medium sweet potatoes, scrubbed
- Cinnamon Butter
- Salted Garlic Herb Butter

Directions:
1. Preheat the toaster oven to 450ºF. Line a 15x10-inch baking pan with foil.
2. Prick each sweet potato several times with a fork and place on baking pan.
3. Bake 45 to 1 hour or until fork tender. Serve with Cinnamon Butter or Salted Garlic Herb Butter.

Cinnamon Pita Chips

Servings: 4
Cooking Time: 6 Minutes
Ingredients:
- 2 tablespoons sugar
- 2 teaspoons cinnamon
- 2 whole 6-inch pitas, whole grain or white
- oil for misting or cooking spray

Directions:
1. Mix sugar and cinnamon together.
2. Cut each pita in half and each half into 4 wedges. Break apart each wedge at the fold.
3. Mist one side of pita wedges with oil or cooking spray. Sprinkle them all with half of the cinnamon sugar.
4. Turn the wedges over, mist the other side with oil or cooking spray, and sprinkle with the remaining cinnamon sugar.
5. Place pita wedges in air fryer oven and air-fry at 330°F for 2 minutes.
6. Cook 2 more minutes. If needed cook 2 more minutes, until crisp. Watch carefully because at this point they will cook very quickly.

Turkey Burger Sliders

Servings: 8
Cooking Time: 7 Minutes
Ingredients:
- 1 pound ground turkey
- ¼ teaspoon curry powder
- 1 teaspoon Hoisin sauce
- ½ teaspoon salt
- 8 slider buns
- ½ cup slivered red onions
- ½ cup slivered green or red bell pepper
- ½ cup fresh chopped pineapple (or pineapple tidbits from kids' fruit cups, drained)
- light cream cheese, softened

Directions:
1. Combine turkey, curry powder, Hoisin sauce, and salt and mix together well.
2. Shape turkey mixture into 8 small patties.
3. Place patties in air fryer oven and air-fry at 360°F for 7 minutes, until patties are well done and juices run clear.
4. Place each patty on the bottom half of a slider bun and top with onions, peppers, and pineapple. Spread the remaining bun halves with cream cheese to taste, place on top, and serve.

Ham And Cheese Palmiers

Servings: 30
Cooking Time: 60 Minutes
Ingredients:
- 1 (9½ by 9-inch) sheet puff pastry, thawed
- 2 tablespoons Dijon mustard
- 2 teaspoons minced fresh thyme
- 2 ounces Parmesan cheese, grated (1 cup)
- 4 ounces thinly sliced deli ham

Directions:
1. Roll puff pastry into 12-inch square on lightly floured counter. Brush evenly with mustard; sprinkle with thyme and Parmesan; pressing gently to adhere, and lay ham evenly over top. Roll up opposite sides of pastry until they meet in middle. Wrap pastry log in plastic wrap and refrigerate until firm, about 1 hour.
2. Adjust toaster oven rack to middle position, select air-fry or convection setting, and preheat the toaster oven to 400 degrees. Line large and small rimmed baking sheets with parchment paper. Using sharp knife, trim ends of log, then slice into ⅓-inch-thick pieces. Space desired number of palmiers at least 1 inch apart on prepared small sheet; space remaining palmiers evenly on prepared large sheet. Re-shape palmiers as needed.
3. Bake small sheet of palmiers until golden brown and crisp, 15 to 25 minutes. Transfer palmiers to wire rack and let cool for 15 minutes before serving. (Palmiers can be held at room temperature for up to 6 hours before serving.)
4. Freeze remaining large sheet of palmiers until firm, about 1 hour. Transfer palmiers to 1-gallon zipper-lock bag and freeze for up to 1 month. Cook frozen palmiers as directed; do not thaw

Beef Pork And Lamb

Pretzel-coated Pork Tenderloin

Servings: 4
Cooking Time: 10 Minutes
Ingredients:
- 1 Large egg white(s)
- 2 teaspoons Dijon mustard (gluten-free, if a concern)
- 1½ cups (about 6 ounces) Crushed pretzel crumbs
- 1 pound (4 sections) Pork tenderloin, cut into ¼-pound (4-ounce) sections
- Vegetable oil spray

Directions:
1. Preheat the toaster oven to 350°F .
2. Set up and fill two shallow soup plates or small pie plates on your counter: one for the egg white(s), whisked with the mustard until foamy; and one for the pretzel crumbs.
3. Dip a section of pork tenderloin in the egg white mixture and turn it to coat well, even on the ends. Let any excess egg white mixture slip back into the rest, then set the pork in the pretzel crumbs. Roll it several times, pressing gently, until the pork is evenly coated, even on the ends. Generously coat the pork section with vegetable oil spray, set it aside, and continue coating and spraying the remaining sections.
4. Set the pork sections in the air fryer oven with at least ¼ inch between them. Air-fry undisturbed for 10 minutes, or until an instant-read meat thermometer inserted into the center of one section registers 145°F.
5. Use kitchen tongs to transfer the pieces to a wire rack. Cool for 3 to 5 minutes before serving.

Pork Cutlets With Almond-lemon Crust

Servings: 3
Cooking Time: 14 Minutes
Ingredients:
- ¾ cup Almond flour
- ¾ cup Plain dried bread crumbs (gluten-free, if a concern)
- 1½ teaspoons Finely grated lemon zest
- 1¼ teaspoons Table salt
- ¾ teaspoon Garlic powder
- ¾ teaspoon Dried oregano
- 1 Large egg white(s)
- 2 tablespoons Water
- 3 6-ounce center-cut boneless pork loin chops (about ¾ inch thick)
- Olive oil spray

Directions:
1. Preheat the toaster oven to 375°F .
2. Mix the almond flour, bread crumbs, lemon zest, salt, garlic powder, and dried oregano in a large bowl until well combined.
3. Whisk the egg white(s) and water in a shallow soup plate or small pie plate until uniform.
4. Dip a chop in the egg white mixture, turning it to coat all sides, even the ends. Let any excess egg white mixture slip back into the rest, then set it in the almond flour mixture. Turn it several times, pressing gently to coat it evenly. Generously coat the chop with olive oil spray, then set aside to dip and coat the remaining chop(s).
5. Set the chops in the air fryer oven with as much air space between them as possible. Air-fry undisturbed for 12 minutes, or until browned and crunchy. You may need to add 2 minutes to the cooking time if the machine is at 360°F.
6. Use kitchen tongs to transfer the chops to a wire rack. Cool for a few minutes before serving.

Spicy Flank Steak With Fresh Tomato-corn Salsa

Servings: 4
Cooking Time: 20 Minutes
Ingredients:
- 2 large tomatoes, chopped
- 1 cup fresh (or canned) corn
- ½ English cucumber, chopped
- ¼ red onion, chopped
- 1 tablespoon jalapeño pepper, chopped
- 1 tablespoon fresh cilantro, chopped
- Sea salt, for seasoning
- Freshly ground black pepper, for seasoning
- 1 pound extra-lean beef flank steak, trimmed of fat
- Olive oil, for brushing
- 1 teaspoon garlic powder
- 1 teaspoon chili powder

Directions:
1. Preheat the toaster oven to 450°F on BROIL for 5 minutes.

2. In a small bowl, stir the tomato, corn, cucumber, onion, jalapeño, and cilantro, and season with salt and pepper.
3. Rub the steak all over with the oil and then season with garlic powder, chili powder, salt, and pepper.
4. Place the air-fryer basket in the baking tray and arrange the steak in the basket.
5. In position 2, broil for 20 minutes, turning halfway through, until browned and with an internal temperature of 140°F, for medium-rare.
6. Let the steak rest for 10 minutes and then cut it very thinly against the grain.
7. Serve with the salsa.

Beer-baked Pork Tenderloin

Servings: 4
Cooking Time: 40 Minutes
Ingredients:
- 1 pound lean pork tenderloin, fat trimmed off
- 3 garlic cloves, minced
- 1 cup good-quality dark ale or beer
- 2 bay leaves
- Salt and freshly cracked black pepper
- Spiced apple slices

Directions:
1. Preheat the toaster oven to 400° F.
2. Place the tenderloin in an 8½ × 8½ × 4-inch ovenproof baking dish. Sprinkle the minced garlic over the pork, pour over the beer, add the bay leaves, and season to taste with the salt and pepper. Cover with aluminum foil.
3. BAKE, covered, for 40 minutes, or until the meat is tender. Discard the bay leaves and serve sliced with the liquid. Garnish with the spiced apple slices.

Skirt Steak Fajitas

Servings: 4
Cooking Time: 30 Minutes
Ingredients:
- 2 tablespoons olive oil
- ¼ cup lime juice
- 1 clove garlic, minced
- ½ teaspoon ground cumin
- ½ teaspoon hot sauce
- ½ teaspoon salt
- 2 tablespoons chopped fresh cilantro
- 1 pound skirt steak
- 1 onion, sliced
- 1 teaspoon chili powder
- 1 red pepper, sliced
- 1 green pepper, sliced
- salt and freshly ground black pepper
- 8 flour tortillas
- shredded lettuce, crumbled Queso Fresco (or grated Cheddar cheese), sliced black olives, diced tomatoes, sour cream and guacamole for serving

Directions:
1. Combine the olive oil, lime juice, garlic, cumin, hot sauce, salt and cilantro in a shallow dish. Add the skirt steak and turn it over several times to coat all sides. Pierce the steak with a needle-style meat tenderizer or paring knife. Marinate the steak in the refrigerator for at least 3 hours, or overnight. When you are ready to cook, remove the steak from the refrigerator and let it sit at room temperature for 30 minutes.
2. Preheat the toaster oven to 400°F.
3. Toss the onion slices with the chili powder and a little olive oil and transfer them to the air fryer oven. Air-fry at 400°F for 5 minutes. Add the red and green peppers to the air fryer oven with the onions, season with salt and pepper and air-fry for 8 more minutes, until the onions and peppers are soft. Transfer the vegetables to a dish and cover with aluminum foil to keep warm.
4. Place the skirt steak in the air fryer oven and pour the marinade over the top. Air-fry at 400°F for 12 minutes. Flip the steak over and air-fry at 400°F for an additional 5 minutes. (The time needed for your steak will depend on the thickness of the skirt steak. 17 minutes should bring your steak to roughly medium.) Transfer the cooked steak to a cutting board and let the steak rest for a few minutes. If the peppers and onions need to be heated, return them to the air fryer oven for just 1 to 2 minutes.
5. Thinly slice the steak at an angle, cutting against the grain of the steak. Serve the steak with the onions and peppers, the warm tortillas and the fajita toppings on the side so that everyone can make their own fajita.

Spanish Pork Skewers

Servings: 4
Cooking Time: 16 Minutes
Ingredients:
- 1 pound pork tenderloin, cut into ¾- to 1-inch cubes
- 2 tablespoons olive oil
- 1 teaspoon ground cumin
- ½ teaspoon smoked paprika
- ½ teaspoon dried thyme leaves
- ½ teaspoon kosher salt, plus more for seasoning
- ⅛ teaspoon red pepper flakes
- 2 cloves garlic, minced

- 1 red bell pepper, cut into ¾- to 1-inch squares
- 1 small red onion, cut into ¾- to 1-inch wedges
- Freshly ground black pepper
- Nonstick cooking spray
- 2 tablespoons unsalted butter
- 1 tablespoon sherry or balsamic vinegar
- 1 teaspoon packed dark brown sugar

Directions:
1. Place the pork cubes in a medium bowl. Drizzle 1 tablespoon of oil over the pork. Stir the cumin, paprika, thyme, ½ teaspoon salt, the pepper flakes, and garlic in a small bowl. Sprinkle the seasonings over the pork. Stir to coat the pork evenly. Cover and refrigerate for at least 4 hours or up to overnight.
2. Place the bell pepper and onion pieces in a medium bowl. Drizzle with the remaining tablespoon olive oil and season with salt and pepper. Toss to coat evenly.
3. Alternately thread the pork and vegetables onto skewers. Spray a 12 x 12-inch baking pan with nonstick cooking spray. Place the filled skewers on the prepared pan. Place the pan in the toaster oven, positioning the skewers about 3 to 4 inches below the heating element. (Depending on your oven, you may need to set the rack to the middle position.)
4. Set the toaster oven on broil. Broil for 10 minutes. Turn the skewers. Broil for an additional 5 minutes, or until the vegetables are tender and a meat thermometer registers 145°F. Do not overcook.
5. Meanwhile, combine the butter, vinegar, and brown sugar in a small, glass, microwave-safe bowl. Season with salt and pepper. Microwave on High (100 percent) power for 45 seconds or until the butter melts and the mixture begins to bubble. Stir to dissolve the sugar.
6. Lightly brush the vinegar mixture over the skewers. Broil for 1 minute or until the skewers are browned.

Albóndigas

Servings: 4
Cooking Time: 15 Minutes
Ingredients:
- 1 pound Lean ground pork
- 3 tablespoons Very finely chopped trimmed scallions
- 3 tablespoons Finely chopped fresh cilantro leaves
- 3 tablespoons Plain panko bread crumbs (gluten-free, if a concern)
- 3 tablespoons Dry white wine, dry sherry, or unsweetened apple juice
- 1½ teaspoons Minced garlic
- 1¼ teaspoons Mild smoked paprika
- ¾ teaspoon Dried oregano
- ¾ teaspoon Table salt
- ¼ teaspoon Ground black pepper
- Olive oil spray

Directions:
1. Preheat the toaster oven to 400°F.
2. Mix the ground pork, scallions, cilantro, bread crumbs, wine or its substitute, garlic, smoked paprika, oregano, salt, and pepper in a bowl until the herbs and spices are evenly distributed in the mixture.
3. Lightly coat your clean hands with olive oil spray, then form the ground pork mixture into balls, using 2 tablespoons for each one. Spray your hands frequently so that the meat mixture doesn't stick.
4. Set the balls in the air fryer oven so that they're not touching, even if they're close together. Air-fry undisturbed for 15 minutes, or until well browned and an instant-read meat thermometer inserted into one or two balls registers 165°F.
5. Use a nonstick-safe spatula and kitchen tongs for balance to gently transfer the fragile balls to a wire rack to cool for 5 minutes before serving.

Calf's Liver

Servings: 4
Cooking Time: 5 Minutes
Ingredients:
- 1 pound sliced calf's liver
- salt and pepper
- 2 eggs
- 2 tablespoons milk
- ½ cup whole wheat flour
- 1½ cups panko breadcrumbs
- ½ cup plain breadcrumbs
- ½ teaspoon salt
- ¼ teaspoon pepper
- oil for misting or cooking spray

Directions:
1. Cut liver slices crosswise into strips about ½-inch wide. Sprinkle with salt and pepper to taste.
2. Beat together egg and milk in a shallow dish.
3. Place wheat flour in a second shallow dish.
4. In a third shallow dish, mix together panko, plain breadcrumbs, ½ teaspoon salt, and ¼ teaspoon pepper.
5. Preheat the toaster oven to 390°F.
6. Dip liver strips in flour, egg wash, and then breadcrumbs, pressing in coating slightly to make crumbs stick.

7. Cooking half the liver at a time, place strips in air fryer oven in a single layer, close but not touching. Air-fry at 390°F for 5 minutes or until done to your preference.
8. Repeat step 7 to cook remaining liver.

Indian Fry Bread Tacos

Servings: 4
Cooking Time: 20 Minutes
Ingredients:
- 1 cup all-purpose flour
- 1½ teaspoons salt, divided
- 1½ teaspoons baking powder
- ¼ cup milk
- ¼ cup warm water
- ½ pound lean ground beef
- One 14.5-ounce can pinto beans, drained and rinsed
- 1 tablespoon taco seasoning
- ½ cup shredded cheddar cheese
- 2 cups shredded lettuce
- ¼ cup black olives, chopped
- 1 Roma tomato, diced
- 1 avocado, diced
- 1 lime

Directions:
1. In a large bowl, whisk together the flour, 1 teaspoon of the salt, and baking powder. Make a well in the center and add in the milk and water. Form a ball and gently knead the dough four times. Cover the bowl with a damp towel, and set aside.
2. Preheat the toaster oven to 380°F.
3. In a medium bowl, mix together the ground beef, beans, and taco seasoning. Crumble the meat mixture into the air fryer oven and air-fry for 5 minutes; toss the meat and cook an additional 2 to 3 minutes, or until cooked fully. Place the cooked meat in a bowl for taco assembly; season with the remaining ½ teaspoon salt as desired.
4. On a floured surface, place the dough. Cut the dough into 4 equal parts. Using a rolling pin, roll out each piece of dough to 5 inches in diameter. Spray the dough with cooking spray and place in the air fryer oven, working in batches as needed. Air-fry for 3 minutes, flip over, spray with cooking spray, and air-fry for an additional 1 to 3 minutes, until golden and puffy.
5. To assemble, place the fry breads on a serving platter. Equally divide the meat and bean mixture on top of the fry bread. Divide the cheese, lettuce, olives, tomatoes, and avocado among the four tacos. Squeeze lime over the top prior to serving.

Pork Taco Gorditas

Servings: 4
Cooking Time: 21 Minutes
Ingredients:
- 1 pound lean ground pork
- 2 tablespoons chili powder
- 2 tablespoons ground cumin
- 1 teaspoon dried oregano
- 2 teaspoons paprika
- 1 teaspoon garlic powder
- ½ cup water
- 1 (15-ounce) can pinto beans, drained and rinsed
- ½ cup taco sauce
- salt and freshly ground black pepper
- 2 cups grated Cheddar cheese
- 5 (12-inch) flour tortillas
- 4 (8-inch) crispy corn tortilla shells
- 4 cups shredded lettuce
- 1 tomato, diced
- ⅓ cup sliced black olives
- sour cream, for serving
- tomato salsa, for serving

Directions:
1. Preheat the toaster oven to 400°F.
2. Place the ground pork in the air fryer oven and air-fry at 400°F for 10 minutes, stirring a few times during the cooking process to gently break up the meat. Combine the chili powder, cumin, oregano, paprika, garlic powder and water in a small bowl. Stir the spice mixture into the browned pork. Stir in the beans and taco sauce and air-fry for an additional minute. Transfer the pork mixture to a bowl. Season to taste with salt and freshly ground black pepper.
3. Sprinkle ½ cup of the shredded cheese in the center of four of the flour tortillas, making sure to leave a 2-inch border around the edge free of cheese and filling. Divide the pork mixture among the four tortillas, placing it on top of the cheese. Place a crunchy corn tortilla on top of the pork and top with shredded lettuce, diced tomatoes, and black olives. Cut the remaining flour tortilla into 4 quarters. These quarters of tortilla will serve as the bottom of the gordita. Place one quarter tortilla on top of each gordita and fold the edges of the bottom flour tortilla up over the sides, enclosing the filling. While holding the seams down, brush the bottom of the gordita with olive oil and place the seam side down on the countertop while you finish the remaining three gorditas.
4. Preheat the toaster oven to 380°F.
5. Air-fry one gordita at a time. Transfer the gordita carefully to the air fryer oven, seam side down. Brush or spray the top tortilla with oil and air-fry for 5 minutes.

Carefully turn the gordita over and air-fry for an additional 5 minutes, until both sides are browned. When finished air frying all four gorditas, layer them back into the air fryer oven for an additional minute to make sure they are all warm before serving with sour cream and salsa.

Sloppy Joes

Servings: 4
Cooking Time: 17 Minutes
Ingredients:
- oil for misting or cooking spray
- 1 pound very lean ground beef
- 1 teaspoon onion powder
- ⅓ cup ketchup
- ¼ cup water
- ½ teaspoon celery seed
- 1 tablespoon lemon juice
- 1½ teaspoons brown sugar
- 1¼ teaspoons low-sodium Worcestershire sauce
- ½ teaspoon salt (optional)
- ½ teaspoon vinegar
- ⅛ teaspoon dry mustard
- hamburger or slider buns

Directions:
1. Spray air fryer oven with nonstick cooking spray or olive oil.
2. Break raw ground beef into small chunks and pile into air fryer oven.
3. Air-fry at 390°F for 5 minutes. Stir to break apart and cook 3 minutes. Stir and cook 4 minutes longer or until meat is well done.
4. Remove meat from air fryer oven, drain, and use a knife and fork to crumble into small pieces.
5. Give your air fryer oven a quick rinse to remove any bits of meat.
6. Place all the remaining ingredients except the buns in a 6 x 6-inch baking pan and mix together.
7. Add meat and stir well.
8. Air-fry at 330°F for 5 minutes. Stir and air-fry for 2 minutes.
9. Scoop onto buns.

Vietnamese Beef Lettuce Wraps

Servings: 4
Cooking Time: 12 Minutes
Ingredients:
- ⅓ cup low-sodium soy sauce
- 2 teaspoons fish sauce
- 2 teaspoons brown sugar
- 1 tablespoon chili paste
- juice of 1 lime
- 2 cloves garlic, minced
- 2 teaspoons fresh ginger, minced
- 1 pound beef sirloin
- Sauce
- ⅓ cup low-sodium soy sauce
- juice of 2 limes
- 1 tablespoon mirin wine
- 2 teaspoons chili paste
- Serving
- 1 head butter lettuce
- ½ cup julienned carrots
- ½ cup julienned cucumber
- ½ cup sliced radishes, sliced into half moons
- 2 cups cooked rice noodles
- ⅓ cup chopped peanuts

Directions:
1. Combine the soy sauce, fish sauce, brown sugar, chili paste, lime juice, garlic and ginger in a bowl. Slice the beef into thin slices, then cut those slices in half. Add the beef to the marinade and marinate for 1 to 3 hours in the refrigerator. When you are ready to cook, remove the steak from the refrigerator and let it sit at room temperature for 30 minutes.
2. Preheat the toaster oven to 400°F.
3. Transfer the beef and marinade to the air fryer oven. Air-fry at 400°F for 12 minutes.
4. While the beef is cooking, prepare a wrap-building station. Combine the soy sauce, lime juice, mirin wine and chili paste in a bowl and transfer to a little pouring vessel. Separate the lettuce leaves from the head of lettuce and put them in a serving bowl. Place the carrots, cucumber, radish, rice noodles and chopped peanuts all in separate serving bowls.
5. When the beef has finished cooking, transfer it to another serving bowl and invite your guests to build their wraps. To build the wraps, place some beef in a lettuce leaf and top with carrots, cucumbers, some rice noodles and chopped peanuts. Drizzle a little sauce over top, fold the lettuce around the ingredients and enjoy!

Lamb Burger With Feta And Olives

Servings: 3
Cooking Time: 16 Minutes
Ingredients:
- 2 teaspoons olive oil
- ⅓ onion, finely chopped
- 1 clove garlic, minced
- 1 pound ground lamb
- 2 tablespoons fresh parsley, finely chopped
- 1½ teaspoons fresh oregano, finely chopped
- ½ cup black olives, finely chopped
- ⅓ cup crumbled feta cheese
- ½ teaspoon salt
- freshly ground black pepper
- 4 thick pita breads
- toppings and condiments

Directions:
1. Preheat a medium skillet over medium-high heat on the stovetop. Add the olive oil and cook the onion until tender, but not browned – about 4 to 5 minutes. Add the garlic and air-fry for another minute. Transfer the onion and garlic to a mixing bowl and add the ground lamb, parsley, oregano, olives, feta cheese, salt and pepper. Gently mix the ingredients together.
2. Divide the mixture into 3 or 4 equal portions and then form the hamburgers, being careful not to over-handle the meat. One good way to do this is to throw the meat back and forth between your hands like a baseball, packing the meat each time you catch it. Flatten the balls into patties, making an indentation in the center of each patty. Flatten the sides of the patties as well to make it easier to fit them into the air fryer oven.
3. Preheat the toaster oven to 370°F.
4. If you don't have room for all four burgers, air-fry two or three burgers at a time for 8 minutes at 370°F. Flip the burgers over and air-fry for another 8 minutes. If you cooked your burgers in batches, return the first batch of burgers to the air fryer oven for the last two minutes of cooking to re-heat. This should give you a medium-well burger. If you'd prefer a medium-rare burger, shorten the cooking time to about 13 minutes. Remove the burgers to a resting plate and let the burgers rest for a few minutes before dressing and serving.
5. While the burgers are resting, toast the pita breads in the air fryer oven for 2 minutes. Tuck the burgers into the toasted pita breads, or wrap the pitas around the burgers and serve with a tzatziki sauce or some mayonnaise.

Steak With Herbed Butter

Servings: 2
Cooking Time: 16 Minutes
Ingredients:
- 4 tablespoons unsalted butter, softened
- 1 tablespoon minced flat-leaf (Italian) parsley
- 1 tablespoon chopped fresh chives
- 2 cloves garlic, minced
- 1 teaspoon Worcestershire sauce
- 2 beef strip steaks, cut about 1½ inches thick
- 1 tablespoon olive oil
- Kosher salt and freshly ground black pepper

Directions:
1. Combine the butter, parsley, chives, garlic, and Worcestershire sauce in a small bowl until well blended; set aside.
2. Preheat the toaster oven to broil.
3. Brush the steaks with olive oil and season with salt and pepper. Place the steak on the broiler rack set over the broiler pan. Place the pan in the toaster oven, positioning the steaks about 3 to 4 inches below the heating element. (Depending on your oven and the thickness of the steak, you may need to set the rack to the middle position.) Broil for 6 minutes, turn the steaks over, and broil for an additional 7 minutes. If necessary to reach the desired doneness, turn the steaks over again and broil for an additional 3 minutes or until you reach your desired doneness.
4. Spread the herb butter generously over the steaks. Allow the steaks to stand for 5 to 10 minutes before slicing and serving.

Glazed Meatloaf

Servings: 4
Cooking Time: 60 Minutes
Ingredients:
- 2 pounds extra-lean ground beef
- ½ cup fine bread crumbs
- 1 large egg
- 1 medium carrot, shredded
- 2 teaspoons minced garlic
- ¼ cup milk
- 1 tablespoon Italian seasoning
- ½ teaspoon sea salt
- ⅛ teaspoon freshly ground black pepper
- ½ cup ketchup
- 1 tablespoon dark brown sugar
- 1 teaspoon apple cider vinegar

Directions:

1. Place the rack in position 1 and preheat the toaster oven to 375°F on BAKE for 5 minutes.
2. In a large bowl, mix the ground beef, bread crumbs, egg, carrot, garlic, milk, Italian seasoning, salt, and pepper until well combined.
3. Press the mixture into a 9-by-5-inch loaf pan.
4. In a small bowl, stir the ketchup, brown sugar, and vinegar. Set aside.
5. Bake for 40 minutes.
6. Take the meatloaf out and spread the glaze over the top. Bake an additional 20 minutes until cooked through, with an internal temperature of 165°F. Serve.

Lamb Koftas Meatballs

Servings: 3
Cooking Time: 8 Minutes
Ingredients:
- 1 pound ground lamb
- 1 teaspoon ground cumin
- 1 teaspoon ground coriander
- 2 tablespoons chopped fresh mint
- 1 egg, beaten
- ½ teaspoon salt
- freshly ground black pepper

Directions:
1. Combine all ingredients in a bowl and mix together well. Divide the mixture into 10 portions. Roll each portion into a ball and then by cupping the meatball in your hand, shape it into an oval.
2. Preheat the toaster oven to 400°F.
3. Air-fry the koftas for 8 minutes.
4. Serve warm with the cucumber-yogurt dip.

Slow Cooked Carnitas

Servings: 6
Cooking Time: 360 Minutes
Ingredients:
- 1 pork shoulder (5 pounds), bone-in
- 2½ teaspoons kosher salt
- 1½ teaspoons black pepper
- 1½ teaspoons ground cumin
- 1 teaspoon dried oregano
- ¼ teaspoon ground coriander
- 2 bay leaves
- 6 garlic cloves
- 1 small onion, quartered
- 1 cinnamon stick
- 1 full orange peel (no white)
- 2 oranges, juiced
- 1 lime, juiced

Directions:
1. Season the pork shoulder with salt, pepper, cumin, oregano, and coriander.
2. Place the seasoned pork shoulder in a large pot along with any seasoning that did not stick to the pork.
3. Add in the bay leaves, garlic cloves, onion, cinnamon stick, and orange peel.
4. Squeeze in the juice of two oranges and one lime and cover with foil.
5. Insert the wire rack at low position in the Air Fryer Toaster Oven, then place the pot on the rack.
6. Select the Slow Cook function and press Start/Pause.
7. Remove carefully when done, uncover, and remove the bone.
8. Shred the carnitas and use them in tacos, burritos, or any other way you please.

Chipotle-glazed Meat Loaf

Servings: 4
Cooking Time: 65 Minutes
Ingredients:
- 1 ½ pounds lean ground beef
- ¼ cup finely chopped onion
- ½ cup crushed tortilla chips
- 1 teaspoon ground cumin
- ½ teaspoon chili powder
- ½ teaspoon garlic powder
- ½ teaspoon kosher salt
- ¼ teaspoon freshly ground black pepper
- 3 tablespoons chopped pickled jalapeños
- 3 tablespoons chunky salsa
- 1 large egg
- ⅓ cup ketchup
- 3 ½ teaspoons minced chipotle chilies in adobo sauce

Directions:
1. Preheat the toaster oven to 375 °F. Line a 12 x 12-inch baking pan with aluminum foil.
2. Combine the ground beef, onion, tortilla chips, cumin, chili powder, garlic powder, salt, pepper, pickled jalapeños, salsa, and egg in a large bowl, stirring until blended well. Shape the meat mixture into a 9 x 5-inch loaf and place on the prepared pan.
3. Bake, uncovered, for 30 minutes. Carefully remove the meat loaf from the oven and spoon off any collected grease from the pan.
4. Place the ketchup in a small bowl and stir in the chipotle chilies in adobo sauce. Spread the ketchup mixture on top of

the meat loaf. Continue to bake for an additional 25 to 35 minutes or until a meat thermometer registers 160 °F. Let stand for 10 minutes before slicing.

Italian Meatballs

Servings: 4
Cooking Time: 12 Minutes
Ingredients:
- 12 ounces lean ground beef
- 4 ounces Italian sausage, casing removed
- ½ cup breadcrumbs
- 1 cup grated Parmesan cheese
- 1 egg
- 2 tablespoons milk
- 2 teaspoons Italian seasoning
- ½ teaspoon onion powder
- ½ teaspoon garlic powder
- Pinch of red pepper flakes

Directions:
1. In a large bowl, place all the ingredients and mix well. Roll out 24 meatballs.
2. Preheat the toaster oven to 360°F.
3. Place the meatballs in the air fryer oven and air-fry for 12 minutes, tossing every 4 minutes. Using a food thermometer, check to ensure the internal temperature of the meatballs is 165°F.

Chicken Fried Steak

Servings: 4
Cooking Time: 15 Minutes
Ingredients:
- 2 eggs
- ½ cup buttermilk
- 1½ cups flour
- ¾ teaspoon salt
- ½ teaspoon pepper
- 1 pound beef cube steaks
- salt and pepper
- oil for misting or cooking spray

Directions:
1. Beat together eggs and buttermilk in a shallow dish.
2. In another shallow dish, stir together the flour, ½ teaspoon salt, and ¼ teaspoon pepper.
3. Season cube steaks with remaining salt and pepper to taste. Dip in flour, buttermilk egg wash, and then flour again.
4. Spray both sides of steaks with oil or cooking spray.
5. Cooking in 2 batches, place steaks in air fryer oven in single layer. Air-fry at 360°F for 10 minutes. Spray tops of steaks with oil and cook 5 minutes or until meat is well done.
6. Repeat to cook remaining steaks.

Red Curry Flank Steak

Servings: 4
Cooking Time: 18 Minutes
Ingredients:
- 3 tablespoons red curry paste
- ¼ cup olive oil
- 2 teaspoons grated fresh ginger
- 2 tablespoons soy sauce
- 2 tablespoons rice wine vinegar
- 3 scallions, minced
- 1½ pounds flank steak
- fresh cilantro (or parsley) leaves

Directions:
1. Mix the red curry paste, olive oil, ginger, soy sauce, rice vinegar and scallions together in a bowl. Place the flank steak in a shallow glass dish and pour half the marinade over the steak. Pierce the steak several times with a fork or meat tenderizer to let the marinade penetrate the meat. Turn the steak over, pour the remaining marinade over the top and pierce the steak several times again. Cover and marinate the steak in the refrigerator for 6 to 8 hours.
2. When you are ready to cook, remove the steak from the refrigerator and let it sit at room temperature for 30 minutes.
3. Preheat the toaster oven to 400°F.
4. Cut the flank steak in half so that it fits more easily into the air fryer oven and transfer both pieces to the air fryer oven. Pour the marinade over the steak. Air-fry for 18 minutes, depending on your preferred degree of doneness of the steak (12 minutes = medium rare). Flip the steak over halfway through the cooking time.
5. When your desired degree of doneness has been reached, remove the steak to a cutting board and let it rest for 5 minutes before slicing. Thinly slice the flank steak against the grain of the meat. Transfer the slices to a serving platter, pour any juice from the bottom of the air fryer oven over the sliced flank steak and sprinkle the fresh cilantro on top.

Minted Lamb Chops

Servings: 4
Cooking Time: 15 Minutes
Ingredients:
- Mint mixture:
- 4 tablespoons finely chopped fresh mint
- 2 tablespoons nonfat yogurt
- 1 tablespoon olive oil
- Salt and freshly ground black pepper to taste
- 4 lean lamb chops, fat trimmed, approximately ¾ inch thick
- 1 tablespoon balsamic vinegar

Directions:
1. Combine the mint mixture ingredients in a small bowl, stirring well to blend. Set aside. Place the lamp chops on a broiling rack with a pan underneath.
2. BROIL the lamb chops for 10 minutes, or until they are slightly pink. Remove from the oven and brush one side liberally with balsamic vinegar. Turn the chops over with tongs and spread with the mint mixture, using all of the mixture.
3. BROIL again for 5 minutes, or until lightly browned.

Almond And Sun-dried Tomato Crusted Pork Chops

Servings: 4
Cooking Time: 10 Minutes
Ingredients:
- ½ cup oil-packed sun-dried tomatoes
- ½ cup toasted almonds
- ¼ cup grated Parmesan cheese
- ½ cup olive oil
- 2 tablespoons water
- ½ teaspoon salt
- freshly ground black pepper
- 4 center-cut boneless pork chops (about 1¼ pounds)

Directions:
1. Place the sun-dried tomatoes into a food processor and pulse them until they are coarsely chopped. Add the almonds, Parmesan cheese, olive oil, water, salt and pepper. Process all the ingredients into a smooth paste. Spread most of the paste (leave a little in reserve) onto both sides of the pork chops and then pierce the meat several times with a needle-style meat tenderizer or a fork. Let the pork chops sit and marinate for at least 1 hour (refrigerate if marinating for longer than 1 hour).
2. Preheat the toaster oven to 370°F.
3. Brush a little olive oil on the bottom of the air fryer oven. Transfer the pork chops into the air fryer oven, spooning a little more of the sun-dried tomato paste onto the pork chops if there are any gaps where the paste may have been rubbed off. Air-fry the pork chops at 370°F for 10 minutes, turning the chops over halfway through the cooking process.
4. When the pork chops have finished cooking, transfer them to a serving plate and serve with mashed potatoes and vegetables for a hearty meal.

Italian Sausage & Peppers

Servings: 6
Cooking Time: 25 Minutes
Ingredients:
- 1 6-ounce can tomato paste
- ⅔ cup water
- 1 8-ounce can tomato sauce
- 1 teaspoon dried parsley flakes
- ½ teaspoon garlic powder
- ⅛ teaspoon oregano
- ½ pound mild Italian bulk sausage
- 1 tablespoon extra virgin olive oil
- ½ large onion, cut in 1-inch chunks
- 4 ounces fresh mushrooms, sliced
- 1 large green bell pepper, cut in 1-inch chunks
- 8 ounces spaghetti, cooked
- Parmesan cheese for serving

Directions:
1. In a large saucepan or skillet, stir together the tomato paste, water, tomato sauce, parsley, garlic, and oregano. Heat on stovetop over very low heat while preparing meat and vegetables.
2. Break sausage into small chunks, about ½-inch pieces. Place in air fryer oven baking pan.
3. Air-fry at 390°F for 5 minutes. Stir. Cook 7 minutes longer or until sausage is well done. Remove from pan, drain on paper towels, and add to the sauce mixture.
4. If any sausage grease remains in baking pan, pour it off or use paper towels to soak it up. (Be careful handling that hot pan!)
5. Place olive oil, onions, and mushrooms in pan and stir. Air-fry for 5 minutes or just until tender. Using a slotted spoon, transfer onions and mushrooms from baking pan into the sauce and sausage mixture.
6. Place bell pepper chunks in air fryer oven baking pan and air-fry for 8 minutes or until tender. When done, stir into sauce with sausage and other vegetables.
7. Serve over cooked spaghetti with plenty of Parmesan cheese.

Better-than-chinese-take-out Pork Ribs

Servings: 3
Cooking Time: 35 Minutes
Ingredients:
- 1½ tablespoons Hoisin sauce (gluten-free, if a concern)
- 1½ tablespoons Regular or low-sodium soy sauce or gluten-free tamari sauce
- 1½ tablespoons Shaoxing (Chinese cooking rice wine), dry sherry, or white grape juice
- 1½ teaspoons Minced garlic
- ¾ teaspoon Ground dried ginger
- ¾ teaspoon Ground white pepper
- 1½ pounds Pork baby back rib rack(s), cut into 2-bone pieces

Directions:
1. Mix the hoisin sauce, soy or tamari sauce, Shaoxing or its substitute, garlic, ginger, and white pepper in a large bowl. Add the rib sections and stir well to coat. Cover and refrigerate for at least 2 hours or up to 24 hours, stirring the rib sections in the marinade occasionally.
2. Preheat the toaster oven to 350°F. Set the ribs in their bowl on the counter as the machine heats.
3. When the machine is at temperature, set the rib pieces on their sides in a single layer in the air fryer oven with as much air space between them as possible. Air-fry for 35 minutes, turning and rearranging the pieces once, until deeply browned and sizzling.
4. Use kitchen tongs to transfer the rib pieces to a large serving bowl or platter. Wait a minute or two before serving them so the meat can reabsorb some of its own juices.

Steak Pinwheels With Pepper Slaw And Minneapolis Potato Salad

Servings: 4
Cooking Time: 16 Minutes
Ingredients:
- Brushing mixture:
- ½ cup cold strong brewed coffee
- 2 tablespoons molasses
- 1 tablespoon tomato paste
- 2 garlic cloves, minced
- 1 tablespoon olive oil
- Garlic powder
- 1 teaspoon butcher's pepper
- 1 pound lean, boneless beefsteak, flattened to ⅛-inch thickness with a meat mallet or rolling pin (place steak between 2 sheets of heavy-duty plastic wrap)

Directions:
1. Combine the brushing mixture ingredients in a small bowl and set aside.
2. Cut the steak into 2 × 3-inch strips, brush with the mixture, and roll up, securing the edges with toothpicks. Brush again with the mixture and place in an oiled or nonstick 8½ × 8½ × 2-inch square baking (cake) pan.
3. BROIL for 8 minutes, then turn with tongs, brush with the mixture again, and broil for another 8 minutes, or until browned.

Lamb Curry

Servings: 4
Cooking Time: 40 Minutes
Ingredients:
- 1 pound lean lamb for stewing, trimmed and cut into 1 × 1-inch pieces
- 1 small onion, chopped
- 3 garlic cloves, minced
- 2 plum tomatoes, chopped
- ½ cup dry white wine
- 2 tablespoons curry powder
- Salt and cayenne to taste

Directions:
1. Preheat the toaster oven to 400° F.
2. Combine all the ingredients in an 8½ × 8½ × 4-inch ovenproof baking dish. Adjust the seasonings.
3. BAKE, covered, for 40 minutes, or until the meat is tender and the onion is cooked.

Crispy Smoked Pork Chops

Servings: 3
Cooking Time: 8 Minutes
Ingredients:
- ⅔ cup All-purpose flour or tapioca flour
- 1 Large egg white(s)
- 2 tablespoons Water
- 1½ cups Corn flake crumbs (gluten-free, if a concern)
- 3 ½-pound, ½-inch-thick bone-in smoked pork chops

Directions:
1. Preheat the toaster oven to 375°F.
2. Set up and fill three shallow soup plates or small pie plates on your counter: one for the flour; one for the egg white(s), whisked with the water until foamy; and one for the corn flake crumbs.

3. Set a chop in the flour and turn it several times, coating both sides and the edges. Gently shake off any excess flour, then set it in the beaten egg white mixture. Turn to coat both sides as well as the edges. Let any excess egg white slip back into the rest, then set the chop in the corn flake crumbs. Turn it several times, pressing gently to coat the chop evenly on both sides and around the edge. Set the chop aside and continue coating the remaining chop(s) in the same way.

4. Set the chops in the air fryer oven with as much air space between them as possible. Air-fry undisturbed for 8 minutes, or until the coating is crunchy and the chops are heated through.

5. Use kitchen tongs to transfer the chops to a wire rack and cool for a couple of minutes before serving.

Easy Tex-mex Chimichangas

Servings: 2
Cooking Time: 8 Minutes
Ingredients:
- ¼ pound Thinly sliced deli roast beef, chopped
- ½ cup (about 2 ounces) Shredded Cheddar cheese or shredded Tex-Mex cheese blend
- ¼ cup Jarred salsa verde or salsa rojo
- ½ teaspoon Ground cumin
- ½ teaspoon Dried oregano
- 2 Burrito-size (12-inch) flour tortilla(s), not corn tortillas (gluten-free, if a concern)
- ⅔ cup Canned refried beans
- Vegetable oil spray

Directions:
1. Preheat the toaster oven to 375°F.
2. Stir the roast beef, cheese, salsa, cumin, and oregano in a bowl until well mixed.
3. Lay a tortilla on a clean, dry work surface. Spread ⅓ cup of the refried beans in the center lower third of the tortilla(s), leaving an inch on either side of the spread beans.
4. For one chimichanga, spread all of the roast beef mixture on top of the beans. For two, spread half of the roast beef mixture on each tortilla.
5. At either "end" of the filling mixture, fold the sides of the tortilla up and over the filling, partially covering it. Starting with the unfolded side of the tortilla just below the filling, roll the tortilla closed. Fold and roll the second filled tortilla, as necessary.
6. Coat the exterior of the tortilla(s) with vegetable oil spray. Set the chimichanga(s) seam side down in the air fryer oven, with at least ½ inch air space between them if you're working with two. Air-fry undisturbed for 8 minutes, or until the tortilla is lightly browned and crisp.
7. Use kitchen tongs to gently transfer the chimichanga(s) to a wire rack. Cool for at last 5 minutes or up to 20 minutes before serving.

Cilantro-crusted Flank Steak

Servings: 2
Cooking Time: 16 Minutes
Ingredients:
- Coating:
- 2 tablespoons chopped onion
- 1 tablespoon olive oil
- 2 tablespoons plain nonfat yogurt
- 1 plum tomato
- ½ cup fresh cilantro leaves
- 2 tablespoons cooking sherry
- ¼ teaspoon hot sauce
- 1 teaspoon garlic powder
- ½ teaspoon chili powder
- Salt and freshly ground black pepper
- 2 8-ounce flank steaks

Directions:
1. Process the coating ingredients in a blender or food processor until smooth. Spread half of the coating mixture on top of the flank steaks. Place the steaks on a broiling rack with a pan underneath.
2. BROIL for 8 minutes. Turn with tongs, spread the remaining mixture on the steaks, and broil again for 8 minutes, or until done to your preference.

Lime-ginger Pork Tenderloin

Servings: 4
Cooking Time: 26 Minutes
Ingredients:
- ½ cup packed dark brown sugar
- Juice of ½ lime
- 2 teaspoons fresh ginger, peeled and grated
- 1 teaspoon minced garlic
- 2 (1-pound) extra-lean pork tenderloins, trimmed of fat
- Sea salt, for seasoning
- Freshly ground black pepper, for seasoning
- 1 tablespoon olive oil

Directions:
1. Preheat the toaster oven to 400°F on CONVECTION BAKE for 5 minutes.
2. In a small bowl, stir the sugar, lime juice, ginger, and garlic together.
3. Lightly season the pork tenderloins all over with salt and pepper.

4. Heat the oil in a large skillet over medium-high heat. Brown the pork on all sides, about 6 minutes in total.
5. Place the air-fryer basket in the baking tray and place the tenderloins in the basket.
6. Brush the pork all over with the ginger-lime mixture.
7. In position 2, bake for 20 minutes, basting the pork at 10 minutes, until it reaches an internal temperature of about 145°F.
8. Let the pork rest for 10 minutes and serve.

Barbecued Broiled Pork Chops

Servings: 2
Cooking Time: 16 Minutes
Ingredients:
- Barbecue sauce mixture:
- 1 tablespoon ketchup
- ¼ cup dry red wine
- 1 tablespoon vegetable oil
- ⅛ teaspoon smoked flavoring (liquid smoke)
- 1 teaspoon chili powder
- 1 teaspoon ground cumin
- 1 teaspoon brown sugar
- ¼ teaspoon butcher's pepper
- 2 large (6- to 8-ounce) lean pork chops, approximately ¾ to 1 inch thick

Directions:
1. Combine the barbecue sauce mixture ingredients in a small bowl. Brush the chops with the sauce and place on a broiling rack with a pan underneath.
2. BROIL 8 minutes, turn with tongs, and broil for another 8 minutes, or until the meat is cooked to your preference.

Seasoned Boneless Pork Sirloin Chops

Servings: 2
Cooking Time: 16 Minutes
Ingredients:
- Seasoning mixture:
- ½ teaspoon ground cumin
- ¼ teaspoon turmeric
- Pinch of ground cardamom
- Pinch of grated nutmeg
- 1 teaspoon vegetable oil
- 1 teaspoon Pickapeppa sauce
- 2½- to ¾-pound boneless lean pork sirloin chops

Directions:
1. Combine the seasoning mixture ingredients in a small bowl and brush on both sides of the chops. Place the chops on the broiling rack with a pan underneath.
2. BROIL 8 minutes, remove the chops, turn, and brush with the mixture. Broil again for 8 minutes, or until the chops are done to your preference.

Spicy Little Beef Birds

Servings: 2
Cooking Time: 12 Minutes
Ingredients:
- Spicy mixture:
- 1 tablespoon olive oil
- 1 tablespoon brown mustard
- 1 teaspoon chili powder
- 1 teaspoon garlic powder
- 1 teaspoon hot sauce
- 1 tablespoon barbecue sauce or salsa
- Salt and freshly ground black pepper to taste
- ½ to ¾ pound pepper steaks, cut into 3 × 4-inch strips

Directions:
1. Blend the spicy mixture ingredients in a small bowl and brush both sides of the beef strips.
2. Roll up the strips lengthwise and fasten with toothpicks near each end. Place the beef rolls in an oiled or nonstick 8½ × 8½ × 2-inch square baking (cake) pan.
3. BROIL for 6 minutes, remove from the oven, and turn with tongs. Brush with the spicy mixture and broil again for 6 minutes, or until done to your preference.

Beef-stuffed Bell Peppers

Servings: 4
Cooking Time: 30 Minutes
Ingredients:
- 4 medium red or yellow bell peppers
- 1 pound extra-lean ground beef
- ½ sweet onion, finely chopped
- 2 teaspoons minced garlic
- 1 cup marinara sauce
- 1 cup ready-made brown or wild rice
- 1 cup fresh kale, chopped
- 1 teaspoon dried basil
- Sea salt, for seasoning
- Freshly ground black pepper, for seasoning
- 1 cup Swiss cheese, shredded

Directions:
1. Preheat the toaster oven to 350°F on AIR FRY for 5 minutes.

2. Cut the top off the peppers and scoop the seeds and membranes out. Set the pepper tops aside.
3. Place a large skillet over medium-high heat and brown the beef, about 10 minutes.
4. Add the onion and garlic and sauté until softened, about 4 minutes.
5. Add the marinara sauce, rice, kale, and basil, stirring to combine. Remove from the heat and season with salt and pepper.
6. Place the air-fryer basket in the baking tray and place the peppers in the basket, hollow-side up.
7. Evenly divide the filling among the peppers. You can place the pepper tops cut-side up and place the pepper bottoms in the tops to balance them, so that they do not tip over.
8. In position 1, air fry for 15 minutes until the peppers are tender. Top with the cheese and air fry for 2 more minutes more to melt the cheese. Serve.

Barbeque Ribs

Servings: 4
Cooking Time: 35 Minutes
Ingredients:
- 2 pounds pork spareribs or baby back ribs, silver skin removed
- 2 tablespoons brown sugar
- 1 teaspoon chili powder
- 1 teaspoon dry mustard
- Sea salt, for seasoning
- Freshly ground black pepper, for seasoning
- Oil spray (hand-pumped)
- 1 cup barbeque sauce

Directions:
1. Preheat the toaster oven to 375°F on AIR FRY for 5 minutes.
2. Cut the ribs into 4 bone sections or to fit in the basket.
3. In a small bowl, combine the brown sugar, chili powder, and mustard, and rub it all over the ribs.
4. Season the ribs with salt and pepper.
5. Place the air-fryer basket in the baking tray and spray it generously with the oil.
6. Arrange the ribs in the basket. There can be overlap if necessary.
7. In position 2, air fry for 35 minutes, turning halfway through, until the ribs are tender, browned, and crisp.
8. Baste the ribs with the barbeque sauce and serve.

Beef And Spinach Braciole

Servings: 4
Cooking Time: 92 Minutes
Ingredients:
- 7-inch oven-safe baking pan or casserole
- ½ onion, finely chopped
- 1 teaspoon olive oil
- ⅓ cup red wine
- 2 cups crushed tomatoes
- 1 teaspoon Italian seasoning
- ½ teaspoon garlic powder
- ¼ teaspoon crushed red pepper flakes
- 2 tablespoons chopped fresh parsley
- 2 top round steaks (about 1½ pounds)
- salt and freshly ground black pepper
- 2 cups fresh spinach, chopped
- 1 clove minced garlic
- ½ cup roasted red peppers, julienned
- ½ cup grated pecorino cheese
- ¼ cup pine nuts, toasted and rough chopped
- 2 tablespoons olive oil

Directions:
1. Preheat the toaster oven to 400°F.
2. Toss the onions and olive oil together in a 7-inch metal baking pan or casserole dish. Air-fry at 400°F for 5 minutes, stirring a couple times during the cooking process. Add the red wine, crushed tomatoes, Italian seasoning, garlic powder, red pepper flakes and parsley and stir. Cover the pan tightly with aluminum foil, lower the air fryer oven temperature to 350°F and continue to air-fry for 15 minutes.
3. While the sauce is simmering, prepare the beef. Using a meat mallet, pound the beef until it is ¼-inch thick. Season both sides of the beef with salt and pepper. Combine the spinach, garlic, red peppers, pecorino cheese, pine nuts and olive oil in a medium bowl. Season with salt and freshly ground black pepper. Spread the mixture evenly over the steaks. Starting at one of the short ends, roll the beef around the filling, tucking in the sides as you roll to ensure the filling is completely enclosed. Secure the beef rolls with toothpicks.
4. Remove the baking pan with the sauce from the air fryer oven and set it aside. Preheat the toaster oven to 400°F.
5. Brush or spray the beef rolls with a little olive oil and air-fry at 400°F for 12 minutes, rotating the beef during the cooking process for even browning. When the beef is browned, submerge the rolls into the sauce in the baking pan,

cover the pan with foil and return it to the air fryer oven. Air-fry at 250°F for 60 minutes.
6. Remove the beef rolls from the sauce. Cut each roll into slices and serve with pasta, ladling some of the sauce overtop.

Kielbasa Sausage With Pierogies And Caramelized Onions

Servings: 3
Cooking Time: 30 Minutes
Ingredients:
- 1 Vidalia or sweet onion, sliced
- olive oil
- salt and freshly ground black pepper
- 2 tablespoons butter, cut into small cubes
- 1 teaspoon sugar
- 1 pound light Polish kielbasa sausage, cut into 2-inch chunks
- 1 (13-ounce) package frozen mini pierogies
- 2 teaspoons vegetable or olive oil
- chopped scallions

Directions:
1. Preheat the toaster oven to 400°F.
2. Toss the sliced onions with a little olive oil, salt and pepper and transfer them to the air fryer oven. Dot the onions with pieces of butter and air-fry at 400°F for 2 minutes. Then sprinkle the sugar over the onions and stir. Pour any melted butter from the bottom of the air fryer oven over the onions (do this over the sink – some of the butter will spill through the pan). Continue to air-fry for another 13 minutes, stirring the pan every few minutes to cook the onions evenly.
3. Add the kielbasa chunks to the onions and toss. Air-fry for another 5 minutes. Transfer the kielbasa and onions to a bowl and cover with aluminum foil to keep warm.
4. Toss the frozen pierogies with the vegetable or olive oil and transfer them to the air fryer oven. Air-fry at 400°F for 8 minutes.
5. When the pierogies have finished cooking, return the kielbasa and onions to the air fryer oven and gently toss with the pierogies. Air-fry for 2 more minutes and then transfer everything to a serving platter. Garnish with the chopped scallions and serve hot with the spicy sour cream sauce below.
6. Kielbasa Sausage with Pierogies and Caramelized Onions

Mustard-herb Lamb Chops

Servings: 2
Cooking Time: 15 Minutes
Ingredients:
- 2 tablespoons Dijon mustard
- 1 teaspoon minced garlic
- ¼ cup bread crumbs
- 1 teaspoon dried Italian herbs
- Zest of 1 lemon
- 4 lamb loin chops (about 1 pound), room temperature
- Sea salt, for seasoning
- Freshly ground black pepper, for seasoning
- Oil spray (hand-pumped)

Directions:
1. Preheat the toaster oven to 425°F on CONVECTION BAKE for 5 minutes.
2. Line the baking tray with parchment or aluminum foil.
3. In a small bowl, stir the mustard and garlic until blended.
4. In another small bowl, stir the bread crumbs, herbs, and lemon zest until mixed.
5. Lightly season the lamb chops on both sides with salt and pepper. Brush the mustard mixture over a chop and dredge it in the bread crumb mixture to lightly bread the lamb. Set the lamb on the baking tray and repeat with the other chops.
6. Spray the chops lightly with the oil, and in position 2, bake for 15 minutes until browned and the internal temperature is 130°F for medium-rare.
7. Rest the lamb for 5 minutes, then serve.

Crunchy Fried Pork Loin Chops

Servings: 3
Cooking Time: 12 Minutes
Ingredients:
- 1 cup All-purpose flour or tapioca flour
- 1 Large egg(s), well beaten
- 1½ cups Seasoned Italian-style dried bread crumbs (gluten-free, if a concern)
- 3 4- to 5-ounce boneless center-cut pork loin chops
- Vegetable oil spray

Directions:
1. Preheat the toaster oven to 350°F.
2. Set up and fill three shallow soup plates or small pie plates on your counter: one for the flour, one for the beaten egg(s), and one for the bread crumbs.
3. Dredge a pork chop in the flour, coating both sides as well as around the edge. Gently shake off any excess, then dip the chop in the egg(s), again coating both sides and the edge. Let any excess egg slip back into the rest, then set the chop in the bread crumbs, turning it and pressing gently to coat well on both sides and the edge. Coat the pork chop all over with vegetable oil spray and set aside so you can dredge, coat, and spray the additional chop(s).
4. Set the chops in the air fryer oven with as much air space between them as possible. Air-fry undisturbed for 12 minutes, or until brown and crunchy and an instant-read meat thermometer inserted into the center of a chop registers 145°F.
5. Use kitchen tongs to transfer the chops to a wire rack. Cool for 5 minutes before serving

Poultry

Pecan Turkey Cutlets

Servings: 4
Cooking Time: 12 Minutes
Ingredients:
- ¾ cup panko breadcrumbs
- ¼ teaspoon salt
- ¼ teaspoon pepper
- ¼ teaspoon dry mustard
- ¼ teaspoon poultry seasoning
- ½ cup pecans
- ¼ cup cornstarch
- 1 egg, beaten
- 1 pound turkey cutlets, ½-inch thick
- salt and pepper
- oil for misting or cooking spray

Directions:
1. Place the panko crumbs, ¼ teaspoon salt, ¼ teaspoon pepper, mustard, and poultry seasoning in food processor. Process until crumbs are finely crushed. Add pecans and process in short pulses just until nuts are finely chopped. Go easy so you don't overdo it!
2. Preheat the toaster oven to 360°F.
3. Place cornstarch in one shallow dish and beaten egg in another. Transfer coating mixture from food processor into a third shallow dish.
4. Sprinkle turkey cutlets with salt and pepper to taste.
5. Dip cutlets in cornstarch and shake off excess. Then dip in beaten egg and roll in crumbs, pressing to coat well. Spray both sides with oil or cooking spray.
6. Place 2 cutlets in air fryer oven in a single layer and air-fry for 12 minutes or until juices run clear.
7. Repeat step 6 to cook remaining cutlets.

Roasted Game Hens With Vegetable Stuffing

Servings: 2
Cooking Time: 50 Minutes
Ingredients:
- Stuffing:
- 1 cup multigrain bread crumbs
- 2 tablespoons chopped onion
- 1 carrot, shredded
- 1 celery stalk, shredded
- 1 garlic clove, minced
- 2 tablespoons chopped fresh parsley
- Salt and freshly ground black pepper to taste
- 2 whole game hens (thawed or fresh), giblets removed, rinsed, and patted dry with paper towels

Directions:
1. Preheat the toaster oven to 350° F.
2. Combine the stuffing ingredients in a medium bowl. Stuff the cavities of the game hens and place them in a baking dish.
3. BAKE, covered, for 45 minutes, or until the meat is tender and the juices run clear when the breast is pierced with a fork.
4. BROIL, uncovered, for 8 minutes, or until lightly browned.

Italian Roasted Chicken Thighs

Servings: 6
Cooking Time: 14 Minutes
Ingredients:
- 6 boneless chicken thighs
- ½ teaspoon dried oregano
- ½ teaspoon garlic powder
- ½ teaspoon sea salt
- ½ teaspoon black pepper
- ¼ teaspoon crushed red pepper flakes

Directions:
1. Pat the chicken thighs with paper towel.
2. In a small bowl, mix the oregano, garlic powder, salt, pepper, and crushed red pepper flakes. Rub the spice mixture onto the chicken thighs.
3. Preheat the toaster oven to 400°F.
4. Place the chicken thighs in the air fryer oven and spray with cooking spray. Air-fry for 10 minutes, turn over, and cook another 4 minutes. When cooking completes, the internal temperature should read 165°F.

Chicken Fajitas

Servings: 4
Cooking Time: 15 Minutes
Ingredients:
- FOR THE FAJITAS
- ½ teaspoon ground cumin
- ½ teaspoon garlic powder
- ¼ teaspoon smoked paprika
- ¼ teaspoon onion powder
- ¼ teaspoon chili powder
- 1 pound boneless, skinless chicken breast, cut into ¼-inch strips
- 1 red bell pepper, cut into thin slices
- 1 green bell pepper, cut into thin slices
- 1 small red onion, cut into thin slices
- 2 tablespoons olive oil
- 8 (6-inch) tortillas
- OPTIONAL TOPPINGS
- Salsa
- Sour cream
- Pickled jalapeños
- Shredded lettuce

Directions:
1. Preheat the toaster oven to 375°F on AIR FRY for 5 minutes.
2. Place the air-fryer basket in the baking tray.
3. In a large bowl, stir the cumin, garlic powder, paprika, onion powder, and chili powder until well mixed. Add the chicken, bell peppers, onion, and oil, and toss to coat evenly.
4. Spread the chicken and veggies on the baking sheet.
5. In position 2, air fry for 15 minutes, tossing them halfway through, until cooked and the vegetables are lightly browned.
6. Serve tucked into the tortillas with your favorite toppings.

Chicken Breast With Chermoula Sauce

Servings: 4
Cooking Time: 15 Minutes
Ingredients:
- Chicken Ingredients
- 2 boneless skinless chicken breasts 1 tablespoon olive oil
- 1 teaspoon salt
- 1 teaspoon pepper
- Chermoula Ingredients
- 1 cup fresh cilantro
- 1 cup fresh parsley
- ¼ cup fresh mint
- ½ teaspoon red chili flakes
- ½ teaspoon cumin seeds
- ½ teaspoon coriander seeds
- 3 garlic cloves, peeled
- ½ cup extra virgin olive oil
- 1 lemon, zested and juiced
- ¾ teaspoons smoked paprika
- ¾ teaspoons salt

Directions:
1. Combine all the chermoula sauce ingredients in a blender or food processor. Pulse until smooth. Taste and add salt if needed. Place into a bowl and set aside.
2. Slice the chicken breast in half lengthwise and lightly pound with a meat tenderizer until both halves are about
3. ½-inch thick.
4. Preheat the toaster oven to 430°F.
5. Line the food tray with foil, then place the chicken breasts on the tray. Drizzle chicken with olive oil and season with salt and pepper.
6. Insert the food tray at top position in the preheated oven.
7. Select the Air Fry function, adjust time to 15 minutes, and press Start/Pause.
8. Remove when the chicken breast reaches an internal temperature of 160°F. Allow the chicken to rest for 5 minutes.
9. Brush the chermoula sauce over the chicken, or serve chicken with chermoula sauce on the side.

Orange-glazed Roast Chicken

Servings: 6
Cooking Time: 100 Minutes
Ingredients:
- 1 3-pound whole chicken, rinsed and patted dry with paper towels
- Brushing mixture:
- 2 tablespoons orange juice concentrate
- 1 tablespoon soy sauce
- 1 tablespoon toasted sesame oil
- 1 teaspoon ground ginger
- Salt and freshly ground black pepper to taste

Directions:
1. Preheat the toaster oven to 400° F.
2. Place the chicken, breast side up, in an oiled or nonstick 8½ × 8½ × 2-inch square (cake) pan and brush with the mixture, which has been combined in a small bowl, reserving the remaining mixture. Cover with aluminum foil.

3. BAKE for 1 hour and 20 minutes. Uncover and brush the chicken with remaining mixture.
4. BAKE, uncovered, for 20 minutes, or until the breast is tender when pierced with a fork and golden brown.

Sweet-and-sour Chicken

Servings: 6
Cooking Time: 10 Minutes
Ingredients:
- 1 cup pineapple juice
- 1 cup plus 3 tablespoons cornstarch, divided
- ¼ cup sugar
- ¼ cup ketchup
- ¼ cup apple cider vinegar
- 2 tablespoons soy sauce or tamari
- 1 teaspoon garlic powder, divided
- ¼ cup flour
- 1 tablespoon sesame seeds
- ½ teaspoon salt
- ¼ teaspoon ground black pepper
- 2 large eggs
- 2 pounds chicken breasts, cut into 1-inch cubes
- 1 red bell pepper, cut into 1-inch pieces
- 1 carrot, sliced into ¼-inch-thick rounds

Directions:
1. In a medium saucepan, whisk together the pineapple juice, 3 tablespoons of the cornstarch, the sugar, the ketchup, the apple cider vinegar, the soy sauce or tamari, and ½ teaspoon of the garlic powder. Cook over medium-low heat, whisking occasionally as the sauce thickens, about 6 minutes. Stir and set aside while preparing the chicken.
2. Preheat the toaster oven to 370°F.
3. In a medium bowl, place the remaining 1 cup of cornstarch, the flour, the sesame seeds, the salt, the remaining ½ teaspoon of garlic powder, and the pepper.
4. In a second medium bowl, whisk the eggs.
5. Working in batches, place the cubed chicken in the cornstarch mixture to lightly coat; then dip it into the egg mixture, and return it to the cornstarch mixture. Shake off the excess and place the coated chicken in the air fryer oven. Spray with cooking spray and air-fry for 5 minutes, and spray with more cooking spray. Cook an additional 3 to 5 minutes, or until completely cooked and golden brown.
6. On the last batch of chicken, add the bell pepper and carrot to the air fryer oven and cook with the chicken.
7. Place the cooked chicken and vegetables into a serving bowl and toss with the sweet-and-sour sauce to serve.

Hot Thighs

Servings: 4
Cooking Time: 40 Minutes
Ingredients:
- 6 skinless, boneless chicken thighs
- ¼ cup fresh lemon juice
- Seasonings:
- 1 teaspoon garlic powder
- ¼ teaspoon cayenne
- ½ teaspoon chili powder
- 1 teaspoon onion powder
- Salt and freshly ground black pepper to taste

Directions:
1. Preheat the toaster oven to 450° F.
2. Brush the chicken thighs liberally with the lemon juice. Set aside.
3. Combine the seasonings in a small bowl and transfer to a paper or plastic bag. Add the thighs and shake well to coat. Remove from the bag and place in an oiled or nonstick 8½ × 8½ × 2-inch square (cake) pan. Cover the pan with aluminum foil.
4. BAKE, covered, for 20 minutes. Turn the pieces with tongs and bake again for another 20 minutes, or until the meat is tender and lightly browned.

I Forgot To Thaw—garlic Capered Chicken Thighs

Servings: 4
Cooking Time: 50 Minutes
Ingredients:
- 6 frozen skinless, boneless chicken thighs
- Garlic mixture:
- 3 garlic cloves, minced
- ¾ cup dry white wine
- 2 tablespoons capers
- ½ teaspoon paprika
- ¼ teaspoon ground cumin
- Salt and freshly ground black pepper to taste

Directions:
1. Preheat the toaster oven to 400° F.
2. Thaw the chicken as directed. Separate the pieces and add the garlic mixture, which has been combined in a small bowl, stirring well to coat. Cover the dish with aluminum foil.
3. BAKE for 30 minutes, or until the chicken is tender. Remove the cover and turn the chicken pieces, spooning the sauce over them.

4. BROIL for 8 minutes, or until the chicken is lightly browned.

Chicken Hand Pies

Servings: 8
Cooking Time: 10 Minutes
Ingredients:
- ¾ cup chicken broth
- ¾ cup frozen mixed peas and carrots
- 1 cup cooked chicken, chopped
- 1 tablespoon cornstarch
- 1 tablespoon milk
- salt and pepper
- 1 8-count can organic flaky biscuits
- oil for misting or cooking spray

Directions:
1. In a medium saucepan, bring chicken broth to a boil. Stir in the frozen peas and carrots and air-fry for 5 minutes over medium heat. Stir in chicken.
2. Mix the cornstarch into the milk until it dissolves. Stir it into the simmering chicken broth mixture and cook just until thickened.
3. Remove from heat, add salt and pepper to taste, and let cool slightly.
4. Lay biscuits out on wax paper. Peel each biscuit apart in the middle to make 2 rounds so you have 16 rounds total. Using your hands or a rolling pin, flatten each biscuit round slightly to make it larger and thinner.
5. Divide chicken filling among 8 of the biscuit rounds. Place remaining biscuit rounds on top and press edges all around. Use the tines of a fork to crimp biscuit edges and make sure they are sealed well.
6. Spray both sides lightly with oil or cooking spray.
7. Cook in a single layer, 4 at a time, at 330°F for 10 minutes or until biscuit dough is cooked through and golden brown.

Buffalo Egg Rolls

Servings: 8
Cooking Time: 9 Minutes
Ingredients:
- 1 teaspoon water
- 1 tablespoon cornstarch
- 1 egg
- 2½ cups cooked chicken, diced or shredded (see opposite page)
- ⅓ cup chopped green onion
- ⅓ cup diced celery
- ⅓ cup buffalo wing sauce
- 8 egg roll wraps
- oil for misting or cooking spray
- Blue Cheese Dip
- 3 ounces cream cheese, softened
- ⅓ cup blue cheese, crumbled
- 1 teaspoon Worcestershire sauce
- ¼ teaspoon garlic powder
- ¼ cup buttermilk (or sour cream)

Directions:
1. Mix water and cornstarch in a small bowl until dissolved. Add egg, beat well, and set aside.
2. In a medium size bowl, mix together chicken, green onion, celery, and buffalo wing sauce.
3. Divide chicken mixture evenly among 8 egg roll wraps, spooning ½ inch from one edge.
4. Moisten all edges of each wrap with beaten egg wash.
5. Fold the short ends over filling, then roll up tightly and press to seal edges.
6. Brush outside of wraps with egg wash, then spritz with oil or cooking spray.
7. Place 4 egg rolls in air fryer oven.
8. Air-fry at 390°F for 9 minutes or until outside is brown and crispy.
9. While the rolls are cooking, prepare the Blue Cheese Dip. With a fork, mash together cream cheese and blue cheese.
10. Stir in remaining ingredients.
11. Dip should be just thick enough to slightly cling to egg rolls. If too thick, stir in buttermilk or milk 1 tablespoon at a time until you reach the desired consistency.
12. Cook remaining 4 egg rolls as in steps 7 and 8.
13. Serve while hot with Blue Cheese Dip, more buffalo wing sauce, or both.

Spice-rubbed Split Game Hen

Servings: 2
Cooking Time: 48 Minutes
Ingredients:
- Spice rub mixture:
- 1 teaspoon ground cumin
- 1 teaspoon garlic powder
- 1 teaspoon onion powder
- 1 teaspoon paprika
- 1 teaspoon ground coriander
- 1 teaspoon salt (optional)
- 1 Cornish game hen, split

Directions:
1. Preheat the toaster oven to 400° F.

2. Mix all the spices together in a small bowl and rub each half of the game hen well and on both sides to coat evenly. Place the pieces skin side down in a baking dish. Cover the dish with aluminum foil.
3. BAKE for 20 minutes. Turn the pieces over and bake, covered, for another 20 minutes, or until the meat is tender. Remove from the oven and uncover.
4. BROIL 8 minutes, or until browned to your preference.

Light And Lovely Loaf

Servings: 4
Cooking Time: 30 Minutes
Ingredients:
- 2 cups ground chicken or turkey breast
- 1 egg
- ½ cup grated carrot
- ½ cup grated celery
- 1 tablespoon finely chopped onion
- ½ teaspoon garlic powder
- Salt and freshly ground black pepper to taste

Directions:
1. Preheat the toaster oven to 400° F.
2. Blend all ingredients in a bowl, mixing well, and transfer to an oiled or nonstick regular-size 4½ × 8½ × 2¼-inch loaf pan
3. BAKE, uncovered, for 30 minutes, until lightly browned.

Pickle Brined Fried Chicken

Servings: 4
Cooking Time: 47 Minutes
Ingredients:
- 4 bone-in, skin-on chicken legs, cut into drumsticks and thighs (about 3½ pounds)
- pickle juice from a 24-ounce jar of kosher dill pickles
- ½ cup flour
- salt and freshly ground black pepper
- 2 eggs
- 1 cup fine breadcrumbs
- 1 teaspoon salt
- 1 teaspoon freshly ground black pepper
- ½ teaspoon ground paprika
- ⅛ teaspoon ground cayenne pepper
- vegetable or canola oil in a spray bottle

Directions:
1. Place the chicken in a shallow dish and pour the pickle juice over the top. Cover and transfer the chicken to the refrigerator to brine in the pickle juice for 3 to 8 hours.
2. When you are ready to cook, remove the chicken from the refrigerator to let it come to room temperature while you set up a dredging station. Place the flour in a shallow dish and season well with salt and freshly ground black pepper. Whisk the eggs in a second shallow dish. In a third shallow dish, combine the breadcrumbs, salt, pepper, paprika and cayenne pepper.
3. Preheat the toaster oven to 370°F.
4. Remove the chicken from the pickle brine and gently dry it with a clean kitchen towel. Dredge each piece of chicken in the flour, then dip it into the egg mixture, and finally press it into the breadcrumb mixture to coat all sides of the chicken. Place the breaded chicken on a plate or baking sheet and spray each piece all over with vegetable oil.
5. Air-fry the chicken in two batches. Place two chicken thighs and two drumsticks into the air fryer oven. Air-fry for 10 minutes. Then, gently turn the chicken pieces over and air-fry for another 10 minutes. Remove the chicken pieces and let them rest on plate – do not cover. Repeat with the second batch of chicken, air-frying for 20 minutes, turning the chicken over halfway through.
6. Lower the temperature of the air fryer oven to 340°F. Place the first batch of chicken on top of the second batch already in the air fryer oven and air-fry for an additional 7 minutes. Serve warm and enjoy.

Foiled Rosemary Chicken Breasts

Servings: 2
Cooking Time: 30 Minutes
Ingredients:
- 2 skinless, boneless chicken breast halves
- Sauce:
- 3 tablespoons dry white wine
- 1 tablespoon Dijon mustard
- 2 tablespoons nonfat plain yogurt
- Salt and freshly ground black pepper to taste
- 2 rosemary sprigs

Directions:
1. Preheat the toaster oven to 400° F.
2. Place each breast on a 12 × 12-inch square of heavy-duty aluminum foil (or regular foil doubled) and turn up the edges of the foil.
3. Mix together the sauce ingredients and spoon over the chicken breasts. Lay a rosemary sprig on each breast. Bring up the edges of the foil and fold to form a sealed packet.
4. BAKE for 25 minutes or until juices run clear when the meat is pierced with a fork. Remove the rosemary sprigs.
5. BROIL for 5 minutes, or until lightly browned. Replace the sprigs and serve.

Pesto-crusted Chicken

Servings: 2
Cooking Time: 31 Minutes
Ingredients:
- Pesto:
- 1 cup fresh cilantro, parsley, and basil leaves
- 3 tablespoons nonfat plain yogurt
- ¼ cup pine nuts, walnut, or pecans
- 3 tablespoons grated Parmesan cheese
- 2 peeled garlic cloves
- 1 tablespoon lemon juice
- 3 tablespoons olive oil
- Salt and freshly ground black pepper to taste
- 2 skinless, boneless chicken breast halves

Directions:
1. Preheat the toaster oven to 450° F.
2. Blend the pesto ingredients in a blender or food processor until smooth. Set aside.
3. Place the chicken breast halves in an oiled or nonstick 8½ × 8½ × 2-inch square (cake) pan. With a butter knife or spatula, spread the mixture liberally on both sides of each chicken breast. Cover the dish with aluminum foil.
4. BAKE, covered, for 25 minutes, or until the chicken is tender. Remove from the oven and uncover.
5. BROIL for 6 minutes, or until the pesto coating is lightly browned.

Chicken Potpie

Servings: 4
Cooking Time: 48 Minutes
Ingredients:
- Pie filling:
- 1 tablespoon unbleached flour
- ½ cup evaporated skim milk
- 4 skinless, boneless chicken thighs, cut into 1-inch cubes
- 1 cup potatoes, peeled and cut into ½-inch pieces
- ½ cup frozen green peas
- ½ cup thinly sliced carrot
- 2 tablespoons chopped onion
- ½ cup chopped celery
- 1 teaspoon garlic powder
- Salt and freshly ground black pepper to taste
- 8 sheets phyllo pastry, thawed Olive oil

Directions:
1. Preheat the toaster oven to 400° F.
2. Whisk the flour into the milk until smooth in a 1-quart 8½ × 8½ × 4-inch ovenproof baking dish. Add the remaining filling ingredients and mix well. Adjust the seasonings to taste. Cover the dish with aluminum foil.
3. BAKE for 40 minutes, or until the carrot, potatoes, and celery are tender. Remove from the oven and uncover.
4. Place one sheet of phyllo pastry on top of the baked pie-filling mixture, bending the edges to fit the shape of the baking dish. Brush the sheet with olive oil. Add another sheet on top of it and brush with oil. Continue adding the remaining sheets, brushing each one, until the crust is completed. Brush the top with oil.
5. BAKE for 6 minutes, or until the phyllo pastry is browned.

Chicken Cutlets With Broccoli Rabe And Roasted Peppers

Servings: 2
Cooking Time: 10 Minutes
Ingredients:
- ½ bunch broccoli rabe
- olive oil, in a spray bottle
- salt and freshly ground black pepper
- ⅔ cup roasted red pepper strips
- 2 (4-ounce) boneless, skinless chicken breasts
- 2 tablespoons all-purpose flour
- 1 egg, beaten
- ⅓ cup seasoned breadcrumbs
- 2 slices aged provolone cheese

Directions:
1. Bring a medium saucepot of salted water to a boil on the stovetop. Blanch the broccoli rabe for 3 minutes in the boiling water and then drain. When it has cooled a little, squeeze out as much water as possible, drizzle a little olive oil on top, season with salt and black pepper and set aside. Dry the roasted red peppers with a clean kitchen towel and set them aside as well.
2. Place each chicken breast between 2 pieces of plastic wrap. Use a meat pounder to flatten the chicken breasts to about ½-inch thick. Season the chicken on both sides with salt and pepper.
3. Preheat the toaster oven to 400°F.
4. Set up a dredging station with three shallow dishes. Place the flour in one dish, the egg in a second dish and the breadcrumbs in a third dish. Coat the chicken on all sides with the flour. Shake off any excess flour and dip the chicken into the egg. Let the excess egg drip off and coat both sides of the chicken in the breadcrumbs. Spray the chicken with olive oil on both sides and transfer to the air fryer oven.

5. Air-fry the chicken at 400°F for 5 minutes. Turn the chicken over and air-fry for another minute. Then, top the chicken breast with the broccoli rabe and roasted peppers. Place a slice of the provolone cheese on top and secure it with a toothpick or two.
6. Air-fry at 360° for 3 to 4 minutes to melt the cheese and warm everything together.

Jerk Turkey Meatballs

Servings: 7
Cooking Time: 8 Minutes
Ingredients:
- 1 pound lean ground turkey
- ¼ cup chopped onion
- 1 teaspoon minced garlic
- ½ teaspoon dried thyme
- ¼ teaspoon ground cinnamon
- 1 teaspoon cayenne pepper
- ½ teaspoon paprika
- ½ teaspoon salt
- ⅛ teaspoon black pepper
- ¼ teaspoon red pepper flakes
- 2 teaspoons brown sugar
- 1 large egg, whisked
- ⅓ cup panko breadcrumbs
- 2⅓ cups cooked brown Jasmine rice
- 2 green onions, chopped
- ¾ cup sweet onion dressing

Directions:
1. Preheat the toaster oven to 350°F.
2. In a medium bowl, mix the ground turkey with the onion, garlic, thyme, cinnamon, cayenne pepper, paprika, salt, pepper, red pepper flakes, and brown sugar. Add the whisked egg and stir in the breadcrumbs until the turkey starts to hold together.
3. Using a 1-ounce scoop, portion the turkey into meatballs. You should get about 28 meatballs.
4. Spray the air fryer oven with olive oil spray.
5. Place the meatballs into the air fryer oven and air-fry for 5 minutes, rotate the meatball, and cook another 2 to 4 minutes (or until the internal temperature of the meatballs reaches 165°F).
6. Remove the meatballs from the air fryer oven and repeat for the remaining meatballs.
7. Serve warm over a bed of rice with chopped green onions and spicy Caribbean jerk dressing.

Coconut Chicken With Apricot-ginger Sauce

Servings: 4
Cooking Time: 8 Minutes
Ingredients:
- 1½ pounds boneless, skinless chicken tenders, cut in large chunks (about 1¼ inches)
- salt and pepper
- ½ cup cornstarch
- 2 eggs
- 1 tablespoon milk
- 3 cups shredded coconut (see below)
- oil for misting or cooking spray
- Apricot-Ginger Sauce
- ½ cup apricot preserves
- 2 tablespoons white vinegar
- ¼ teaspoon ground ginger
- ¼ teaspoon low-sodium soy sauce
- 2 teaspoons white or yellow onion, grated or finely minced

Directions:
1. Mix all ingredients for the Apricot-Ginger Sauce well and let sit for flavors to blend while you cook the chicken.
2. Season chicken chunks with salt and pepper to taste.
3. Place cornstarch in a shallow dish.
4. In another shallow dish, beat together eggs and milk.
5. Place coconut in a third shallow dish. (If also using panko breadcrumbs, as suggested below, stir them to mix well.)
6. Spray air fryer oven with oil or cooking spray.
7. Dip each chicken chunk into cornstarch, shake off excess, and dip in egg mixture.
8. Shake off excess egg mixture and roll lightly in coconut or coconut mixture. Spray with oil.
9. Place coated chicken chunks in air fryer oven in a single layer, close together but without sides touching.
10. Air-fry at 360°F for 4 minutes, stop, and turn chunks over.
11. Cook an additional 4 minutes or until chicken is done inside and coating is crispy brown.
12. Repeat steps 9 through 11 to cook remaining chicken chunks.

Rotisserie-style Chicken

Servings: 4
Cooking Time: 75 Minutes
Ingredients:
- 1 (3-pound) whole chicken
- 1 teaspoon sea salt
- 1 teaspoon paprika
- 1 teaspoon dried thyme
- 1 teaspoon dried rosemary
- ¼ teaspoon freshly ground black pepper
- 2 tablespoons olive oil

Directions:
1. Preheat the toaster oven to 375°F on CONVECTION BAKE for 5 minutes.
2. Line the baking tray with foil.
3. Pat the chicken dry with paper towels and season all over with the salt, paprika, thyme, rosemary, and pepper. Place the chicken on the baking tray and drizzle with olive oil.
4. In position 1, bake for 1 hour and 15 minutes, until golden brown and the internal temperature of a thigh reads 165°F.
5. Let the chicken rest for 10 minutes and serve.

Quick Chicken For Filling

Servings: 2
Cooking Time: 8 Minutes
Ingredients:
- 1 pound chicken tenders, skinless and boneless
- ½ teaspoon ground cumin
- ½ teaspoon garlic powder
- cooking spray

Directions:
1. Sprinkle raw chicken tenders with seasonings.
2. Spray air fryer oven lightly with cooking spray to prevent sticking.
3. Place chicken in air fryer oven in single layer.
4. Air-fry at 390°F for 4 minutes, turn chicken strips over, and air-fry for an additional 4 minutes.
5. Test for doneness. Thick tenders may require an additional minute or two.

Tandoori Chicken

Servings: 4
Cooking Time: 30 Minutes
Ingredients:
- 1 cup plain Greek yogurt
- ¼ sweet onion, finely chopped
- 2 teaspoons garam masala
- 1 teaspoon minced garlic
- 1 teaspoon fresh ginger, peeled and grated
- ½ teaspoon ground cumin
- ½ teaspoon ground coriander
- ¼ teaspoon sea salt
- ⅛ teaspoon cayenne powder
- 4 (4-ounce) skinless, boneless chicken breasts
- Oil spray (hand-pumped)

Directions:
1. Preheat the toaster oven to 375°F on AIR FRY for 5 minutes.
2. In a medium bowl, whisk the yogurt, onion, garam masala, garlic, ginger, cumin, coriander, salt, and cayenne until well blended. Add the chicken breast, turning to coat.
3. Cover the bowl and refrigerate for at least 3 hours to overnight.
4. Place the air-fryer basket in the baking tray and spray it generously with the oil.
5. Place the chicken breasts in the basket after shaking off the excess marinade. Discard the remaining marinade.
6. In position 2, air fry for 25 to 30 minutes, turning halfway through, until browned with an internal temperature of 165°F. Serve.

Gluten-free Nutty Chicken Fingers

Servings: 4
Cooking Time: 10 Minutes
Ingredients:
- ½ cup gluten-free flour
- ½ teaspoon garlic powder
- ¼ teaspoon onion powder
- ¼ teaspoon black pepper
- ¼ teaspoon salt
- 1 cup walnuts, pulsed into coarse flour
- ½ cup gluten-free breadcrumbs
- 2 large eggs
- 1 pound boneless, skinless chicken tenders

Directions:
1. Preheat the toaster oven to 400°F.
2. In a medium bowl, mix the flour, garlic, onion, pepper, and salt. Set aside.
3. In a separate bowl, mix the walnut flour and breadcrumbs.
4. In a third bowl, whisk the eggs.
5. Liberally spray the air fryer oven with olive oil spray.
6. Pat the chicken tenders dry with a paper towel. Dredge the tenders one at a time in the flour, then dip them in the

egg, and toss them in the breadcrumb coating. Repeat until all tenders are coated.

7. Set each tender in the air fryer oven, leaving room on each side of the tender to allow for flipping.

8. When the air fryer oven is full, cook 5 minutes, flip, and cook another 5 minutes. Check the internal temperature after cooking completes; it should read 165°F. If it does not, cook another 2 to 4 minutes.

9. Remove the tenders and let cool 5 minutes before serving. Repeat until all the tenders are cooked.

Parmesan Crusted Chicken Cordon Bleu

Servings: 2
Cooking Time: 14 Minutes
Ingredients:
- 2 (6-ounce) boneless, skinless chicken breasts
- salt and freshly ground black pepper
- 1 tablespoon Dijon mustard
- 4 slices Swiss cheese
- 4 slices deli-sliced ham
- ¼ cup all-purpose flour
- 1 egg, beaten
- ¾ cup panko breadcrumbs
- ⅓ cup grated Parmesan cheese
- olive oil, in a spray bottle

Directions:
1. Butterfly the chicken breasts. Place the chicken breast on a cutting board and press down on the breast with the palm of your hand. Slice into the long side of the chicken breast, parallel to the cutting board, but not all the way through to the other side. Open the chicken breast like a "book". Place a piece of plastic wrap over the chicken breast and gently pound it with a meat mallet to make it evenly thick.

2. Season the chicken with salt and pepper. Spread the Dijon mustard on the inside of each chicken breast. Layer one slice of cheese on top of the mustard, then top with the 2 slices of ham and the other slice of cheese.

3. Starting with the long edge of the chicken breast, roll the chicken up to the other side. Secure it shut with 1 or 2 toothpicks.

4. Preheat the toaster oven to 350°F.

5. Set up a dredging station with three shallow dishes. Place the flour in the first dish. Place the beaten egg in the second shallow dish. Combine the panko breadcrumbs and Parmesan cheese together in the third shallow dish. Dip the stuffed and rolled chicken breasts in the flour, then the beaten egg and then roll in the breadcrumb-cheese mixture to cover on all sides. Press the crumbs onto the chicken breasts with your hands to make sure they are well adhered. Spray the chicken breasts with olive oil and transfer to the air fryer oven.

6. Air-fry at 350°F for 14 minutes, flipping the breasts over halfway through the cooking time. Let the chicken rest for a few minutes before removing the toothpicks, slicing and serving.

Harissa Lemon Whole Chicken

Servings: 6
Cooking Time: 60 Minutes
Ingredients:
- 2 teaspoons kosher salt
- ½ teaspoon freshly ground black pepper
- ½ teaspoon ground cumin
- 2 garlic cloves
- 6 tablespoons harissa paste
- ½ lemon, juiced
- 1 whole lemon, zested
- 1 (5 pound) whole chicken

Directions:
1. Place salt, pepper, cumin, garlic cloves, harissa paste, lemon juice, and lemon zest in a food processor and pulse until they form a smooth puree.

2. Rub the puree all over the chicken, especially inside the cavity, and cover with plastic wrap.

3. Marinate for 1 hour at room temperature.

4. Preheat the toaster oven to 350°F.

5. Place the marinated chicken on the food tray, then insert the tray at low position in the preheated oven.

6. Select the Roast function, then press Start/Pause.

7. Remove when done, tent chicken with foil, and allow it to rest for 20 minutes before serving.

Sesame Chicken Breasts

Servings: 2
Cooking Time: 20 Minutes
Ingredients:
- Mixture:
- 2 tablespoons sesame oil
- 2 teaspoons soy sauce
- 2 teaspoons balsamic vinegar
- 2 skinless, boneless chicken breast filets
- 3 tablespoons sesame seeds

Directions:

1. Combine the mixture ingredients in a small bowl and brush the filets liberally. Reserve the mixture. Place the filets on a broiling rack with a pan underneath.
2. BROIL 15 minutes, or until the meat is tender and the juices, when the meat is pierced, run clear. Remove from the oven and brush the filets with the remaining mixture. Place the sesame seeds on a plate and press the chicken breast halves into the seeds, coating well.
3. BROIL for 5 minutes, or until the sesame seeds are browned.

Crispy Curry Chicken Tenders

Servings: 4
Cooking Time: 14 Minutes
Ingredients:
- 1 pound boneless skinless chicken tenders
- ¼ cup plain yogurt
- 2 tablespoons thai red curry paste
- 1½ teaspoons salt, divided
- ½ teaspoon pepper
- 1¾ cups panko breadcrumbs
- 1 teaspoon granulated garlic
- 1 teaspoon granulated onion
- Olive oil or avocado oil spray

Directions:
1. Whisk together the yogurt, curry paste, 1 teaspoon of salt, and pepper in a large bowl. Add the chicken tenders and toss to coat. Cover bowl with plastic wrap and marinate in the fridge for 6-8 hours.
2. Combine the panko breadcrumbs, ½ teaspoon salt, garlic, and onion. Remove chicken tenders from the marinade and coat individually in the panko mixture.
3. Preheat the toaster oven to 430°F.
4. Spray both sides of each chicken tender well with olive oil or avocado oil spray, then place into the fry basket.
5. Insert the fry basket at mid position in the preheated oven.
6. Select the Air Fry and Shake functions, adjust time to 14 minutes, and press Start/Pause.
7. Flip chicken tenders halfway through cooking. The Shake Reminder will let you know when.
8. Remove when chicken tenders are golden and crispy.

Oven-crisped Chicken

Servings: 4
Cooking Time: 35 Minutes
Ingredients:
- Coating mixture:
- 1 cup cornmeal
- ¼ cup wheat germ
- 1 teaspoon paprika
- 1 teaspoon garlic powder
- Salt and butcher's pepper to taste
- 3 tablespoons olive oil
- 1 tablespoon spicy brown mustard
- 6 skinless, boneless chicken thighs

Directions:
1. Preheat the toaster oven to 375° F.
2. Combine the coating mixture ingredients in a small bowl and transfer to a plate, spreading the mixture evenly over the plate's surface. Set aside.
3. Whisk together the oil and mustard in a bowl. Add the chicken pieces and toss to coat thoroughly. Press both sides of each piece into the coating mixture to coat well. Chill in the refrigerator for 10 minutes. Transfer the chicken pieces to a broiling rack with a pan underneath.
4. BAKE, uncovered, for 35 minutes, or until the meat is tender and the coating is crisp and golden brown or browned to your preference.

Chicken Wellington

Servings: 4
Cooking Time: 30 Minutes
Ingredients:
- 2 small (5- to 6-ounce) boneless, skinless chicken breast halves
- Kosher salt and freshly ground black pepper
- 2 teaspoons Italian seasoning
- 2 tablespoons olive oil
- 3 tablespoons unsalted butter, softened
- 3 ounces cream cheese, softened (about ⅓ cup)
- ¾ cup shredded Monterey Jack cheese
- ¼ cup grated Parmesan cheese
- 1 cup frozen (loose-pack) chopped spinach, thawed and squeezed dry
- ¾ cup chopped canned artichoke hearts, drained
- ½ teaspoon garlic powder
- 1 sheet frozen puff pastry, about 9 inches square, thawed (½ of a 17.3-ounce package)
- 1 large egg, lightly beaten

Directions:
1. Preheat the toaster oven to 425° F. Line a 12 x 12-inch baking pan with parchment paper.
2. Cut the chicken breasts in half lengthwise. Season each piece with the salt, pepper, and Italian seasoning. Fold the thinner end under the larger piece to make the chicken breasts into a rounded shape. Secure with toothpicks.

3. Heat a large skillet over medium-high heat. Add the olive oil and heat. Add the chicken breasts and brown well, turning to brown evenly. Remove from the skillet and set aside to cool. Remove the toothpicks.

4. Stir the butter, cream cheese, Monterey Jack, and Parmesan in a large bowl. Stir in the spinach, artichoke hearts, and garlic powder. Season with salt and pepper.

5. Roll out the puff pastry sheet on a lightly floured board until it makes a 12-inch square. Cut into four equal pieces. Spread one-fourth of the spinach-artichoke mixture on the surface of each pastry square to within ½ inch of all four edges. Place the chicken in the center of each. Gently fold the puff pastry up over the chicken and pinch the edges to seal tightly.

6. Place each chicken bundle, seam side down, on the prepared pan. Brush the top of each bundle lightly with the beaten egg. Bake for 25 to 30 minutes, or until the pastry is golden brown and crisp and a meat thermometer inserted into the chicken reaches 165°F.

Sesame Orange Chicken

Servings: 2
Cooking Time: 9 Minutes
Ingredients:
- 1 pound boneless, skinless chicken breasts, cut into cubes
- salt and freshly ground black pepper
- ¼ cup cornstarch
- 2 eggs, beaten
- 1½ cups panko breadcrumbs
- vegetable or peanut oil, in a spray bottle
- 12 ounces orange marmalade
- 1 tablespoon soy sauce
- 1 teaspoon minced ginger
- 2 tablespoons hoisin sauce
- 1 tablespoon sesame oil
- sesame seeds, toasted

Directions:
1. Season the chicken pieces with salt and pepper. Set up a dredging station. Put the cornstarch in a zipper-sealable plastic bag. Place the beaten eggs in a bowl and put the panko breadcrumbs in a shallow dish. Transfer the seasoned chicken to the bag with the cornstarch and shake well to completely coat the chicken on all sides. Remove the chicken from the bag, shaking off any excess cornstarch and dip the pieces into the egg. Let any excess egg drip from the chicken and transfer into the breadcrumbs, pressing the crumbs onto the chicken pieces with your hands. Spray the chicken pieces with vegetable or peanut oil.

2. Preheat the toaster oven to 400°F.

3. Combine the orange marmalade, soy sauce, ginger, hoisin sauce and sesame oil in a saucepan. Bring the mixture to a boil on the stovetop, lower the heat and simmer for 10 minutes, until the sauce has thickened. Set aside and keep warm.

4. Transfer the coated chicken to the air fryer oven and air-fry at 400°F for 9 minutes, rotate a few times during the cooking process to help the chicken cook evenly.

5. Right before serving, toss the browned chicken pieces with the sesame orange sauce. Serve over white rice with steamed broccoli. Sprinkle the sesame seeds on top.

Poblano Bake

Servings: 4
Cooking Time: 11 Minutes
Ingredients:
- 2 large poblano peppers (approx. 5½ inches long excluding stem)
- ¾ pound ground turkey, raw
- ¾ cup cooked brown rice
- 1 teaspoon chile powder
- ½ teaspoon ground cumin
- ½ teaspoon garlic powder
- 4 ounces sharp Cheddar cheese, grated
- 1 8-ounce jar salsa, warmed

Directions:
1. Slice each pepper in half lengthwise so that you have four wide, flat pepper halves.

2. Remove seeds and membrane and discard. Rinse inside and out.

3. In a large bowl, combine turkey, rice, chile powder, cumin, and garlic powder. Mix well.

4. Divide turkey filling into 4 portions and stuff one into each of the 4 pepper halves. Press lightly to pack down.

5. Place 2 pepper halves in air fryer oven and air-fry at 390°F for 10 minutes or until turkey is well done.

6. Top each pepper half with ¼ of the grated cheese. Cook 1 more minute or just until cheese melts.

7. Repeat steps 5 and 6 to cook remaining pepper halves.

8. To serve, place each pepper half on a plate and top with ¼ cup warm salsa.

Sticky Soy Chicken Thighs

Servings: 2
Cooking Time: 20 Minutes
Ingredients:
- 2 tablespoons less-sodium soy sauce
- 1 tablespoon olive oil
- 1 tablespoon honey
- 1 tablespoon balsamic vinegar
- 1 tablespoon chili sauce
- Juice of 1 lime
- 1 teaspoon minced garlic
- 1 teaspoon ginger, peeled and grated
- 2 bone-in, skin-on chicken thighs
- Oil spray (hand-pumped)
- 1 scallion, both white and green parts, thinly sliced, for garnish
- 2 teaspoons sesame seeds, for garnish

Directions:
1. Preheat the toaster oven to 400°F on AIR FRY for 5 minutes.
2. In a large bowl, combine the soy sauce, olive oil, honey, balsamic vinegar, chili sauce, lime juice, garlic, and ginger. Add the chicken thighs to the bowl and toss to coat. Cover the bowl and refrigerate for 30 minutes.
3. Place the air-fryer basket in the baking tray and generously spray with oil.
4. Place the thighs in the basket, and in position 2, air fry for 20 minutes until cooked through and the thighs are browned and lightly caramelized, with an internal temperature of 165°F.
5. Garnish the chicken with the scallion and sesame seeds and serve.

Chicken In Mango Sauce

Servings: 2
Cooking Time: 40 Minutes
Ingredients:
- 2 skinless and boneless chicken breast halves
- 1 tablespoon capers
- 1 tablespoon raisins
- Mango mixture:
- 1 cup mango pieces
- 1 teaspoon balsamic vinegar
- ½ teaspoon garlic powder
- 1 teaspoon fresh ginger, peeled and minced
- ½ teaspoon soy sauce
- ½ teaspoon curry powder
- 1 tablespoon pimientos, minced
- Salt and pepper to taste

Directions:
1. Preheat the toaster oven to 375° F.
2. Process the mango mixture ingredients in a food processor or blender until smooth. Transfer to an oiled or nonstick 8½ × 8½ × 2-inch square (cake) pan and add the capers, raisins, and pimientos, stirring well to blend. Add the chicken breasts and spoon the mixture over the breasts to coat well.
3. BAKE for 40 minutes. Serve the breasts with the sauce.

Guiltless Bacon

Servings: 4
Cooking Time: 10 Minutes
Ingredients:
- 6 slices lean turkey bacon, placed on a broiling pan

Directions:
1. BROIL 5 minutes, turn the pieces, and broil again for 5 more minutes, or until done to your preference. Press the slices between paper towels and serve immediately.

Chicken Souvlaki Gyros

Servings: 4
Cooking Time: 18 Minutes
Ingredients:
- ¼ cup extra-virgin olive oil
- 1 clove garlic, crushed
- 1 tablespoon Italian seasoning
- ½ teaspoon paprika
- ½ lemon, sliced
- ¼ teaspoon salt
- 1 pound boneless, skinless chicken breasts
- 4 whole-grain pita breads
- 1 cup shredded lettuce
- ½ cup chopped tomatoes
- ¼ cup chopped red onion
- ¼ cup cucumber yogurt sauce

Directions:
1. In a large resealable plastic bag, combine the olive oil, garlic, Italian seasoning, paprika, lemon, and salt. Add the chicken to the bag and secure shut. Vigorously shake until all the ingredients are combined. Set in the fridge for 2 hours to marinate.
2. When ready to cook, preheat the toaster oven to 360°F.
3. Liberally spray the air fryer oven with olive oil mist. Remove the chicken from the bag and discard the leftover marinade. Place the chicken into the air fryer oven, allowing enough room between the chicken breasts to flip.

4. Air-fry for 10 minutes, flip, and cook another 8 minutes.
5. Remove the chicken from the air fryer oven when it has cooked (or the internal temperature of the chicken reaches 165°F). Let rest 5 minutes. Then thinly slice the chicken into strips.
6. Assemble the gyros by placing the pita bread on a flat surface and topping with chicken, lettuce, tomatoes, onion, and a drizzle of yogurt sauce.
7. Serve warm.

Teriyaki Chicken Drumsticks

Servings: 2
Cooking Time: 17 Minutes
Ingredients:
- 2 tablespoons soy sauce
- ¼ cup dry sherry
- 1 tablespoon brown sugar
- 2 tablespoons water
- 1 tablespoon rice wine vinegar
- 1 clove garlic, crushed
- 1-inch fresh ginger, peeled and sliced
- pinch crushed red pepper flakes
- 4 to 6 bone-in, skin-on chicken drumsticks
- 1 tablespoon cornstarch
- fresh cilantro leaves

Directions:
1. Make the marinade by combining the soy sauce, dry sherry, brown sugar, water, rice vinegar, garlic, ginger and crushed red pepper flakes. Pour the marinade over the chicken legs, cover and let the chicken marinate for 1 to 4 hours in the refrigerator.
2. Preheat the toaster oven to 380°F.
3. Transfer the chicken from the marinade to the air fryer oven, transferring any extra marinade to a small saucepan. Air-fry at 380°F for 8 minutes. Flip the chicken over and continue to air-fry for another 6 minutes, watching to make sure it doesn't brown too much.
4. While the chicken is cooking, bring the reserved marinade to a simmer on the stovetop. Dissolve the cornstarch in 2 tablespoons of water and stir this into the saucepan. Bring to a boil to thicken the sauce. Remove the garlic clove and slices of ginger from the sauce and set aside.
5. When the time is up on the air fryer oven, brush the thickened sauce on the chicken and air-fry for 3 more minutes. Remove the chicken from the air fryer oven and brush with the remaining sauce.
6. Serve over rice and sprinkle the cilantro leaves on top.

Philly Chicken Cheesesteak Stromboli

Servings: 2
Cooking Time: 28 Minutes
Ingredients:
- ½ onion, sliced
- 1 teaspoon vegetable oil
- 2 boneless, skinless chicken breasts, partially frozen and sliced very thin on the bias (about 1 pound)
- 1 tablespoon Worcestershire sauce
- salt and freshly ground black pepper
- ½ recipe of Blue Jean Chef pizza dough, or 14 ounces of store-bought pizza dough
- 1½ cups grated Cheddar cheese
- ½ cup Cheese Whiz® (or other jarred cheese sauce), warmed gently in the microwave
- tomato ketchup for serving

Directions:
1. Preheat the toaster oven to 400°F.
2. Toss the sliced onion with oil and air-fry for 8 minutes, stirring halfway through the cooking time. Add the sliced chicken and Worcestershire sauce to the air fryer oven, and toss to evenly distribute the ingredients. Season the mixture with salt and freshly ground black pepper and air-fry for 8 minutes, stirring a couple of times during the cooking process. Remove the chicken and onion from the air fryer oven and let the mixture cool a little.
3. On a lightly floured surface, roll or press the pizza dough out into a 13-inch by 11-inch rectangle, with the long side closest to you. Sprinkle half of the Cheddar cheese over the dough leaving an empty 1-inch border from the edge farthest away from you. Top the cheese with the chicken and onion mixture, spreading it out evenly. Drizzle the cheese sauce over the meat and sprinkle the remaining Cheddar cheese on top.
4. Start rolling the stromboli away from you and toward the empty border. Make sure the filling stays tightly tucked inside the roll. Finally, tuck the ends of the dough in and pinch the seam shut. Place the seam side down and shape the Stromboli into a U-shape to fit in the air-fry oven. Cut 4 small slits with the tip of a sharp knife evenly in the top of the dough and lightly brush the stromboli with a little oil.
5. Preheat the toaster oven to 370°F.
6. Spray or brush the air fryer oven with oil and transfer the U-shaped stromboli to the air fryer oven. Air-fry for 12 minutes, turning the stromboli over halfway through the cooking time. (Use a plate to invert the stromboli out of the air fryer oven and then slide it back into the air fryer oven off the plate.)

7. To remove, carefully flip stromboli over onto a cutting board. Let it rest for a couple of minutes before serving. Slice the stromboli into 3-inch pieces and serve with ketchup for dipping, if desired.

Fiesta Chicken Plate

Servings: 4
Cooking Time: 15 Minutes
Ingredients:
- 1 pound boneless, skinless chicken breasts (2 large breasts)
- 2 tablespoons lime juice
- 1 teaspoon cumin
- ½ teaspoon salt
- ½ cup grated Pepper Jack cheese
- 1 16-ounce can refried beans
- ½ cup salsa
- 2 cups shredded lettuce
- 1 medium tomato, chopped
- 2 avocados, peeled and sliced
- 1 small onion, sliced into thin rings
- sour cream
- tortilla chips (optional)

Directions:
1. Split each chicken breast in half lengthwise.
2. Mix lime juice, cumin, and salt together and brush on all surfaces of chicken breasts.
3. Place in air fryer oven and air-fry at 390°F for 15 minutes, until well done.
4. Divide the cheese evenly over chicken breasts and air-fry for an additional minute to melt cheese.
5. While chicken is cooking, heat refried beans on stovetop or in microwave.
6. When ready to serve, divide beans among 4 plates. Place chicken breasts on top of beans and spoon salsa over. Arrange the lettuce, tomatoes, and avocados artfully on each plate and scatter with the onion rings.
7. Pass sour cream at the table and serve with tortilla chips if desired.

Chicken-fried Steak With Gravy

Servings: 2
Cooking Time: 16 Minutes
Ingredients:
- FOR THE STEAK
- Oil spray (hand-pumped)
- 1 cup all-purpose flour
- 1 teaspoon garlic powder
- 1 teaspoon onion powder
- 1 teaspoon smoked paprika
- 2 large eggs
- 2 (½-pound) cube steaks
- Sea salt, for seasoning
- Freshly ground black pepper, for seasoning
- FOR THE GRAVY
- 2 tablespoons salted butter
- 2 tablespoons all-purpose flour
- 1½ cups whole milk
- ¼ cup heavy (whipping) cream
- Sea salt, for seasoning
- Freshly ground black pepper, for seasoning

Directions:
1. To make the steak
2. Preheat the toaster oven to 400°F on AIR FRY for 5 minutes.
3. Place the air-fryer basket in the baking tray and spray it generously with the oil.
4. In a medium bowl, stir the flour, garlic powder, onion powder, and paprika until well blended.
5. In a medium bowl, beat the eggs and place them next to the flour.
6. Season the steaks all over with salt and pepper.
7. Dredge a steak in the egg and then in the flour mixture, making sure it is well coated. Shake off any excess flour.
8. Place the steak in the basket and repeat the process with the other steak.
9. Spray the tops of the steaks with the oil.
10. In position 2, air fry for 9 minutes until golden brown and crispy. Turn the steaks over, spray the second side with the oil, and air fry for an additional 7 minutes.
11. Set the steaks aside to rest for 5 minutes.
12. To make the gravy
13. While the steak is air frying, melt the butter in a medium saucepan over medium-high heat.
14. Whisk in the flour and cook for 2 minutes until lightly browned.
15. Whisk in the milk until the gravy is creamy and thick, about 5 minutes. Whisk in the cream and season with salt and pepper.
16. Serve the steak topped with the gravy.

Lunch And Dinner

Favorite Baked Ziti

Servings: 4
Cooking Time: 30 Minutes
Ingredients:
- 2 tablespoons olive oil
- 1 small onion, diced
- 3 cloves garlic, minced
- ¼ teaspoon red pepper flakes
- 1 pound lean ground beef
- ½ teaspoon kosher salt
- ¼ cup dry red wine
- 1 (14.5-ounce) can crushed tomatoes
- 1 tablespoon tomato paste
- 16 ounces ziti, uncooked
- Nonstick cooking spray
- ⅓ cup grated Parmesan cheese
- 1 ½ cups shredded mozzarella cheese
- 2 ounces fresh mozzarella cheese, cut into cubes (about ½ cup)

Directions:
1. Heat the olive oil in a large skillet over medium-high heat. Add the onion and cook, stirring frequently, until tender, 3 to 4 minutes. Stir in the garlic and red pepper flakes. Add the ground beef and salt. Cook, breaking up the ground beef, until the meat is brown and cooked through. Drain well, if needed, and return to the skillet.
2. Add the wine and cook for 2 minutes. Add the tomatoes, tomato paste, and ¾ cup water. Reduce the heat and simmer, uncovered, for 20 to 25 minutes, stirring occasionally.
3. Cook the ziti according to the package directions, except reduce the cooking time to 7 minutes. The ziti will be harder than Al Dente, which is what you want. Drain and rinse under cold water. Transfer to a large bowl.
4. Preheat the toaster oven to 425 ºF. Spray an 11 x 7 x 2 ½-inch baking dish with nonstick cooking spray. Spoon about 1 cup of the meat sauce into the prepared dish. Add half of the ziti in an even layer. Spoon about half of the remaining sauce over the ziti. Sprinkle with half the Parmesan and all the shredded mozzarella. Add the remaining half of ziti and cover with the remaining sauce. Sprinkle the remaining Parmesan on top.
5. Bake, covered, for 20 minutes. Remove from the oven and add the cubes of fresh mozzarella. Bake, uncovered, for an additional 10 minutes. If desired, turn to broil for a few minutes to make the top crispy and brown.
6. Remove from the oven and let stand for 10 minutes before serving.

Quick Pan Pizza

Servings: 8
Cooking Time: 22 Minutes
Ingredients:
- 1 can (13.8 oz.) refrigerator pizza crust, cut in half
- 2 tablespoons oil, divided
- 2/3 cup Slow Cooker Marinara Sauce, divided
- 2 cups shredded mozzarella cheese, divided
- 18 slices pepperoni, divided
- 1 small green pepper, sliced into rings, divided
- 2 large mushrooms, sliced, divided

Directions:
1. Preheat the toaster oven to 425°F. Spray baking pan with nonstick cooking spray.
2. Press half of dough into pan. Brush with 1 tablespoon oil.
3. Bake 8 to 9 minutes or until light brown.
4. Top baked crust with 1/3 cup sauce, 1 cup shredded mozzarella cheese and half of the pepperoni, green pepper and mushrooms.
5. Bake an additional 11 to 13 minutes or until cheese is melted and crust is brown. Repeat to make second pizza.

Sage, Chicken + Mushroom Pasta Casserole

Servings: 6
Cooking Time: 35 Minutes
Ingredients:
- Nonstick cooking spray
- 8 ounces bow-tie pasta, uncooked
- 4 tablespoons unsalted butter
- 8 ounces button or white mushrooms, sliced
- 3 tablespoons all-purpose flour
- Kosher salt and freshly ground black pepper
- 2 cups whole milk
- ½ cup dry white wine
- 2 tablespoons minced fresh sage
- 1 ½ cups chopped cooked chicken
- 1 cup shredded fontina, Monterey Jack, or Swiss cheese
- ½ cup shredded Parmesan cheese

Directions:

1. Preheat the toaster oven to 350°F. Spray a 2-quart baking pan with nonstick cooking spray.
2. Cook the pasta according to the package directions; drain and set aside.
3. Melt the butter in a large skillet over medium-high heat. Add the mushrooms and cook, stirring frequently, until the liquid has evaporated, 7 to 10 minutes. Blend in the flour and cook, stirring constantly, for 1 minute. Season with salt and pepper. Gradually stir in the milk and wine. Cook, stirring constantly, until the mixture bubbles and begins to thicken. Remove from the heat. Stir in the sage, cooked pasta, chicken, and fontina. Season with salt and pepper.
4. Spoon into the prepared pan. Cover and bake for 25 to 30 minutes. Uncover, sprinkle with the Parmesan, and bake for an additional 5 minutes or until the cheese is melted.
5. Remove from the oven and let stand for 5 to 10 minutes before serving.

Kashaburgers

Servings: 4
Cooking Time: 50 Minutes
Ingredients:
- 1 cup kasha
- 2 tablespoons minced onion or scallions
- 1 tablespoon minced garlic
- ½ cup multigrain bread crumbs
- 1 egg
- ¼ teaspoon paprika
- ½ teaspoon chili powder
- ¼ teaspoon sesame oil
- 1 tablespoon vegetable oil
- Salt and freshly ground black pepper to taste

Directions:
1. Preheat the toaster oven to 400° F.
2. Combine 2 cups water and the kasha in a 1-quart 8½ × 8½ × 4-inch ovenproof baking dish.
3. BAKE, uncovered, for 30 minutes, or until the grains are cooked. Remove from the oven and add all the other ingredients, stirring to mix well. When the mixture is cooled, shape into 4 to 6 patties and place on a rack with a broiling pan underneath.
4. BROIL for 20 minutes, turn with a spatula, then broil for another 10 minutes, or until browned.

Pea Soup

Servings: 6
Cooking Time: 55 Minutes
Ingredients:
- 1 cup dried split peas, ground in a blender to a powderlike consistency
- 3 strips lean turkey bacon, uncooked and chopped
- ¼ cup grated carrots
- ¼ cup grated celery
- 2 tablespoons grated onion
- ½ teaspoon garlic powder
- Salt and freshly ground black pepper to taste
- Garnish:
- 2 tablespoons chopped fresh chives

Directions:
1. Preheat the toaster oven to 400° F.
2. Combine all the ingredients in a 1-quart 8½ × 8½ × 4-inch ovenproof baking dish, mixing well. Adjust the seasonings.
3. BAKE, covered, for 35 minutes. Remove from the oven and stir.
4. BAKE, covered, for another 20 minutes, or until the soup is thickened. Ladle the soup into individual soup bowls and garnish each with chopped fresh chives.

French Onion Soup

Servings: 4
Cooking Time: 46 Minutes
Ingredients:
- 1 cup finely chopped onions
- 1 teaspoon toasted sesame oil
- 1 tablespoon vegetable oil
- 2 ½ cup dry white wine
- 3 teaspoons soy sauce
- ½ teaspoon garlic powder
- Freshly ground black pepper to taste
- 4 French bread rounds, sliced 1 inch thick
- 4 tablespoons grated Parmesan cheese
- 1 tablespoon chopped fresh parsley

Directions:
1. Place the onions, sesame oil, and vegetable oil in an 8½ × 8½ × 2-inch square baking (cake) pan.
2. BROIL for 10 minutes, stirring every 3 minutes until the onions are tender. Remove from the oven and transfer to a 1-quart 8½ × 8½ × 4-inch ovenproof baking dish. Add 2 cups water, the wine, and the soy sauce. Add the garlic powder and pepper and adjust the seasonings.
3. BAKE, covered, at 400° F. for 30 minutes. Remove from the oven, uncover, and add the 4 bread rounds, letting them float on top of the soup. Sprinkle each with 1 tablespoon Parmesan cheese.
4. BROIL, uncovered, for 6 minutes, or until the cheese is lightly browned. With tongs, transfer the bread rounds to 4

individual soup bowls. Ladle the soup on top of the bread rounds. Garnish with the parsley and serve immediately.

Italian Stuffed Zucchini Boats

Servings: 6
Cooking Time: 26 Minutes
Ingredients:
- 6 small zucchini, halved lengthwise
- 1 pound bulk hot sausage
- 1 small onion, chopped
- 2 cloves garlic, minced
- 1 small Roma tomato, seeded and chopped
- 1/4 cup Parmesan cheese
- 3 tablespoons tomato paste
- 2 teaspoons dried Italian seasoning
- 1 teaspoon salt
- 1/2 teaspoon coarse black pepper
- 1 cup shredded mozzarella cheese
- Sliced fresh basil

Directions:
1. Preheat the toaster oven to 350°F. Spray a 13x9-inch baking pan with nonstick cooking spray.
2. Scoop out center of zucchini halves. Reserve 1 1/2 cups. Place zucchini boats in baking pan.
3. In a large skillet over medium-high heat, cook sausage, stirring to crumble, about 6 minutes or until browned. Remove sausage to a medium bowl.
4. Add onion and garlic to skillet, cook until onion is translucent. Stir in reserved zucchini, sausage, tomatoes, Parmesan cheese, tomato paste, Italian seasoning, salt and black pepper.
5. Spoon mixture into the zucchini boats.
6. Bake for 20 minutes. Remove from oven and top with mozzarella cheese.
7. Bake an additional 5 to 6 minutes or until cheese is melted.
8. Sprinkle with sliced fresh basil before serving.

Crunchy Baked Chicken Tenders

Servings: 3-4
Cooking Time: 18 Minutes
Ingredients:
- 2/3 cup seasoned panko breadcrumbs
- 2/3 cup cheese crackers, crushed
- 2 teaspoons melted butter
- 2 large eggs, beaten
- Salt and pepper
- 1 1/2 pounds chicken tenders
- Barbecue sauce

Directions:
1. Preheat the toaster oven to 450°F. Spray the toaster oven baking pan with nonstick cooking spray.
2. In medium bowl, combine breadcrumbs, cheese cracker crumbs and butter.
3. In another medium bowl, mix eggs, salt and pepper.
4. Dip chicken tenders in eggs and dredge in breadcrumb mixture.
5. Place on pan.
6. Bake for 15 to 18 minutes, turning once. Serve with barbecue sauce for dipping.

Herbal Summer Casserole

Servings: 4
Cooking Time: 45 Minutes
Ingredients:
- 4 small yellow (summer) squashes, cut into ¾-inch slices
- 1 green bell pepper, seeded and chopped
- 1 tablespoon roasted garlic, mashed in 1 tablespoon olive oil
- ¼ cup seasoned bread crumbs
- ¼ cup grated Parmesan cheese
- ¼ cup chopped fresh parsley
- 2 tablespoons chopped fresh cilantro
- 2 tablespoons chopped onion
- 2 plum tomatoes, chopped
- 2 carrots, peeled and cut into ¼-inch slices
- 4 tablespoons fresh lemon juice
- ½ teaspoon caraway seeds
- ¼ teaspoon celery seed
- Salt and freshly ground black pepper to taste

Directions:
1. Preheat the toaster oven to 400° F.
2. Combine all the ingredients in a 1-quart 8½ × 8½ × 4-inch ovenproof baking dish, mixing well. Cover the dish with aluminum foil.
3. BAKE, covered, for 45 minutes, or until the vegetables are tender.

Gardener's Rice

Servings: 4
Cooking Time: 40 Minutes
Ingredients:
- ½ cup rice
- 2 tablespoons finely chopped scallions
- 2 small zucchini, finely chopped
- 1 bell pepper, finely chopped
- 1 small tomato, finely chopped
- ¼ cup frozen peas
- ¼ cup frozen corn
- 1 teaspoon ground cumin
- ½ teaspoon dried oregano or
- 1 teaspoon chopped fresh oregano
- Salt and freshly ground black pepper to taste

Directions:
1. Preheat the toaster oven to 400° F.
2. Combine all the ingredients with ¼ cups water in a 1-quart 8½ × 8½ × 4-inch ovenproof baking dish, stirring well to blend. Adjust the seasonings to taste. Cover with aluminum foil.
3. BAKE, covered, for 30 minutes, or until the rice and vegetables are almost cooked. Remove from the oven, uncover, and let stand for 10 minutes to complete the cooking. Fluff once more and adjust the seasonings before serving.

Inspirational Personal Pizza

Servings: 1
Cooking Time: 30 Minutes
Ingredients:
- 1 9-inch ready-made pizza crust
- 1 teaspoon olive oil
- 2 tablespoons tomato paste
- 4 ounces (½ cup) ground lean turkey breast
- 2 tablespoons sliced marinated artichokes
- 2 tablespoons pitted and chopped kalamata olives
- 2 tablespoons crumbled feta cheese
- 1 tablespoon chopped fresh basil leaves
- 1 tablespoon chopped fresh oregano leaves
- 2 tablespoons grated Parmesan cheese
- ¼ teaspoon red pepper flakes

Directions:
1. Preheat the toaster oven to 375°F.
2. Brush the pizza crust with the olive oil and spread on the tomato paste. Add all the other ingredients. Place the pizza on the toaster oven rack.
3. BAKE for 30 minutes, or until the topping is cooked and the crust is lightly browned.

Parmesan Crusted Tilapia

Servings: 2
Cooking Time: 14 Minutes
Ingredients:
- 2 ounces Parmesan cheese
- 1/4 cup Italian seasoned Panko bread crumbs
- 1/2 teaspoon Italian seasoning
- 1/4 teaspoon ground black pepper
- 1 tablespoon mayonnaise
- 2 tilapia fillets or other white fish fillets (about 4 ounces each)

Directions:
1. Preheat the toaster oven to 425°F. Spray baking pan with nonstick cooking spray.
2. Using a spiralizer, grate Parmesan cheese and place in a large resealable plastic bag. Add Panko bread crumbs, Italian seasoning and black pepper. Seal and shake bag.
3. Spread mayonnaise on both sides of fish fillets. Add fish to bag and shake until coated with crumb mixture.
4. Press remaining crumbs from bag onto fish. Place on prepared baking pan.
5. Bake until fish flakes easily with a fork, 12 to 14 minutes.

Moroccan Couscous

Servings: 4
Cooking Time: 22 Minutes
Ingredients:
- 1 cup couscous
- 2 tablespoons finely chopped scallion
- 2 tablespoons finely chopped bell pepper
- 1 plum tomato, finely chopped
- 2 tablespoons chopped pitted black olives
- 1 tablespoon olive oil
- ¼ teaspoon ground cumin
- ¼ teaspoon ground cinnamon
- ¼ teaspoon turmeric Pinch of cayenne
- Salt and freshly ground black pepper to taste

Directions:
1. Preheat the toaster oven to 400° F.
2. Combine all the ingredients with ¼ cups water in a 1-quart 8½ × 8½ × 4-inch ovenproof baking dish. Adjust the seasonings to taste. Cover with aluminum foil.

3. BAKE, covered, for 12 minutes. Remove from the heat and fluff with a fork. Cover again and let stand for 10 minutes. Fluff once more before serving.

Healthy Southwest Stuffed Peppers

Servings: 6
Cooking Time: 30 Minutes
Ingredients:
- 1 tablespoon oil
- 1 small onion, chopped
- 1 garlic clove, minced
- 1/2 pound ground turkey
- 1/2 cup drained black beans
- 1/2 cup whole kernel corn
- 1 jar (16 oz.) medium salsa, divided
- 1/2 cup cooked white rice
- 1/2 teaspoon chili powder
- 1/2 teaspoon salt
- 1/4 teaspoon ground cumin
- 1/4 teaspoon black pepper
- 3 medium peppers, halved lengthwise leaving stem on, seeded
- 1/3 cup shredded Monterey Jack cheese, divided
- Sour cream
- Chopped fresh cilantro

Directions:
1. Preheat the toaster oven to 350°F. Spray baking pan with nonstick cooking spray.
2. In a large skillet over medium-high, heat oil. Add onion and garlic, cook for 2 to 3 minutes.
3. Add turkey to skillet, cook, stirring frequently, for 6 to 8 minutes or until turkey is cooked through.
4. Stir black beans, corn, 1/2 cup salsa, rice, chili powder, salt, cumin and pepper into turkey mixture.
5. Fill each pepper half with turkey mixture, dividing mixture evenly among peppers.
6. Top each pepper half with remaining salsa.
7. Bake 20 minutes. Sprinkle with cheese and bake an additional 10 minutes or until heated through.
8. Top with sour cream and cilantro.

Chicken Noodle Soup

Servings: 4
Cooking Time: 45 Minutes
Ingredients:
- 1 cup egg noodles, uncooked
- 1 skinless, boneless chicken breast filet, cut into 1-inch pieces
- 1 carrot, peeled and chopped
- 1 celery stalk, chopped
- 1 plum tomato, chopped
- 1 small onion, peeled and chopped
- 1 tablespoon chopped fresh parsley
- 1 teaspoon dried basil
- Salt and freshly ground black pepper to taste

Directions:
1. Preheat the toaster oven to 400° F.
2. Combine all the ingredients with 3 cups water in a 1-quart 8½ × 8½ × 4-inch ovenproof baking dish.
3. BAKE, covered, for 45 minutes, or until the vegetables and chicken are tender.

Pesto Pizza

Servings: 1
Cooking Time: 20 Minutes
Ingredients:
- Topping:
- ½ cup chopped fresh basil
- 1 tablespoon pine nuts (pignoli)
- 1 tablespoon olive oil
- 2 tablespoons shredded Parmesan cheese
- 1 garlic clove, minced
- ½ teaspoon dried oregano or 1 tablespoon chopped fresh oregano
- 1 plum tomato, chopped
- Salt and pepper to taste
- 1 9-inch ready-made pizza crust
- 2 tablespoons shredded low-fat mozzarella

Directions:
1. Preheat the toaster oven to 375° F.
2. Combine the topping ingredients in a small bowl.
3. Process the mixture in a blender or food processor until smooth. Spread the mixture on the pizza crust, then sprinkle with the mozzarella cheese. Place the pizza crust on the toaster oven rack.
4. BAKE for 20 minutes, or until the cheese is melted and the crust is brown.

Parmesan Artichoke Pizza

Servings: 6
Cooking Time: 15 Minutes
Ingredients:
- CRUST
- ¾ cup warm water (110°F)
- 1 ½ teaspoons active dry yeast
- ¼ teaspoon sugar
- 1 tablespoon olive oil
- 1 teaspoon table salt
- ⅓ cup whole wheat flour
- 1 ½ to 1 ⅔ cups bread flour
- TOPPINGS
- 2 tablespoons olive oil
- 1 teaspoon Italian seasoning
- 1 clove garlic, minced
- ½ cup whole milk ricotta cheese, at room temperature
- ⅔ cup drained, chopped marinated artichokes
- ¼ cup chopped red onion
- 3 tablespoons minced fresh basil
- ½ cup shredded Parmesan cheese
- ⅓ cup shredded mozzarella cheese

Directions:
1. Make the Crust: Place the warm water, yeast, and sugar in a large mixing bowl for a stand mixer. Stir, then let stand for 3 to 5 minutes or until bubbly.
2. Stir in the olive oil, salt, whole wheat flour, and 1 ½ cups bread flour. If the dough is too sticky, stir in an additional 1 to 2 tablespoons bread flour. Beat with the flat (paddle) beater at medium-speed for 5 minutes (or knead by hand for 5 to 7 minutes or until the dough is smooth and elastic). Place in a greased large bowl, turn the dough over, cover with a clean towel, and let stand for 30 to 45 minutes, or until starting to rise.
3. Stir the olive oil, Italian seasoning, and garlic in a small bowl; set aside.
4. Preheat the toaster oven to 450°F. Place a 12-inch pizza pan in the toaster oven while it is preheating.
5. Turn the dough onto a lightly floured surface and pull or roll the dough to make a 12-inch circle. Carefully transfer the crust to the hot pan.
6. Brush the olive oil mixture over the crust. Spread the ricotta evenly over the crust. Top with the artichokes, red onions, fresh basil, Parmesan, and mozzarella. Bake for 13 to 15 minutes, or until the crust is golden brown and the cheese is melted. Let stand for 5 minutes before cutting.

Family Favorite Pizza

Servings: 6
Cooking Time: 22 Minutes
Ingredients:
- CRUST
- ½ cup warm water (about 110 °F)
- 1 teaspoon active dry yeast
- 1 ½ cups all-purpose flour, plus more for kneading
- 1 teaspoon kosher salt
- ½ teaspoon olive oil
- TOPPINGS
- Pizza sauce
- 2 cups shredded Italian blend cheese or mozzarella cheese
- ¼ cup grated Parmesan cheese
- Optional toppings: pepperoni slices, cooked crumbled or sliced sausage, vegetables, or other favorite pizza toppings

Directions:
1. Make the Crust: Pour the water into a medium bowl and sprinkle with the yeast. Let stand for 5 minutes until the yeast is foamy. Add the flour, salt, and olive oil. Mix until a dough forms. Turn the dough out on a floured surface and knead until a ball forms that springs back when you poke a finger into it, about 5 minutes. If the dough is too sticky, add a tablespoon of flour and knead into the dough. Cover the dough and allow to rest for 10 minutes.
2. Preheat the toaster oven to 450°F. Place a 12-inch pizza pan in the toaster oven while it is preheating.
3. Stretch and roll the dough into an 11 ½-inch round. If the dough starts to shrink back, let it rest for 5 to 10 more minutes and then continue to roll. Carefully remove the hot pan from the toaster oven and place the pizza crust on the hot pan. Top with the desired amount of sauce. Layer cheese and any of your favorite pizza toppings over the pizza.
4. Bake for 18 to 22 minutes, or until the crust is golden brown and the cheese is melted. Let stand for 5 minutes before cutting.

Honey Bourbon–glazed Pork Chops With Sweet Potatoes + Apples

Servings: 2
Cooking Time: 42 Minutes
Ingredients:
- Nonstick cooking spray
- 2 medium sweet potatoes, peeled and quartered
- 2 tablespoons bourbon
- 2 tablespoons honey

- 1 tablespoon canola or vegetable oil
- ½ teaspoon onion powder
- ½ teaspoon dry mustard
- ¼ teaspoon dried thyme leaves
- Kosher salt and freshly ground black pepper
- 2 bone-in pork chops, cut about ¾ inch thick
- 1 Granny Smith apple, not peeled, cored and cut into ½-inch wedges

Directions:
1. Preheat the toaster oven to 375°F. Spray a 12 x 12-inch baking pan with nonstick cooking spray.
2. Place the sweet potatoes on one side of the prepared pan. Spray with nonstick cooking spray. Bake, uncovered, for 20 minutes.
3. Meanwhile, stir the bourbon, honey, oil, onion powder, mustard, and thyme in a small bowl. Season with salt and pepper and set aside.
4. Turn the potatoes over. Place the pork chops on the other end of the pan in a single layer. Arrange the apple wedges around the potatoes and pork chops, stacking the apples as needed. Brush the bourbon mixture generously over all. Bake for 15 to 18 minutes or until the pork is done as desired and a meat thermometer registers a minimum of 145°F.
5. For additional browning, set the toaster oven to Broil and broil for 2 to 4 minutes, or until the edges are brown as desired.
6. Transfer to a serving platter. Spoon any drippings over the meat and vegetables. Let stand for 5 minutes before serving.

Crab Chowder

Servings: 4
Cooking Time: 40 Minutes
Ingredients:
- 1 6-ounce can lump crabmeat, drained and chopped, or ½ pound fresh crabmeat, cleaned and chopped
- 1 cup skim milk or low-fat soy milk
- 1 cup fat-free half-and-half
- 2 tablespoons unbleached flour
- ¼ cup chopped onion
- ½ cup peeled and diced potato
- 1 carrot, peeled and chopped
- 1 celery stalk, chopped
- 2 garlic cloves, minced
- 2 tablespoons chopped fresh parsley
- ½ teaspoon ground cumin
- 1 teaspoon paprika
- Salt and butcher's pepper to taste

Directions:
1. Preheat the toaster oven to 400° F.
2. Whisk together the milk, half-and-half, and flour in a bowl. Transfer the mixture to a 1-quart 8½ × 8½ × 4-inch ovenproof baking dish. Add all the other ingredients, mixing well. Adjust the seasonings to taste.
3. BAKE, covered, for 40 minutes, or until the vegetables are tender.

Chicken Thighs With Roasted Rosemary Root Vegetables

Servings: 2
Cooking Time: 70 Minutes
Ingredients:
- 2 sprigs fresh rosemary
- 1 small turnip, peeled and cut into 1 1/2-inch cubes
- 1 parsnip, peeled and cut into 1/2-inch slices
- 1 small onion, quartered
- 1 large sweet potato, peeled and cut into 1-inch cubes
- 2 cloves garlic, peeled
- 2 tablespoons olive oil
- 1 teaspoon salt, divided
- 1/2 teaspoon coarse pepper, divided
- 1/2 teaspoon rotisserie chicken seasoning
- 4 chicken thighs with bone and skin

Directions:
1. Place rack on bottom position of toaster oven. Preheat the toaster oven to 425°F.
2. Spray the toaster oven baking pan with nonstick cooking spray. Place rosemary sprigs on pan.
3. In a large bowl, mix turnip. parsnip, onion, sweet potato, garlic, oil, 1/2 teaspoon salt and 1/4 teaspoon pepper until vegetables are coated with oil. Add to baking pan.
4. Bake 30 minutes. Stir vegetables.
5. Sprinkle remaining salt, pepper and rotisserie chicken seasoning over chicken pieces.
6. Place chicken on top of vegetables in pan. Continue baking for an additional 35 to 40 minutes or until chicken reaches 165°F when tested with a meat thermometer and vegetables are roasted.

Connecticut Garden Chowder

Servings: 4
Cooking Time: 60 Minutes
Ingredients:
- Soup:
- ½ cup peeled and shredded potato
- ½ cup shredded carrot
- ½ cup shredded celery 2 plum tomatoes, chopped
- 1 small zucchini, shredded
- 2 bay leaves
- ¼ teaspoon sage
- 1 teaspoon garlic powder
- Salt and butcher's pepper to taste
- Chowder base:
- 2 tablespoons reduced-fat cream cheese, at room temperature
- ½ cup fat-free half-and-half
- 2 tablespoons unbleached flour
- 2 tablespoons chopped fresh parsley

Directions:
1. Preheat the toaster oven to 375° F.
2. Combine the soup ingredients in a 1-quart 8½ × 8½ × 4-inch ovenproof baking dish, mixing well. Adjust the seasonings to taste.
3. BAKE, covered, for 40 minutes, or until the vegetables are tender.
4. Whisk the chowder mixture ingredients together until smooth. Add the mixture to the cooked soup ingredients and stir well to blend.
5. BAKE, uncovered for 20 minutes, or until the stock is thickened. Ladle the soup into individual soup bowls and garnish with the parsley.

Oven-baked Couscous

Servings: 4
Cooking Time: 10 Minutes
Ingredients:
- 1 10-ounce package couscous
- 2 tablespoons olive oil
- 2 tablespoons canned chickpeas
- 2 tablespoons canned or frozen green peas
- 1 tablespoon chopped fresh parsley
- 3 scallions, chopped
- Salt and pepper to taste

Directions:
1. Preheat the toaster oven to 400° F.
2. Mix together all the ingredients with 2 cups water in a 1-quart 8½ × 8½ × 4-inch ovenproof baking dish. Adjust the seasonings to taste. Cover with aluminum foil.
3. BAKE, covered, for 10 minutes, or until the couscous and vegetables are tender. Adjust the seasonings to taste and fluff with a fork before serving.

Oven-baked Rice

Servings: 2
Cooking Time: 40 Minutes
Ingredients:
- ¼ cup regular rice (not parboiled or precooked)
- Seasonings:
- 1 tablespoon olive oil
- 1 teaspoon dried parsley or
- 1 tablespoon chopped fresh parsley
- 1 teaspoon garlic powder or roasted garlic
- Salt and freshly ground black pepper to taste

Directions:
1. Preheat the toaster oven to 400° F.
2. Combine ¼ cups water and the rice in a 1-quart 8½ × 8½ × 4-inch ovenproof baking dish. Stir well to blend. Cover with aluminum foil.
3. BAKE, covered, for 30 minutes, or until the rice is almost cooked. Add the seasonings, fluff with a fork to combine the seasonings well, then let the rice sit, covered, for 10 minutes. Fluff once more before serving.

Spanish Rice

Servings: 4
Cooking Time: 45 Minutes
Ingredients:
- ¾ cup rice
- 2 tablespoons dry white wine
- 3 tablespoons olive oil
- 1 15-ounce can whole tomatoes
- ¼ cup thinly sliced onions
- 3 tablespoons chopped fresh cilantro
- 4 ½ cup chopped bell pepper
- 5 2 bay leaves
- Salt and a pinch of red pepper flakes to taste

Directions:
1. Preheat the toaster oven to 375° F.
2. Combine all the ingredients with 1 cup water in a 1-quart 8½ × 8½ × 4-inch ovenproof baking dish and adjust the seasonings. Cover with aluminum foil.
3. BAKE, covered, for 45 minutes, or until the rice is cooked, removing the cover after 30 minutes.

Cheesy Chicken–stuffed Shells

Servings: 4
Cooking Time: 40 Minutes
Ingredients:
- Nonstick cooking spray
- 16 jumbo pasta shells
- 1 cup finely diced cooked chicken
- 1 cup whole milk ricotta cheese
- 1 ¼ cups shredded mozzarella cheese
- 1 large egg, slightly beaten
- ⅓ cup grated Parmesan cheese
- 1 teaspoon Italian seasoning
- 2 cloves garlic, minced
- ¼ teaspoon kosher salt
- ¼ teaspoon freshly ground black pepper
- 1 ½ cups marinara sauce

Directions:
1. Preheat the toaster oven to 350 ºF. Spray an 8 x 8-inch square baking pan with nonstick cooking spray.
2. Cook the shells according to the package directions, drain, and rinse with cool water.
3. Combine the chicken, ricotta, ¾ cup of the mozzarella, egg, Parmesan, Italian seasoning, garlic, salt, and pepper in a large bowl.
4. Spread about ¾ cup of the marinara sauce in the prepared pan. Fill each shell with a heaping tablespoon of the chicken-cheese mixture. Place the prepared shells, stuffed side up, in the pan. Pour the remaining marinara over the shells.
5. Cover and bake for 25 to 30 minutes. Sprinkle with the remaining ½ cup mozzarella and bake, uncovered, for an additional 5 to 10 minutes or until the cheese is melted. Remove from the oven and let stand for 5 to 10 minutes before serving.

Lentil And Carrot Soup

Servings: 4
Cooking Time: 40 Minutes
Ingredients:
- ½ cup lentils
- ½ cup dry white wine
- 1 small onion, chopped
- 3 carrots, peeled and finely chopped
- ½ cup fresh mushrooms, cleaned and sliced, or 1 5-ounce can mushroom pieces, well drained
- 3 garlic cloves, minced
- 1 tablespoon chopped fresh parsley
- 1 tablespoon Worcestershire sauce
- Salt and freshly ground black pepper to taste

Directions:
1. Preheat the toaster oven to 375° F.
2. Combine all the ingredients with 2 cups water in a 1-quart 8½ × 8½ × 4-inch ovenproof baking dish. Adjust the seasonings.
3. BAKE for 40 minutes, or until the lentils, carrots, and onions are tender. Ladle into individual soup bowls and serve.

Scalloped Corn Casserole

Servings: 4
Cooking Time: 38 Minutes
Ingredients:
- Casserole mixture:
- 2 15-ounce cans corn
- 1 red bell pepper, chopped
- ¼ cup chopped scallions
- ½ cup fat-free half-and-half
- 2 tablespoons unbleached flour
- 2 eggs
- ½ teaspoon chili powder
- 1 teaspoon ground cumin
- 1 teaspoon garlic powder
- Salt and freshly ground black pepper to taste
- ¼ cup multigrain seasoned bread Crumbs
- 1 tablespoon margarine

Directions:
1. Preheat the toaster oven to 400° F.
2. Combine all the casserole mixture ingredients in a 1-quart 8½ × 8½ × 4-inch ovenproof baking dish, mixing well. Adjust the seasonings to taste. Cover with aluminum foil.
3. BAKE, covered, for 30 minutes, or until the pepper and onions are tender. Remove from the oven and uncover. Sprinkle with the bread crumbs and dot with the margarine.
4. BROIL for 8 minutes, or until the bread crumb topping is lightly browned.

Maple Bacon

Servings: 6
Cooking Time: 16 Minutes
Ingredients:
- 12 slices bacon
- ½ cup packed dark brown sugar
- 2 tablespoons maple syrup
- 1 teaspoon Dijon mustard
- 2 tablespoons red or white wine

Directions:

1. Preheat the toaster oven to 350°F. Line a 12 x 12-inch baking pan with aluminum foil.
2. Place 6 bacon strips on the prepared pan, leaving space between the strips. Bake for 10 minutes or until the bacon is almost crisp. Carefully drain the bacon and return it to the pan.
3. Combine the brown sugar, maple syrup, mustard, and wine in a small bowl. Blend until smooth. Brush the glaze over the bacon. Bake for 8 minutes. Turn the bacon and brush with the glaze. Continue to bake for an additional 6 to 8 minutes, or until golden brown.
4. Repeat with the remaining bacon strips.

Homemade Pizza Sauce

Servings: 1
Cooking Time: 20 Minutes
Ingredients:
- 1 9-inch ready-made pizza crust or 1 homemade pizza crust
- 2 plum tomatoes, chopped
- 1 tablespoon olive oil
- 3 garlic cloves, peeled and chopped ¼ cup chopped onion
- 2 tablespoons tomato paste
- 2 tablespoons dry red wine
- 1 tablespoon chopped fresh basil or 1 teaspoon dried basil
- 1 tablespoon chopped fresh oregano or 1 teaspoon dried oregano
- 1 bay leaf
- Salt and freshly ground black pepper to taste

Directions:
1. Combine all ingredients in an 8½ × 8½ × 2-inch square baking (cake) pan. Adjust the seasonings to taste.
2. BROIL for 20 minutes, or until the onions and tomatoes are tender. Remove the bay leaf and cool before spreading on the pizza crust. Bake the pizza according to instructions on the ready-made crust package or in the homemade pizza crust recipe.

Classic Beef Stew

Servings: 4
Cooking Time: 50 Minutes
Ingredients:
- 1½ cups dark beer
- 4 tablespoons unbleached flour
- 2 cups (approximately 1 pound) lean top round steak, cut into 1-inch cubes
- 1 cup peeled and coarsely chopped carrots
- 1 cup peeled and coarsely chopped potatoes
- ½ cup coarsely chopped onion
- 1 cup fresh or frozen peas
- 2 plum tomatoes, chopped
- 3 garlic cloves, minced
- 4 3 bay leaves
- ¼ teaspoon ground cumin
- Salt and butcher's pepper to taste

Directions:
1. Preheat the toaster oven to 400° F.
2. Whisk together the beer and flour in a 1-quart 8½ × 8½ × 4-inch ovenproof baking dish. Add all the other ingredients and seasonings and mix well, adjusting the seasonings to taste. Cover the dish with aluminum foil.
3. BAKE, covered, for 50 minutes, or until the meat is cooked and the vegetables are tender. Remove the bay leaves before serving.

Salad Lentils

Servings: 4
Cooking Time: 35 Minutes
Ingredients:
- ¼ cup lentils
- 1 tablespoon olive oil
- Salad ingredients:
- 1 celery stalk, trimmed and Chopped
- 1 plum tomato, chopped
- 1 cucumber, peeled, seeded, and chopped
- 1½ cups spinach leaves, pulled into small pieces
- 1 tablespoon balsamic vinegar
- 1 tablespoon olive oil
- ½ teaspoon dried oregano
- 1 tablespoon chopped scallions
- 2 tablespoons sliced pitted black olives
- 1 teaspoon minced roasted garlic

Directions:
1. Preheat the toaster oven to 400° F.
2. Combine the lentils, ¼ cups water, and olive oil in a 1-quart 8½ × 8½ × 4-inch ovenproof baking dish. Cover with aluminum foil.
3. BAKE, covered, for 35 minutes, or until the lentils are tender. When cool, combine with all the salad ingredients in a serving bowl and toss well. Adjust the seasonings, chill, and serve.

Roasted Vegetable Gazpacho

Servings: 4
Cooking Time: 35 Minutes
Ingredients:
- Vegetables and seasonings:
- 1 bell pepper, thinly sliced
- ½ cup chopped celery
- ½ cup frozen or canned corn
- 1 medium onion, thinly sliced
- 1 small yellow squash, cut into 1-inch slices
- 1 small zucchini, cut into 1-inch slices
- 3 garlic cloves, chopped
- ½ teaspoon ground cumin
- 2 tablespoons olive oil
- Salt and freshly ground black pepper to taste
- 1 quart tomato juice
- 1 tablespoon lemon juice
- 3 tablespoons chopped fresh cilantro

Directions:
1. Preheat the toaster oven to 400°F.
2. Combine the vegetables and seasonings in an oiled or nonstick 8½ × 8½ × 2-inch square baking (cake) pan, mixing well.
3. BAKE, covered, for 25 minutes, or until the onions and celery are tender. Remove from the oven, uncover, and turn the vegetable pieces with tongs.
4. BROIL for 10 minutes, or until the vegetables are lightly browned. Remove from the oven and cool. Transfer to a large nonaluminum container and add the tomato juice, lemon juice, and cilantro. Adjust the seasonings.
5. Chill, covered, for several hours, preferably a day or two to enrich the flavor of the stock.

Very Quick Pizza

Servings: 1
Cooking Time: 3 Minutes
Ingredients:
- 2 tablespoons salsa
- 1 6-inch whole wheat pita bread
- 2 tablespoons shredded part-skim, low-moisture mozzarella cheese

Directions:
1. Spread the salsa on the pita bread and sprinkle with the cheese.
2. TOAST once, or until the cheese is melted.

Middle Eastern Roasted Chicken

Servings: 4
Cooking Time: 25 Minutes
Ingredients:
- 3 tablespoons fresh lemon juice
- ¼ cup plus 1 tablespoon olive oil
- 4 cloves garlic, minced
- ½ teaspoon kosher salt
- 1 teaspoon freshly ground black pepper
- 1 teaspoon ground cumin
- 1 teaspoon paprika
- ½ teaspoon turmeric
- ⅛ teaspoon red pepper flakes
- 1 pound boneless, skinless chicken breasts
- 1 large onion, cut into thin wedges

Directions:
1. Whisk the lemon juice, ¼ cup olive oil, garlic, salt, pepper, cumin, paprika, turmeric, and red pepper flakes in a small bowl until blended.
2. Cut the chicken breast lengthwise into thin scaloppine slices. Place the chicken in a nonreactive dish and pour the marinade over the chicken. Turn the chicken to coat thoroughly and evenly. Cover, refrigerate, and marinate for at least 1 hour and up to 10 hours. (The longer the better, as the flavor melds with the chicken.)
3. Remove the chicken from the refrigerator and add the onion to the marinade.
4. Preheat the toaster oven to 425°F. Brush the remaining tablespoon of olive oil over the bottom of a 12 x 12-inch pan. Place the chicken pieces on one side of the baking sheet and the onion wedges on the other side in a single layer. Discard any remaining marinade.
5. Roast for 20 to 25 minutes or until the chicken is browned and a meat thermometer registers 165°F. Remove from the oven and let rest a few minutes, then slice the chicken into thin strips. Toss with the onion and serve.

Baked Tomato Casserole

Servings: 4
Cooking Time: 45 Minutes
Ingredients:
- Casserole mixture:
- 1 medium onion, coarsely chopped
- 3 medium tomatoes, coarsely chopped
- 1 medium green pepper, coarsely chopped
- 2 garlic cloves, minced
- ½ teaspoon crushed oregano
- ½ teaspoon crushed basil

- 1 tablespoon extra virgin olive oil
- 2 tablespoons chopped fresh cilantro
- Salt and freshly ground black pepper
- 3 4 tablespoons grated Parmesan cheese
- ¼ cup multigrain bread crumbs

Directions:
1. Preheat the toaster oven to 400° F.
2. Combine the casserole mixture ingredients in a 1-quart 8½ × 8½ × 4-inch ovenproof baking dish. Adjust the seasonings to taste and cover with aluminum foil.
3. BAKE, covered, for 35 minutes, or until the tomatoes and pepper are tender. Remove from the oven, uncover, and sprinkle with the bread crumbs and Parmesan cheese.
4. BROIL for 10 minutes, or until the topping is lightly browned.

Dijon Salmon With Green Beans Sheet Pan Supper

Servings: 2-3
Cooking Time: 15 Minutes
Ingredients:
- 3/4 pound salmon fillets, cut in portion-size pieces
- 2 tablespoons olive oil
- 1 tablespoon soy sauce
- 1 tablespoon Dijon mustard
- 2 cloves garlic
- 6 ounces thin green beans, trimmed
- 1/2 small red bell pepper, thinly sliced
- 1/2 small yellow bell pepper, thinly sliced
- 1 small leek, white part only, thinly sliced
- Dash coarse black pepper

Directions:
1. Place rack on bottom position of toaster oven. Preheat the toaster oven to 400°F. Spray the toaster oven baking pan with nonstick cooking spray or line the pan with nonstick aluminum foil. Place salmon skin-side down in center of pan.
2. In a food chopper, process olive oil, soy sauce, mustard and garlic until blended and garlic is chopped. Set aside.
3. In a large bowl, combine green beans, bell peppers and leeks. Add 2 tablespoons olive oil mixture and stir until vegetables are coated. Arrange vegetables evenly in pan around salmon.
4. Drizzle salmon with remaining olive oil mixture.
5. Bake until salmon is done to medium-well and vegetables are crisp-tender, about 15 minutes.

One-step Classic Goulash

Servings: 4
Cooking Time: 56 Minutes
Ingredients:
- 1 cup elbow macaroni
- 1 cup (8-ounce can) tomato sauce
- 1 cup very lean ground round or sirloin
- 1 cup peeled and chopped fresh tomato
- ½ cup finely chopped onion
- 1 teaspoon garlic powder
- Salt and freshly ground black pepper
- Topping:
- 1 cup homemade bread crumbs
- 1 tablespoon margarine

Directions:
1. Preheat the toaster oven to 400° F.
2. Combine all the ingredients, except the topping, with 2 cups water in a 1-quart 8½ × 8½ × 4-inch ovenproof baking dish and mix well. Adjust the seasonings to taste. Cover with aluminum foil.
3. BAKE, covered, for 50 minutes, or until the macaroni is cooked, stirring after 25 minutes to distribute the liquid. Uncover, sprinkle with bread crumbs, and dot with margarine.
4. BROIL for 6 minutes, or until the topping is lightly browned.

Classic Tuna Casserole

Servings: 4
Cooking Time: 65 Minutes
Ingredients:
- 1 cup elbow macaroni
- 2 6-ounce cans tuna packed in water, drained well and crumbled
- 1 cup frozen peas 1 6-ounce can button mushrooms, drained
- 1 tablespoon margarine
- Salt and freshly ground black pepper
- 1 cup fat-free half-and-half
- 4 tablespoons unbleached flour
- 1 teaspoon garlic powder
- 1 cup multigrain bread crumbs

Directions:
1. Preheat the toaster oven to 400° F.
2. Combine the macaroni and 3 cups water in a 1-quart 8½ × 8½ × 4-inch ovenproof baking dish, stirring to blend well. Cover with aluminum foil.

3. BAKE, covered, for 35 minutes, or until the macaroni is tender. Remove from the oven and drain well. Return to the baking dish and add the tuna, peas, and mushrooms. Add salt and pepper to taste.

4. Whisk together the half-and-half, flour, and garlic powder in a small bowl until smooth. Add to the macaroni mixture and stir to blend well.

5. BAKE, covered, for 25 minutes. Remove from the oven, sprinkle the top with the bread crumbs, and dot with the margarine. Bake, uncovered, for 10 minutes, or until the top is browned.

Yeast Dough For Two Pizzas

Servings: 8
Cooking Time: 20 Minutes
Ingredients:
- ¼ cup tepid water
- 1 cup tepid skim milk
- ½ teaspoon sugar
- 1 1¼-ounce envelope dry yeast
- 2 cups unbleached flour
- 1 tablespoon olive oil

Directions:

1. Preheat the toaster oven to 400° F.

2. Combine the water, milk, and sugar in a bowl. Add the yeast and set aside for 3 to 5 minutes, or until the yeast is dissolved.

3. Stir in the flour gradually, adding just enough to form a ball of the dough.

4. KNEAD on a floured surface until the dough is satiny, and then put the dough in a bowl in a warm place with a damp towel over the top. In 1 hour or when the dough has doubled in bulk, punch it down and divide it in half. Flatten the dough and spread it out to the desired thickness on an oiled or nonstick 9¾-inch-diameter pie pan. Spread with Homemade Pizza Sauce (recipe follows) and add any desired toppings.

5. BAKE for 20 minutes, or until the topping ingredients are cooked and the cheese is melted.

Fish And Seafood

Tuna Nuggets In Hoisin Sauce

Servings: 4
Cooking Time: 7 Minutes
Ingredients:
- ½ cup hoisin sauce
- 2 tablespoons rice wine vinegar
- 2 teaspoons sesame oil
- 1 teaspoon garlic powder
- 2 teaspoons dried lemongrass
- ¼ teaspoon red pepper flakes
- ½ small onion, quartered and thinly sliced
- 8 ounces fresh tuna, cut into 1-inch cubes
- cooking spray
- 3 cups cooked jasmine rice

Directions:
1. Mix the hoisin sauce, vinegar, sesame oil, and seasonings together.
2. Stir in the onions and tuna nuggets.
3. Spray air fryer oven baking pan with nonstick spray and pour in tuna mixture.
4. Air-fry at 390°F for 3 minutes. Stir gently.
5. Cook 2 minutes and stir again, checking for doneness. Tuna should be barely cooked through, just beginning to flake and still very moist. If necessary, continue cooking and stirring in 1-minute intervals until done.
6. Serve warm over hot jasmine rice.

Maple-crusted Salmon

Servings: 2
Cooking Time: 8 Minutes
Ingredients:
- 12 ounces salmon filets
- ⅓ cup maple syrup
- 1 teaspoon Worcestershire sauce
- 2 teaspoons Dijon mustard or brown mustard
- ½ cup finely chopped walnuts
- ½ teaspoon sea salt
- ½ lemon
- 1 tablespoon chopped parsley, for garnish

Directions:
1. Place the salmon in a shallow baking dish. Top with maple syrup, Worcestershire sauce, and mustard. Refrigerate for 30 minutes.
2. Preheat the toaster oven to 350°F.
3. Remove the salmon from the marinade and discard the marinade.
4. Place the chopped nuts on top of the salmon filets, and sprinkle salt on top of the nuts. Place the salmon, skin side down, in the air fryer oven. Air-fry for 6 to 8 minutes or until the fish flakes in the center.
5. Remove the salmon and plate on a serving platter. Squeeze fresh lemon over the top of the salmon and top with chopped parsley. Serve immediately.

Broiled Scallops

Servings: 6
Cooking Time: 3 Minutes
Ingredients:
- Broiling sauce:
- 2 tablespoons chopped fresh parsley
- 3 shallots, finely chopped
- ¾ cup white wine
- 3 tablespoons margarine, at room
- Temperature
- ½ teaspoon dried thyme
- 3 tablespoons sesame seeds
- Salt and freshly ground black pepper
- 1½ pounds (3 cups) bay scallops, rinsed and drained

Directions:
1. Whisk together the ingredients for the broiling sauce in a small bowl and transfer to a 1-quart 8½ × 8½ × 4-inch ovenproof baking dish. Adjust the seasoning, add the scallops, and spoon the mixture over them.
2. BROIL for 3 minutes, or until all the scallops are opaque instead of translucent. Serve with the sauce.

Classic Crab Cakes

Servings: 4
Cooking Time: 10 Minutes
Ingredients:
- 10 ounces Lump crabmeat, picked over for shell and cartilage
- 6 tablespoons Plain panko bread crumbs (gluten-free, if a concern)
- 6 tablespoons Chopped drained jarred roasted red peppers
- 4 Medium scallions, trimmed and thinly sliced

- ¼ cup Regular or low-fat mayonnaise (not fat-free; gluten-free, if a concern)
- ¼ teaspoon Dried dill
- ¼ teaspoon Dried thyme
- ¼ teaspoon Onion powder
- ¼ teaspoon Table salt
- ⅛ teaspoon Celery seeds
- Up to ⅛ teaspoon Cayenne
- Vegetable oil spray

Directions:
1. Preheat the toaster oven to 400°F.
2. Gently mix the crabmeat, bread crumbs, red pepper, scallion, mayonnaise, dill, thyme, onion powder, salt, celery seeds, and cayenne in a bowl until well combined.
3. Use clean and dry hands to form ½ cup of this mixture into a tightly packed 1-inch-thick, 3- to 4-inch-wide patty. Coat the top and bottom of the patty with vegetable oil spray and set it aside. Continue making 1 more patty for a small batch, 3 more for a medium batch, or 5 more for a larger one, coating them with vegetable oil spray on both sides.
4. Set the patties in one layer in the air fryer oven and air-fry undisturbed for 10 minutes, or until lightly browned and cooked through.
5. Use a nonstick-safe spatula to transfer the crab cakes to a serving platter or plates. Wait a couple of minutes before serving.

Ginger Miso Calamari

Servings: 4
Cooking Time: 10 Minutes
Ingredients:
- 15 ounces calamari, cleaned
- Sauce:
- 2 tablespoons dry white wine
- 2 tablespoons white miso
- 1 tablespoon balsamic vinegar
- 1 teaspoon honey
- 1 teaspoon toasted sesame oil
- 1 teaspoon olive oil
- 1 tablespoon grated fresh ginger
- Salt and white pepper to taste

Directions:
1. Slice the calamari bodies into ½-inch rings, leaving the tentacles uncut. Set aside.
2. Whisk together the sauce ingredients in a bowl. Transfer the mixture to a baking pan and add the calamari, mixing well to coat.
3. BROIL for 20 minutes, turning with tongs every 5 minutes, or until cooked but not rubbery. Serve with the sauce.

Miso-rubbed Salmon Fillets

Servings: 3
Cooking Time: 5 Minutes
Ingredients:
- ¼ cup White (shiro) miso paste (usually made from rice and soy beans)
- 1½ tablespoons Mirin or a substitute
- 2½ teaspoons Unseasoned rice vinegar
- Vegetable oil spray
- 3 6-ounce skin-on salmon fillets

Directions:
1. Preheat the toaster oven to 400°F.
2. Mix the miso, mirin, and vinegar in a small bowl until uniform.
3. Remove from the machine. Generously spray the skin side of each fillet. Pick them up one by one with a nonstick-safe spatula and set them in the baking pan skin side down with as much air space between them as possible. Coat the top of each fillet with the miso mixture, dividing it evenly between them.
4. Return the baking pan to the machine. Air-fry undisturbed for 5 minutes, or until lightly browned and firm.
5. Use a nonstick-safe spatula to transfer the fillets to serving plates. Cool for only a minute or so before serving.

Shrimp, Chorizo And Fingerling Potatoes

Servings: 4
Cooking Time: 16 Minutes
Ingredients:
- ½ red onion, chopped into 1-inch chunks
- 8 fingerling potatoes, sliced into 1-inch slices or halved lengthwise
- 1 teaspoon olive oil
- salt and freshly ground black pepper
- 8 ounces raw chorizo sausage, sliced into 1-inch chunks
- 16 raw large shrimp, peeled, deveined and tails removed
- 1 lime
- ¼ cup chopped fresh cilantro
- chopped orange zest (optional)

Directions:
1. Preheat the toaster oven to 380°F.
2. Combine the red onion and potato chunks in a bowl and toss with the olive oil, salt and freshly ground black pepper.

3. Transfer the vegetables to the air fryer oven and air-fry for 6 minutes.
4. Add the chorizo chunks and continue to air-fry for another 5 minutes.
5. Add the shrimp, season with salt and continue to air-fry for another 5 minutes.
6. Transfer the tossed shrimp, chorizo and potato to a bowl and squeeze some lime juice over the top to taste. Toss in the fresh cilantro, orange zest and a drizzle of olive oil, and season again to taste.
7. Serve with a fresh green salad.

Crunchy And Buttery Cod With Ritz® Cracker Crust

Servings: 2
Cooking Time: 10 Minutes
Ingredients:
- 4 tablespoons butter, melted
- 8 to 10 RITZ® crackers, crushed into crumbs
- 2 (6-ounce) cod fillets
- salt and freshly ground black pepper
- 1 lemon

Directions:
1. Preheat the toaster oven to 380°F.
2. Melt the butter in a small saucepan on the stovetop or in a microwavable dish in the microwave, and then transfer the butter to a shallow dish. Place the crushed RITZ® crackers into a second shallow dish.
3. Season the fish fillets with salt and freshly ground black pepper. Dip them into the butter and then coat both sides with the RITZ® crackers.
4. Place the fish into the air fryer oven and air-fry at 380°F for 10 minutes, flipping the fish over halfway through the cooking time.
5. Serve with a wedge of lemon to squeeze over the top.

Pecan-crusted Tilapia

Servings: 4
Cooking Time: 8 Minutes
Ingredients:
- 1 pound skinless, boneless tilapia filets
- ¼ cup butter, melted
- 1 teaspoon minced fresh or dried rosemary
- 1 cup finely chopped pecans
- 1 teaspoon sea salt
- ¼ teaspoon paprika
- 2 tablespoons chopped parsley
- 1 lemon, cut into wedges

Directions:
1. Pat the tilapia filets dry with paper towels.
2. Pour the melted butter over the filets and flip the filets to coat them completely.
3. In a medium bowl, mix together the rosemary, pecans, salt, and paprika.
4. Preheat the toaster oven to 350°F.
5. Place the tilapia filets into the air fryer oven and top with the pecan coating. Air-fry for 6 to 8 minutes. The fish should be firm to the touch and flake easily when fully cooked.
6. Remove the fish from the air fryer oven. Top the fish with chopped parsley and serve with lemon wedges.

Almond Crab Cakes

Servings: 4
Cooking Time: 10 Minutes
Ingredients:
- 1 pound cooked lump crabmeat, drained and picked over
- ¼ cup ground almonds
- 1 tablespoon Dijon mustard
- 1 scallion, white and green parts, finely chopped
- ½ red bell pepper, finely chopped
- 1 large egg
- 1 teaspoon lemon zest
- Oil spray (hand-pumped)
- 3 tablespoons almond flour

Directions:
1. Preheat the toaster oven to 375°F on AIR FRY for 5 minutes.
2. In a medium bowl, mix the crab meat, almonds, mustard, scallion, bell pepper, egg, and lemon zest until well combined and the mixture holds together when pressed. If the crab cakes do not stick together, add more ground almond.
3. Divide the crab mixture into 8 patties and press them to about 1 inch thick. Place them on a plate, cover, and chill for 30 minutes.
4. Place the air-fryer basket in the baking tray and generously spray with the oil.
5. Place the almond flour on a plate and dredge the crab cakes until they are lightly coated.
6. Place them in the basket and lightly spray both sides with the oil.
7. In position 2, air fry for 10 minutes, turning halfway through, until golden brown. Serve.

Fish Sticks For Kids

Servings: 8
Cooking Time: 6 Minutes
Ingredients:
- 8 ounces fish fillets (pollock or cod)
- salt (optional)
- ½ cup plain breadcrumbs
- oil for misting or cooking spray

Directions:
1. Cut fish fillets into "fingers" about ½ x 3 inches. Sprinkle with salt to taste, if desired.
2. Roll fish in breadcrumbs. Spray all sides with oil or cooking spray.
3. Place in air fryer oven in single layer and air-fry at 390°F for 6 minutes, until golden brown and crispy.

Fish Tacos With Jalapeño-lime Sauce

Servings: 4
Cooking Time: 7 Minutes
Ingredients:
- Fish Tacos
- 1 pound fish fillets
- ¼ teaspoon cumin
- ¼ teaspoon coriander
- ⅛ teaspoon ground red pepper
- 1 tablespoon lime zest
- ¼ teaspoon smoked paprika
- 1 teaspoon oil
- cooking spray
- 6–8 corn or flour tortillas (6-inch size)
- Jalapeño-Lime Sauce
- ½ cup sour cream
- 1 tablespoon lime juice
- ¼ teaspoon grated lime zest
- ½ teaspoon minced jalapeño (flesh only)
- ¼ teaspoon cumin
- Napa Cabbage Garnish
- 1 cup shredded Napa cabbage
- ¼ cup slivered red or green bell pepper
- ¼ cup slivered onion

Directions:
1. Slice the fish fillets into strips approximately ½-inch thick.
2. Put the strips into a sealable plastic bag along with the cumin, coriander, red pepper, lime zest, smoked paprika, and oil. Massage seasonings into the fish until evenly distributed.
3. Spray air fryer oven with nonstick cooking spray and place seasoned fish inside.
4. Air-fry at 390°F for approximately 5 minutes. Distribute fish. Cook an additional 2 minutes, until fish flakes easily.
5. While the fish is cooking, prepare the Jalapeño-Lime Sauce by mixing the sour cream, lime juice, lime zest, jalapeño, and cumin together to make a smooth sauce. Set aside.
6. Mix the cabbage, bell pepper, and onion together and set aside.
7. To warm refrigerated tortillas, wrap in damp paper towels and microwave for 30 to 60 seconds.
8. To serve, spoon some of fish into a warm tortilla. Add one or two tablespoons Napa Cabbage Garnish and drizzle with Jalapeño-Lime Sauce.

Tex-mex Fish Tacos

Servings: 3
Cooking Time: 7 Minutes
Ingredients:
- ¾ teaspoon Chile powder
- ¼ teaspoon Ground cumin
- ¼ teaspoon Dried oregano
- 3 5-ounce skinless mahi-mahi fillets
- Vegetable oil spray
- 3 Corn or flour tortillas
- 6 tablespoons Diced tomatoes
- 3 tablespoons Regular, low-fat, or fat-free sour cream

Directions:
1. Preheat the toaster oven to 400°F.
2. Stir the chile powder, cumin, and oregano in a small bowl until well combined.
3. Coat each piece of fish all over (even the sides and ends) with vegetable oil spray. Sprinkle the spice mixture evenly over all sides of the fillets. Lightly spray them again.
4. When the machine is at temperature, set the fillets in the air fryer oven with as much air space between them as possible. Air-fry undisturbed for 7 minutes, until lightly browned and firm but not hard.
5. Use a nonstick-safe spatula to transfer the fillets to a wire rack. Microwave the tortillas on high for a few seconds, until supple. Put a fillet in each tortilla and top each with 2 tablespoons diced tomatoes and 1 tablespoon sour cream.

Sweet Chili Shrimp

Servings: 4
Cooking Time: 6 Minutes
Ingredients:
- 1 pound jumbo shrimp, peeled and deveined
- ¼ cup sweet chili sauce
- 1 lime, zested and juiced
- 1 tablespoon soy sauce
- 1 tablespoon honey
- 1 tablespoon olive oil
- 1 large garlic clove, minced
- ½ teaspoon salt
- ¼ teaspoon pepper
- 1 green onion, thinly sliced, for garnish

Directions:
1. Place the shrimp in a large bowl. Whisk all the remaining ingredients except the green onion in a separate bowl.
2. Pour sauce over the shrimp and toss to coat.
3. Preheat the toaster Oven to 430°F.
4. Line the food tray with foil, place shrimp on the tray, then insert at top position in the preheated oven.
5. Select the Air Fry function, adjust time to 6 minutes, and press Start/Pause.
6. Remove shrimp and garnish with sliced green onions.

Crab Cakes

Servings: 4
Cooking Time: 9 Minutes
Ingredients:
- 1 pound lump crab meat, checked for shells
- ⅓ cup breadcrumbs
- ¼ cup finely chopped onions
- ¼ cup finely chopped red bell peppers
- ¼ cup finely chopped parsley
- ¼ teaspoon sea salt
- 2 eggs, whisked
- ¾ cup mayonnaise, divided
- ¼ cup sour cream
- 1 lemon, divided
- ¼ cup sweet pickle relish
- 1 tablespoon prepared mustard

Directions:
1. In a large bowl, mix together the crab meat, breadcrumbs, onions, bell peppers, parsley, sea salt, eggs, and ¼ cup of the mayonnaise.
2. Preheat the toaster oven to 380°F.
3. Form 8 patties with the crab cake mixture. Line the air fryer oven with parchment paper and place the crab cakes on the parchment paper. Spray with cooking spray. Air-fry for 4 minutes, turn over the crab cakes, spray with cooking spray, and air-fry for an additional 3 to 5 minutes, or until golden brown and the edges are crispy. Cook in batches as needed.
4. Meanwhile, make the sauce. In a small bowl, mix together the remaining ½ cup of mayonnaise, the sour cream, the juice from ½ of the lemon, the pickle relish, and the mustard.
5. Place the cooked crab cakes on a serving platter and serve with the remaining ½ lemon cut into wedges and the dipping sauce.

Shrimp

Servings: 4
Cooking Time: 8 Minutes
Ingredients:
- 1 pound (26–30 count) shrimp, peeled, deveined, and butterflied (last tail section of shell intact)
- Marinade
- 1 5-ounce can evaporated milk
- 2 eggs, beaten
- 2 tablespoons white vinegar
- 1 tablespoon baking powder
- Coating
- 1 cup crushed panko breadcrumbs
- ½ teaspoon paprika
- ½ teaspoon Old Bay Seasoning
- ¼ teaspoon garlic powder
- oil for misting or cooking spray

Directions:
1. Stir together all marinade ingredients until well mixed. Add shrimp and stir to coat. Refrigerate for 1 hour.
2. When ready to cook, preheat the toaster oven to 390°F.
3. Combine coating ingredients in shallow dish.
4. Remove shrimp from marinade, roll in crumb mixture, and spray with olive oil or cooking spray.
5. Cooking in two batches, place shrimp in air fryer oven in single layer, close but not overlapping. Air-fry at 390°F for 8 minutes, until light golden brown and crispy.
6. Repeat step 5 to cook remaining shrimp.

Coconut-shrimp Po' Boys

Servings: 4
Cooking Time: 5 Minutes
Ingredients:
- ½ cup cornstarch
- 2 eggs
- 2 tablespoons milk
- ¾ cup shredded coconut
- ½ cup panko breadcrumbs
- 1 pound (31–35 count) shrimp, peeled and deveined
- Old Bay Seasoning
- oil for misting or cooking spray
- 2 large hoagie rolls
- honey mustard or light mayonnaise
- 1½ cups shredded lettuce
- 1 large tomato, thinly sliced

Directions:
1. Place cornstarch in a shallow dish or plate.
2. In another shallow dish, beat together eggs and milk.
3. In a third dish mix the coconut and panko crumbs.
4. Sprinkle shrimp with Old Bay Seasoning to taste.
5. Dip shrimp in cornstarch to coat lightly, dip in egg mixture, shake off excess, and roll in coconut mixture to coat well.
6. Spray both sides of coated shrimp with oil or cooking spray.
7. Cook half the shrimp in a single layer at 390°F for 5 minutes.
8. Repeat to cook remaining shrimp.
9. To Assemble
10. Split each hoagie lengthwise, leaving one long edge intact.
11. Place in air fryer oven and air-fry at 390°F for 1 to 2 minutes or until heated through.
12. Remove buns, break apart, and place on 4 plates, cut side up.
13. Spread with honey mustard and/or mayonnaise.
14. Top with shredded lettuce, tomato slices, and coconut shrimp.

Halibut Tacos

Servings: 4
Cooking Time: 15 Minutes
Ingredients:
- Oil spray (hand-pumped)
- 1 teaspoon ground cumin
- ¼ teaspoon sea salt
- ⅛ teaspoon freshly ground black pepper
- 4 (4-ounce) halibut fillets
- 1 tablespoon olive oil
- 1 cup red cabbage, shredded
- 1 carrot, shredded
- 1 scallion, white and green parts, finely chopped
- ¼ cup sour cream
- Juice of 1 lime
- ⅛ teaspoon chili powder
- 4 (8-inch) corn tortillas, room temperature

Directions:
1. Preheat the toaster oven to 350°F on CONVECTION BAKE for 5 minutes.
2. Place the air-fryer basket in the baking tray and spray it generously with the oil.
3. In a small bowl, stir the cumin, salt, and pepper until well blended.
4. Season the fish all over with the seasoning mixture.
5. Place the fish in the basket and drizzle with the olive oil.
6. In position 2, bake for 15 minutes until cooked through and lightly browned.
7. While the fish is cooking, in a medium bowl, toss together the cabbage, carrot, scallion, sour cream, lime juice, and chili powder until very well mixed. Set aside.
8. Divide the fish among the tortillas and top with the slaw. Serve.

Crab-stuffed Peppers

Servings: 4
Cooking Time: 45 Minutes
Ingredients:
- Filling:
- 1½ cups fresh crabmeat, chopped, or 2 6-ounce cans lump crabmeat, drained
- 4 plum tomatoes, chopped
- 2 4-ounce cans sliced mushrooms, drained well
- 4 tablespoons pitted and sliced black olives
- 2 tablespoons olive oil
- 2 garlic cloves, minced
- ½ teaspoon ground cumin
- Salt and freshly ground black pepper to taste
- 4 large bell peppers, tops cut off, seeds and membrane removed
- ½ cup shredded low-fat mozzarella cheese

Directions:
1. Preheat the toaster oven to 375° F.
2. Combine the filling ingredients in a bowl and adjust the seasonings. Spoon the mixture to generously fill each pepper. Place the peppers upright in an 8½ × 8½ × 2-inch oiled or nonstick square (cake) pan.

3. BAKE for 40 minutes, or until the peppers are tender. Remove from the oven and sprinkle the cheese in equal portions on top of the peppers.
4. BROIL 5 minutes, or until the cheese is melted.

Blackened Catfish

Servings: 4
Cooking Time: 8 Minutes
Ingredients:
- 1 teaspoon paprika
- 1 teaspoon garlic powder
- 1 teaspoon onion powder
- 1 teaspoon ground dried thyme
- ½ teaspoon ground black pepper
- ⅛ teaspoon cayenne pepper
- ½ teaspoon dried oregano
- ⅛ teaspoon crushed red pepper flakes
- 1 pound catfish filets
- ½ teaspoon sea salt
- 2 tablespoons butter, melted
- 1 tablespoon extra-virgin olive oil
- 2 tablespoons chopped parsley
- 1 lemon, cut into wedges

Directions:
1. In a small bowl, stir together the paprika, garlic powder, onion powder, thyme, black pepper, cayenne pepper, oregano, and crushed red pepper flakes.
2. Pat the fish dry with paper towels. Season the filets with sea salt and then coat with the blackening seasoning.
3. In a small bowl, mix together the butter and olive oil and drizzle over the fish filets, flipping them to coat them fully.
4. Preheat the toaster oven to 350°F.
5. Place the fish in the air fryer oven and air-fry for 8 minutes, checking the fish for doneness after 4 minutes. The fish will flake easily when cooked.
6. Remove the fish from the air fryer oven. Top with chopped parsley and serve with lemon wedges.

Beer-battered Cod

Servings: 3
Cooking Time: 12 Minutes
Ingredients:
- 1½ cups All-purpose flour
- 3 tablespoons Old Bay seasoning
- 1 Large egg(s)
- ¼ cup Amber beer, pale ale, or IPA
- 3 4-ounce skinless cod fillets
- Vegetable oil spray

Directions:
1. Preheat the toaster oven to 400°F.
2. Set up and fill two shallow soup plates or small pie plates on your counter: one with the flour, whisked with the Old Bay until well combined; and one with the egg(s), whisked with the beer until foamy and uniform.
3. Dip a piece of cod in the flour mixture, turning it to coat on all sides (not just the top and bottom). Gently shake off any excess flour and dip the fish in the egg mixture, turning it to coat. Let any excess egg mixture slip back into the rest, then set the fish back in the flour mixture and coat it again, then back in the egg mixture for a second wash, then back in the flour mixture for a third time. Coat the fish on all sides with vegetable oil spray and set it aside. "Batter" the remaining piece(s) of cod in the same way.
4. Set the coated cod fillets in the air fryer oven with as much space between them as possible. They should not touch. Air-fry undisturbed for 12 minutes, or until brown and crisp.
5. Use kitchen tongs to gently transfer the fish to a wire rack. Cool for only a couple of minutes before serving.

Capered Crab Cakes

Servings: 6
Cooking Time: 30 Minutes
Ingredients:
- 1 pound fresh lump crabmeat, drained and chopped, or 3 5-ounce cans good-quality lump crabmeat
- 1 cup bread crumbs
- ½ cup plain nonfat yogurt
- 1 tablespoon olive oil
- 2 tablespoons capers
- 1 tablespoon garlic powder
- 1 teaspoon hot sauce
- 1 egg, beaten
- 1 tablespoon Worcestershire sauce
- Salt and freshly ground black pepper to taste

Directions:
1. Preheat the toaster oven to 350° F.
2. Combine all the ingredients in a bowl. Shape the mixture into patties approximately 2½ inches wide, adding more bread crumbs if the mixture is too wet and sticky and more yogurt if the mixture is too dry and crumbly. Place the patties in an 8½ × 8½ × 2-inch oiled or nonstick square (cake) pan.
3. BAKE, uncovered, for 25 minutes.
4. BROIL for 5 minutes, until golden brown.

Light Trout Amandine

Servings: 4
Cooking Time: 15 Minutes
Ingredients:
- 1 tablespoon margarine
- ½ cup sliced almonds
- 1 tablespoon lemon juice
- 1 teaspoon Worcestershire sauce
- Salt and freshly ground black pepper
- 4 6-ounce trout fillets
- 2 tablespoons chopped fresh parsley

Directions:
1. Combine the margarine and almonds in an oiled or nonstick 8½ × 8½ × 2-inch square baking (cake) pan.
2. BROIL for 5 minutes, or until the margarine is melted. Remove the pan from the oven and add the lemon juice and Worcestershire sauce. Season to taste with salt and pepper, and stir again to blend well. Add the trout fillets and spoon the mixture over them to coat well.
3. BROIL for 10 minutes, or until the almonds and fillets are lightly browned. Garnish with the chopped parsley before serving.

Crispy Smelts

Servings: 3
Cooking Time: 20 Minutes
Ingredients:
- 1 pound Cleaned smelts
- 3 tablespoons Tapioca flour
- Vegetable oil spray
- To taste Coarse sea salt or kosher salt

Directions:
1. Preheat the toaster oven to 400°F.
2. Toss the smelts and tapioca flour in a large bowl until the little fish are evenly coated.
3. Lay the smelts out on a large cutting board. Lightly coat both sides of each fish with vegetable oil spray.
4. When the machine is at temperature, set the smelts close together in the air fryer oven, with a few even overlapping on top. Air-fry undisturbed for 20 minutes, until lightly browned and crisp.
5. Remove from the machine and turn out the fish onto a wire rack. The smelts will most likely come out as one large block, or maybe in a couple of large pieces. Cool for a minute or two, then sprinkle the smelts with salt and break the block(s) into much smaller sections or individual fish to serve.

Better Fish Sticks

Servings: 3
Cooking Time: 8 Minutes
Ingredients:
- ¾ cup Seasoned Italian-style dried bread crumbs (gluten-free, if a concern)
- 3 tablespoons (about ½ ounce) Finely grated Parmesan cheese
- 10 ounces Skinless cod fillets, cut lengthwise into 1-inch-wide pieces
- 3 tablespoons Regular or low-fat mayonnaise (not fat-free; gluten-free, if a concern)
- Vegetable oil spray

Directions:
1. Preheat the toaster oven to 400°F.
2. Mix the bread crumbs and grated Parmesan in a shallow soup bowl or a small pie plate.
3. Smear the fish fillet sticks completely with the mayonnaise, then dip them one by one in the bread-crumb mixture, turning and pressing gently to make an even and thorough coating. Coat each stick on all sides with vegetable oil spray.
4. Set the fish sticks in the air fryer oven with at least ¼ inch between them. Air-fry undisturbed for 8 minutes, or until golden brown and crisp.
5. Use a nonstick-safe spatula to gently transfer them from the air fryer oven to a wire rack. Cool for only a minute or two before serving.

Spicy Fish Street Tacos With Sriracha Slaw

Servings: 2
Cooking Time: 5 Minutes
Ingredients:
- Sriracha Slaw:
- ½ cup mayonnaise
- 2 tablespoons rice vinegar
- 1 teaspoon sugar
- 2 tablespoons sriracha chili sauce
- 5 cups shredded green cabbage
- ¼ cup shredded carrots
- 2 scallions, chopped
- salt and freshly ground black pepper
- Tacos:
- ½ cup flour
- 1 teaspoon chili powder
- ½ teaspoon ground cumin

- 1 teaspoon salt
- freshly ground black pepper
- ½ teaspoon baking powder
- 1 egg, beaten
- ¼ cup milk
- 1 cup breadcrumbs
- 1 pound mahi-mahi or snapper fillets
- 1 tablespoon canola or vegetable oil
- 6 (6-inch) flour tortillas
- 1 lime, cut into wedges

Directions:
1. Start by making the sriracha slaw. Combine the mayonnaise, rice vinegar, sugar, and sriracha sauce in a large bowl. Mix well and add the green cabbage, carrots, and scallions. Toss until all the vegetables are coated with the dressing and season with salt and pepper. Refrigerate the slaw until you are ready to serve the tacos.
2. Combine the flour, chili powder, cumin, salt, pepper and baking powder in a bowl. Add the egg and milk and mix until the batter is smooth. Place the breadcrumbs in shallow dish.
3. Cut the fish fillets into 1-inch wide sticks, approximately 4-inches long. You should have about 12 fish sticks total. Dip the fish sticks into the batter, coating all sides. Let the excess batter drip off the fish and then roll them in the breadcrumbs, patting the crumbs onto all sides of the fish sticks. Set the coated fish on a plate or baking sheet until all the fish has been coated.
4. Preheat the toaster oven to 400°F.
5. Spray the coated fish sticks with oil on all sides. Spray or brush the inside of the air fryer oven with oil and transfer the fish to the air fryer oven. Place as many sticks as you can in one layer, leaving a little room around each stick. Place any remaining sticks on top, perpendicular to the first layer.
6. Air-fry the fish for 3 minutes. Turn the fish sticks over and air-fry for an additional 2 minutes.
7. While the fish is air-frying, warm the tortilla shells either in a 350°F oven wrapped in foil or in a skillet with a little oil over medium-high heat for a couple minutes. Fold the tortillas in half and keep them warm until the remaining tortillas and fish are ready.
8. To assemble the tacos, place two pieces of the fish in each tortilla shell and top with the sriracha slaw. Squeeze the lime wedge over top and dig in.

Sesame-crusted Tuna Steaks

Servings: 3
Cooking Time: 13 Minutes
Ingredients:

- ½ cup Sesame seeds, preferably a blend of white and black
- 1½ tablespoons Toasted sesame oil
- 3 6-ounce skinless tuna steaks

Directions:
1. Preheat the toaster oven to 400°F.
2. Pour the sesame seeds on a dinner plate. Use ½ tablespoon of the sesame oil as a rub on both sides and the edges of a tuna steak. Set it in the sesame seeds, then turn it several times, pressing gently, to create an even coating of the seeds, including around the steak's edge. Set aside and continue coating the remaining steak(s).
3. When the machine is at temperature, set the steaks in the air fryer oven with as much air space between them as possible. Air-fry undisturbed for 10 minutes for medium-rare (not USDA-approved), or 12 to 13 minutes for cooked through (USDA-approved).
4. Use a nonstick-safe spatula to transfer the steaks to serving plates. Serve hot.

Skewered Salsa Verde Shrimp

Servings: 4
Cooking Time: 8 Minutes
Ingredients:

- 1½ pounds large fresh shrimp, peeled and deveined
- Brushing mixture:
- 1 7-ounce can salsa verde
- 1 teaspoon ground cumin
- ½ teaspoon chopped fresh cilantro or parsley
- 1 teaspoon garlic powder
- 3 tablespoons plain yogurt
- 1 tablespoon olive oil
- Lemon wedges

Directions:
1. Thread the shrimp onto the skewers.
2. Combine the brushing mixture ingredients in a small bowl. Adjust the seasonings and brush the shrimp with the mixture.
3. BROIL the shrimp for 4 minutes. Turn the skewers, brush the shrimp again, and broil for another 4 minutes, or until the shrimp are firm and cooked. Remove the shrimp from the skewers and serve with lemon wedges.

Romaine Wraps With Shrimp Filling

Servings: 4
Cooking Time: 8 Minutes
Ingredients:
- Filling:
- 1 6-ounce can tiny shrimp, drained, or 1 cup fresh shrimp, peeled, cooked, and chopped
- ¾ cup canned chickpeas, mashed into 1 tablespoon olive oil
- 2 tablespoons chopped fresh parsley
- 2 tablespoons grated carrot
- 2 tablespoons chopped bell pepper
- 2 tablespoons minced onion
- 2 tablespoons lemon juice
- 1 teaspoon soy sauce
- Freshly ground black pepper to taste
- 4 large romaine lettuce leaves Olive oil
- 3 tablespoons lemon juice
- 1 teaspoon paprika

Directions:
1. Combine the filling ingredients in a bowl, adjusting the seasonings to taste. Spoon equal portions of the filling into the centers of the romaine leaves. Fold the leaves in half, pressing the filling together, overlap the leaf edges, and skewer with toothpicks to fasten. Carefully place the leaves in an oiled or nonstick 8½ × 8½ × 2-inch square baking (cake) pan. Lightly spray or brush the lettuce rolls with olive oil.
2. BROIL for 8 minutes, or until the filling is cooked and the leaves are lightly browned. Remove from the oven, remove the toothpicks, and drizzle with the lemon juice and sprinkle with paprika.

Flounder Fillets

Servings: 4
Cooking Time: 8 Minutes
Ingredients:
- 1 egg white
- 1 tablespoon water
- 1 cup panko breadcrumbs
- 2 tablespoons extra-light virgin olive oil
- 4 4-ounce flounder fillets
- salt and pepper
- oil for misting or cooking spray

Directions:
1. Preheat the toaster oven to 390°F.
2. Beat together egg white and water in shallow dish.
3. In another shallow dish, mix panko crumbs and oil until well combined and crumbly (best done by hand).
4. Season flounder fillets with salt and pepper to taste. Dip each fillet into egg mixture and then roll in panko crumbs, pressing in crumbs so that fish is nicely coated.
5. Spray air fryer oven with nonstick cooking spray and add fillets. Air-fry at 390°F for 3 minutes.
6. Spray fish fillets but do not turn. Cook 5 minutes longer or until golden brown and crispy. Using a spatula, carefully remove fish from air fryer oven and serve.

Best-dressed Trout

Servings: 2
Cooking Time: 25 Minutes
Ingredients:
- 2 dressed trout
- 1 egg, beaten
- 2 tablespoons finely ground almonds
- 2 tablespoons unbleached flour
- 1 teaspoon paprika or smoked paprika
- Pinch of salt (optional)
- 4 lemon slices, approximately ¼ inch thick
- 1 teaspoon lemon juice

Directions:
1. Preheat the toaster oven to 400° F.
2. Brush the trout (both sides) with the beaten egg. Blend the almonds, flour, paprika, and salt in a bowl and sprinkle both sides of the trout. Insert 2 lemon slices in each trout cavity and place the trout in an oiled or nonstick 8½ × 8½ × 2-inch square baking (cake) pan.
3. BAKE for 20 minutes, or until the meat is white and firm. Remove from the oven and turn the trout carefully with a spatula.
4. BROIL for 5 minutes, or until the trout is lightly browned.

Stuffed Baked Red Snapper

Servings: 2
Cooking Time: 30 Minutes
Ingredients:
- Stuffing mixture:
- 12 medium shrimp, cooked, peeled, and chopped
- 2 tablespoons multigrain bread crumbs
- 1 teaspoon anchovy paste
- ¼ teaspoon paprika
- Salt to taste
- 2 6-ounce red snapper fillets
- 1 egg

- ½ cup fat-free half-and-half
- 2 tablespoons cooking sherry

Directions:
1. Preheat the toaster oven to 350° F.
2. Combine all the stuffing mixture ingredients in a medium bowl and place a mound of mixture on one end of each fillet. Fold over the other fillet end, skewering the edge with toothpicks.
3. Place the rolled fillets in an oiled or nonstick 8½ × 8½ × 2-inch square baking (cake) pan.
4. Whisk the egg in a small bowl until light in color, then whisk in the half-and-half and sherry. Pour over the fillets. Cover the pan with aluminum foil.
5. BAKE for 30 minutes.

Crispy Sweet-and-sour Cod Fillets

Servings: 3
Cooking Time: 12 Minutes

Ingredients:
- 1½ cups Plain panko bread crumbs (gluten-free, if a concern)
- 2 tablespoons Regular or low-fat mayonnaise (not fat-free; gluten-free, if a concern)
- ¼ cup Sweet pickle relish
- 3 4- to 5-ounce skinless cod fillets

Directions:
1. Preheat the toaster oven to 400°F.
2. Pour the bread crumbs into a shallow soup plate or a small pie plate. Mix the mayonnaise and relish in a small bowl until well combined. Smear this mixture all over the cod fillets. Set them in the crumbs and turn until evenly coated on all sides, even on the ends.
3. Set the coated cod fillets in the air fryer oven with as much air space between them as possible. They should not touch. Air-fry undisturbed for 12 minutes, or until browned and crisp.
4. Use a nonstick-safe spatula to transfer the cod pieces to a wire rack. Cool for only a minute or two before serving hot.

Sea Bass With Potato Scales And Caper Aïoli

Servings: 2
Cooking Time: 10 Minutes

Ingredients:
- 2 (6- to 8-ounce) fillets of sea bass
- salt and freshly ground black pepper
- ¼ cup mayonnaise
- 2 teaspoons finely chopped lemon zest
- 1 teaspoon chopped fresh thyme
- 2 fingerling potatoes, very thinly sliced into rounds
- olive oil
- ½ clove garlic, crushed into a paste
- 1 tablespoon capers, drained and rinsed
- 1 tablespoon olive oil
- 1 teaspoon lemon juice, to taste

Directions:
1. Preheat the toaster oven to 400°F.
2. Season the fish well with salt and freshly ground black pepper. Mix the mayonnaise, lemon zest and thyme together in a small bowl. Spread a thin layer of the mayonnaise mixture on both fillets. Start layering rows of potato slices onto the fish fillets to simulate the fish scales. The second row should overlap the first row slightly. Dabbing a little more mayonnaise along the upper edge of the row of potatoes where the next row overlaps will help the potato slices stick. Press the potatoes onto the fish to secure them well and season again with salt. Brush or spray the potato layer with olive oil.
3. Transfer the fish to the air fryer oven and air-fry for 8 to 10 minutes, depending on the thickness of your fillets. 1-inch of fish should take 10 minutes at 400°F.
4. While the fish is cooking, add the garlic, capers, olive oil and lemon juice to the remaining mayonnaise mixture to make the caper aïoli.
5. Serve the fish warm with a dollop of the aïoli on top or on the side.

Sea Scallops

Servings: 4
Cooking Time: 8 Minutes

Ingredients:
- 1½ pounds sea scallops
- salt and pepper
- 2 eggs
- ½ cup flour
- ½ cup plain breadcrumbs
- oil for misting or cooking spray

Directions:
1. Rinse scallops and remove the tough side muscle. Sprinkle to taste with salt and pepper.
2. Beat eggs together in a shallow dish. Place flour in a second shallow dish and breadcrumbs in a third.
3. Preheat the toaster oven to 390°F.
4. Dip scallops in flour, then eggs, and then roll in breadcrumbs. Mist with oil or cooking spray.

5. Place scallops in air fryer oven in a single layer, leaving some space between. You should be able to cook about a dozen at a time.

6. Air-fry at 390°F for 8 minutes, watching carefully so as not to overcook. Scallops are done when they turn opaque all the way through. They will feel slightly firm when pressed with tines of a fork.

7. Repeat step 6 to cook remaining scallops.

Tortilla-crusted Tilapia

Servings: 4
Cooking Time: 12 Minutes
Ingredients:
- 4 (5-ounce) tilapia fillets
- ½ teaspoon ground cumin
- Sea salt, for seasoning
- 1 cup tortilla chips, coarsely crushed
- Oil spray (hand-pumped)
- 1 lime, cut into wedges

Directions:
1. Preheat the toaster oven to 375°F on BAKE for 5 minutes.
2. Line the baking tray with parchment paper.
3. Lightly season the fish with the cumin and salt.
4. Press the tortilla chips onto the top of the fish fillets and place them on the baking sheet.
5. Lightly spray the fish with oil.
6. In position 2, bake until golden and just cooked through, about 12 minutes in total.
7. Serve with the lime wedges.

Almond-crusted Fish

Servings: 4
Cooking Time: 10 Minutes
Ingredients:
- 4 4-ounce fish fillets
- ¾ cup breadcrumbs
- ¼ cup sliced almonds, crushed
- 2 tablespoons lemon juice
- ⅛ teaspoon cayenne
- salt and pepper
- ¾ cup flour
- 1 egg, beaten with 1 tablespoon water
- oil for misting or cooking spray

Directions:
1. Split fish fillets lengthwise down the center to create 8 pieces.
2. Mix breadcrumbs and almonds together and set aside.
3. Mix the lemon juice and cayenne together. Brush on all sides of fish.
4. Season fish to taste with salt and pepper.
5. Place the flour on a sheet of wax paper.
6. Roll fillets in flour, dip in egg wash, and roll in the crumb mixture.
7. Mist both sides of fish with oil or cooking spray.
8. Spray air fryer oven and lay fillets inside.
9. Air-fry at 390°F for 5 minutes, turn fish over, and air-fry for an additional 5 minutes or until fish is done and flakes easily.

Crunchy Clam Strips

Servings: 3
Cooking Time: 8 Minutes
Ingredients:
- ½ pound Clam strips, drained
- 1 Large egg, well beaten
- ½ cup All-purpose flour
- ½ cup Yellow cornmeal
- 1½ teaspoons Table salt
- 1½ teaspoons Ground black pepper
- Up to ¾ teaspoon Cayenne
- Vegetable oil spray

Directions:
1. Preheat the toaster oven to 400°F.
2. Toss the clam strips and beaten egg in a bowl until the clams are well coated.
3. Mix the flour, cornmeal, salt, pepper, and cayenne in a large zip-closed plastic bag until well combined. Using a flatware fork or small kitchen tongs, lift the clam strips one by one out of the egg, letting any excess egg slip back into the rest. Put the strips in the bag with the flour mixture. Once all the strips are in the bag, seal it until the strips are well coated.
4. Use kitchen tongs to pick out the clam strips and lay them on a cutting board (leaving any extra flour mixture in the bag to be discarded). Coat the strips on both sides with vegetable oil spray.
5. When the machine is at temperature, spread the clam strips in the air fryer oven in one layer. They may touch in places, but try to leave as much air space as possible around them. Air-fry undisturbed for 8 minutes, or until brown and crunchy.
6. Gently dump the contents of the air fryer oven onto a serving platter. Cool for just a minute or two before serving hot.

Fried Scallops

Servings: 3
Cooking Time: 6 Minutes
Ingredients:
- ½ cup All-purpose flour or tapioca flour
- 1 Large egg(s), well beaten
- 2 cups Corn flake crumbs (gluten-free, if a concern)
- Up to 2 teaspoons Cayenne
- 1 teaspoon Celery seeds
- 1 teaspoon Table salt
- 1 pound Sea scallops
- Vegetable oil spray

Directions:
1. Preheat the toaster oven to 400°F.
2. Set up and fill three shallow soup plates or small pie plates on your counter: one for the flour; one for the beaten egg(s); and one for the corn flake crumbs, stirred with the cayenne, celery seeds, and salt until well combined.
3. One by one, dip a scallop in the flour, turning it every way to coat it thoroughly. Gently shake off any excess flour, then dip the scallop in the egg(s), turning it again to coat all sides. Let any excess egg slip back into the rest, then set the scallop in the corn flake mixture. Turn it several times, pressing gently to get an even coating on the scallop all around. Generously coat the scallop with vegetable oil spray, then set it aside on a cutting board. Coat the remaining scallops in the same way.
4. Set the scallops in the air fryer oven with as much air space between them as possible. They should not touch. Air-fry undisturbed for 6 minutes, or until lightly browned and firm.
5. Use kitchen tongs to gently transfer the scallops to a wire rack. Cool for only a minute or two before serving.

Snapper With Capers And Olives

Servings: 2
Cooking Time: 10 Minutes
Ingredients:
- 2 tablespoons capers
- ¼ cup pitted and sliced black olives
- 2 tablespoons olive oil
- ½ teaspoon dried oregano
- Salt and freshly ground black pepper to taste
- 2 6-ounce red snapper fillets
- 1 tomato, cut into wedges

Directions:
1. Combine the capers, olives, olive oil, and seasonings in a bowl.
2. Place the fillets in an oiled or nonstick 8½ × 8½ × 2-inch square baking (cake) pan and spoon the caper mixture over them.
3. BROIL for 10 minutes, or until the fish flakes easily with a fork. Serve with the tomato wedges

Vegetables And Vegetarian

Air-fried Potato Salad

Servings: 4
Cooking Time: 15 Minutes
Ingredients:
- 1⅓ pounds Yellow potatoes, such as Yukon Golds, cut into ½-inch chunks
- 1 large Sweet white onion(s), such as Vidalia, chopped into ½-inch pieces
- 1 tablespoon plus 2 teaspoons Olive oil
- ¾ cup Thinly sliced celery
- 6 tablespoons Regular or low-fat mayonnaise (gluten-free, if a concern)
- 2½ tablespoons Apple cider vinegar
- 1½ teaspoons Dijon mustard (gluten-free, if a concern)
- ¾ teaspoon Table salt
- ¼ teaspoon Ground black pepper

Directions:
1. Preheat the toaster oven to 400°F.
2. Toss the potatoes, onion(s), and oil in a large bowl until the vegetables are glistening with oil.
3. When the machine is at temperature, transfer the vegetables to the air fryer oven, spreading them out into as even a layer as you can. Air-fry for 15 minutes, tossing and rearranging the vegetables every 3 minutes so that all surfaces get exposed to the air currents, until the vegetables are tender and even browned at the edges.
4. Pour the contents of the air fryer oven into a serving bowl. Cool for at least 5 minutes or up to 30 minutes. Add the celery, mayonnaise, vinegar, mustard, salt, and pepper. Stir well to coat. The potato salad can be made in advance; cover and refrigerate for up to 4 days.

Asparagus Ronald

Servings: 4
Cooking Time: 25 Minutes
Ingredients:
- 20 asparagus spears, rinsed and hard stem ends cut off
- 1 tablespoon soy sauce
- 3 tablespoons lemon juice
- 3 tablespoons olive oil
- Salt and freshly ground black pepper
- 3 tablespoons crumbled feta cheese

Directions:
1. Preheat the toaster oven to 400° F.
2. Place the asparagus spears in a 1-quart 8½ × 8½ × 4-inch ovenproof baking dish.
3. Drizzle the soy sauce, lemon juice, and olive oil over the asparagus spears. Season to taste with salt and pepper. Cover the dish with aluminum foil.
4. BAKE for 25 minutes, or until tender. Sprinkle with the feta cheese before serving.

Fried Okra

Servings: 4
Cooking Time: 8 Minutes
Ingredients:
- 1 pound okra
- 1 large egg
- 1 tablespoon milk
- 1 teaspoon salt, divided
- ½ teaspoon black pepper, divided
- ¼ teaspoon paprika
- ¼ teaspoon thyme
- ½ cup cornmeal
- ½ cup all-purpose flour

Directions:
1. Preheat the toaster oven to 400°F.
2. Cut the okra into ½-inch rounds.
3. In a medium bowl, whisk together the egg, milk, ½ teaspoon of the salt, and ¼ teaspoon of black pepper. Place the okra into the egg mixture and toss until well coated.
4. In a separate bowl, mix together the remaining ½ teaspoon of salt, the remaining ¼ teaspoon of black pepper, the paprika, the thyme, the cornmeal, and the flour. Working in small batches, dredge the egg-coated okra in the cornmeal mixture until all the okra has been breaded.
5. Place a single layer of okra in the air fryer oven and spray with cooking spray. Air-fry for 4 minutes, toss to check for crispness, and cook another 4 minutes. Repeat in batches, as needed.

Balsamic Sweet Potatoes

Servings: 4
Cooking Time: 40 Minutes
Ingredients:
- 2 medium sweet potatoes, scrubbed (or peeled) and sliced into 1-inch rounds
- 3 tablespoons olive oil
- 2 tablespoons balsamic vinegar
- 2 teaspoons molasses
- ½ teaspoon garlic powder
- Salt and freshly ground black pepper to taste
- 1 tablespoon grated lemon zest

Directions:
1. Preheat the toaster oven to 400° F.
2. Mix the potatoes, oil, balsamic vinegar, molasses, and garlic powder together in an oiled or nonstick 8½ × 8½ × 2-inch square baking (cake) pan. Cover the pan with aluminum foil.
3. BAKE, covered, for 30 minutes, or until tender. Remove the cover.
4. BROIL for 10 minutes, or until the potatoes are lightly browned. Season to taste with salt and pepper and garnish with the lemon zest.

Fried Corn On The Cob

Servings: 2
Cooking Time: 10 Minutes
Ingredients:
- 1½ tablespoons Regular or low-fat mayonnaise (not fat-free; gluten-free, if a concern)
- 1½ teaspoons Minced garlic
- ¼ teaspoon Table salt
- ¾ cup Plain panko bread crumbs (gluten-free, if a concern)
- 3 4-inch lengths husked and de-silked corn on the cob
- Vegetable oil spray

Directions:
1. Preheat the toaster oven to 400°F.
2. Stir the mayonnaise, garlic, and salt in a small bowl until well combined. Spread the panko on a dinner plate.
3. Brush the mayonnaise mixture over the kernels of a piece of corn on the cob. Set the corn in the bread crumbs, then roll, pressing gently, to coat it. Lightly coat with vegetable oil spray. Set it aside, then coat the remaining piece(s) of corn in the same way.
4. Set the coated corn on the cob in the air fryer oven with as much air space between the pieces as possible. Air-fry undisturbed for 10 minutes, or until brown and crisp along the coating.
5. Use kitchen tongs to gently transfer the pieces of corn to a wire rack. Cool for 5 minutes before serving.

Cheesy Potato Skins

Servings: 6
Cooking Time: 54 Minutes
Ingredients:
- 3 6- to 8-ounce small russet potatoes
- 3 Thick-cut bacon strips, halved widthwise (gluten-free, if a concern)
- ¾ teaspoon Mild paprika
- ¼ teaspoon Garlic powder
- ¼ teaspoon Table salt
- ¼ teaspoon Ground black pepper
- ½ cup plus 1 tablespoon (a little over 2 ounces) Shredded Cheddar cheese
- 3 tablespoons Thinly sliced trimmed chives
- 6 tablespoons (a little over 1 ounce) Finely grated Parmesan cheese

Directions:
1. Preheat the toaster oven to 375°F.
2. Prick each potato in four places with a fork (not four places in a line but four places all around the potato). Set the potatoes in the air fryer oven with as much air space between them as possible. Air-fry undisturbed for 45 minutes, or until the potatoes are tender when pricked with a fork.
3. Use kitchen tongs to gently transfer the potatoes to a wire rack. Cool for 15 minutes. Maintain the machine's temperature.
4. Lay the bacon strip halves in the air fryer oven in one layer. They may touch but should not overlap. Air-fry undisturbed for 5 minutes, until crisp. Use those same tongs to transfer the bacon pieces to the wire rack. If there's a great deal of rendered bacon fat in the air fryer oven's bottom or on a tray under the pan attachment, pour this into a bowl, cool, and discard. Don't throw it down the drain!
5. Cut the potatoes in half lengthwise (not just slit them open but actually cut in half). Use a flatware spoon to scoop the hot, soft middles into a bowl, leaving ½ inch of potato all around the inside of the spud next to the skin. Sprinkle the inside of the potato "shells" evenly with paprika, garlic powder, salt, and pepper.
6. Chop the bacon pieces into small bits. Sprinkle these along with the Cheddar and chives evenly inside the potato shells. Crumble 2 to 3 tablespoons of the soft potato insides

over the filling mixture. Divide the grated Parmesan evenly over the tops of the potatoes.
7. Set the stuffed potatoes in the air fryer oven with as much air space between them as possible. Air-fry undisturbed for 4 minutes, until the cheese melts and lightly browns.
8. Use kitchen tongs to gently transfer the stuffed potato halves to a wire rack. Cool for 5 minutes before serving.

Empty-the-refrigerator Roasted Vegetables

Servings: 4
Cooking Time: 35 Minutes
Ingredients:
- 3 cups assorted fresh vegetables, cut into 1 × 1-inch pieces
- 2 garlic cloves, minced
- 2 tablespoons olive oil
- 3 tablespoons dry white wine
- Salt and freshly ground black pepper to taste
- 1 tablespoon chopped fresh basil
- 1 tablespoon chopped fresh oregano
- 1 tablespoon chopped fresh parsley

Directions:
1. Preheat the toaster oven to 400° F.
2. Combine all the ingredients with 2 tablespoons water in a 1-quart 8½ × 8½ × 4-inch ovenproof baking dish, mixing well. Cover the dish with aluminum foil.
3. BAKE, covered, for 25 minutes, until the vegetables are tender. Remove from the oven and stir to blend the vegetables and sauce.
4. BROIL, uncovered, for 10 minutes, or until lightly browned.

Fried Eggplant Slices

Servings: 3
Cooking Time: 12 Minutes
Ingredients:
- 1½ sleeves (about 60 saltines) Saltine crackers
- ¾ cup Cornstarch
- 2 Large egg(s), well beaten
- 1 medium (about ¾ pound) Eggplant, stemmed, peeled, and cut into ¼-inch-thick rounds
- Olive oil spray

Directions:
1. Preheat the toaster oven to 400°F. Also, position the rack in the center of the oven and heat the oven to 175°F.
2. Grind the saltines, in batches if necessary, in a food processor, pulsing the machine and rearranging the saltine pieces every few pulses. Or pulverize the saltines in a large, heavy zip-closed plastic bag with the bottom of a heavy saucepan. In either case, you want small bits of saltines, not just crumbs.
3. Set up and fill three shallow soup plates or small pie plates on your counter: one for the cornstarch, one for the beaten egg(s), and one for the pulverized saltines.
4. Set an eggplant slice in the cornstarch and turn it to coat on both sides. Use a brush to lightly remove any excess. Dip it into the beaten egg(s) and turn to coat both sides. Let any excess egg slip back into the rest, then set the slice in the saltines. Turn several times, pressing gently to coat both sides evenly but not heavily. Coat both sides of the slice with olive oil spray and set it aside. Continue dipping and coating the remaining slices.
5. Set one, two, or maybe three slices in the pan. There should be at least ½ inch between them for proper air flow. Air-fry undisturbed for 12 minutes, or until crisp and browned.
6. Use a nonstick-safe spatula to transfer the slice(s) to a large baking sheet. Slip it into the oven to keep the slices warm as you air-fry more batches, as needed, always transferring the slices to the baking sheet to stay warm.

Rosemary Roasted Potatoes With Lemon

Servings: 12
Cooking Time: 4 Minutes
Ingredients:
- 1 pound small red-skinned potatoes, halved or cut into bite-sized chunks
- 1 tablespoon olive oil
- 1 teaspoon finely chopped fresh rosemary
- ¼ teaspoon salt
- freshly ground black pepper
- 1 tablespoon lemon zest

Directions:
1. Preheat the toaster oven to 400°F.
2. Toss the potatoes with the olive oil, rosemary, salt and freshly ground black pepper.
3. Air-fry for 12 minutes (depending on the size of the chunks), tossing the potatoes a few times throughout the cooking process.
4. As soon as the potatoes are tender to a knifepoint, toss them with the lemon zest and more salt if desired.

Moroccan Cauliflower

Servings: 6
Cooking Time: 15 Minutes
Ingredients:
- 1 tablespoon curry powder
- 2 teaspoons smoky paprika
- ½ teaspoon ground cumin
- ½ teaspoon salt
- 1 head cauliflower, cut into bite-size pieces
- ¼ cup red wine vinegar
- 2 tablespoons extra-virgin olive oil
- 2 tablespoons chopped parsley

Directions:
1. Preheat the toaster oven to 370°F.
2. In a large bowl, mix the curry powder, paprika, cumin, and salt. Add the cauliflower and stir to coat. Pour the red wine vinegar over the top and continue stirring.
3. Place the cauliflower into the air fryer oven; drizzle olive oil over the top.
4. Cook the cauliflower for 5 minutes, toss, and cook another 5 minutes. Raise the temperature to 400°F and continue cooking for 4 to 6 minutes, or until crispy.

Pecan Parmesan Cauliflower

Servings: 4
Cooking Time: 35 Minutes
Ingredients:
- 2½ cups (frozen thawed or fresh) thinly sliced cauliflower florets
- Salt and freshly ground black pepper
- 3 tablespoons freshly grated Parmesan cheese
- ½ cup ground pecans

Directions:
1. Preheat the toaster oven to 400° F.
2. Combine the florets and oil in a 1-quart 8½ × 8½ × 4-inch ovenproof baking dish, tossing to coat well. Season to taste with salt and pepper. Cover the dish with aluminum foil.
3. BAKE for 25 minutes, or until tender. Uncover and sprinkle with the cheese and pecans.
4. BROIL for 10 minutes, or until lightly browned.

Home Fries

Servings: 4
Cooking Time: 20 Minutes
Ingredients:
- 3 pounds potatoes, cut into 1-inch cubes
- ½ teaspoon oil
- salt and pepper

Directions:
1. In a large bowl, mix the potatoes and oil thoroughly.
2. Air-fry at 390°F for 10 minutes and redistribute potatoes.
3. Air-fry for an additional 10 minutes, until brown and crisp.
4. Season with salt and pepper to taste.

Blistered Green Beans

Servings: 3
Cooking Time: 10 Minutes
Ingredients:
- ¾ pound Green beans, trimmed on both ends
- 1½ tablespoons Olive oil
- 3 tablespoons Pine nuts
- 1½ tablespoons Balsamic vinegar
- 1½ teaspoons Minced garlic
- ¾ teaspoon Table salt
- ¾ teaspoon Ground black pepper

Directions:
1. Preheat the toaster oven to 400°F.
2. Toss the green beans and oil in a large bowl until all the green beans are glistening.
3. When the machine is at temperature, pile the green beans into the air fryer oven. Air-fry for 10 minutes, tossing often to rearrange the green beans in the air fryer oven, or until blistered and tender.
4. Dump the contents of the air fryer oven into a serving bowl. Add the pine nuts, vinegar, garlic, salt, and pepper. Toss well to coat and combine. Serve warm or at room temperature.

Lemon-glazed Baby Carrots

Servings: 4
Cooking Time: 33 Minutes
Ingredients:
- Glaze:
- 1 tablespoon margarine
- 2 tablespoons lemon juice
- 1 tablespoon honey
- 1 teaspoon garlic powder
- Salt and freshly ground black pepper to taste
- 2 cups peeled baby carrots (approximately 1 pound)
- 1 tablespoon chopped fresh parsley or cilantro

Directions:
1. Place the glaze ingredients in a 1-quart 8½ × 8½ × 4-inch ovenproof baking dish and broil for 4 minutes, or until

the margarine is melted. Remove from the oven and mix well. Add the carrots and toss to coat. Cover the dish with aluminum foil.
2. BAKE, covered, at 350° F. for 30 minutes, or until the carrots are tender. Garnish with chopped parsley or cilantro and serve immediately.

Baked Stuffed Acorn Squash

Servings: 2
Cooking Time: 25 Minutes
Ingredients:
- Stuffing:
- ¼ cup multigrain bread crumbs
- 1 tablespoon olive oil
- ¼ cup canned or frozen thawed corn
- 2 tablespoons chopped onion
- 1 teaspoon capers
- 1 teaspoon garlic powder
- Salt and freshly ground black pepper
- 1 medium acorn squash, halved and seeds scooped out

Directions:
1. Preheat the toaster oven to 400° F.
2. Combine the stuffing ingredients and season to taste. Fill the squash cavities with the mixture and place in an oiled or nonstick 8½ × 8½ × 2-inch square baking (cake) pan.
3. BAKE for 25 minutes, or until the squash is tender and the stuffing is lightly browned.

Buttery Rolls

Servings: 6
Cooking Time: 14 Minutes
Ingredients:
- 6½ tablespoons Room-temperature whole or low-fat milk
- 3 tablespoons plus 1 teaspoon Butter, melted and cooled
- 3 tablespoons plus 1 teaspoon (or 1 medium egg, well beaten) Pasteurized egg substitute, such as Egg Beaters
- 1½ tablespoons Granulated white sugar
- 1¼ teaspoons Instant yeast
- ¼ teaspoon Table salt
- 2 cups, plus more for dusting All-purpose flour
- Vegetable oil
- Additional melted butter, for brushing

Directions:
1. Stir the milk, melted butter, pasteurized egg substitute (or whole egg), sugar, yeast, and salt in a medium bowl to combine. Stir in the flour just until the mixture makes a soft dough.
2. Lightly flour a clean, dry work surface. Turn the dough out onto the work surface. Knead the dough for 5 minutes to develop the gluten.
3. Lightly oil the inside of a clean medium bowl. Gather the dough into a compact ball and set it in the bowl. Turn the dough over so that its surface has oil on it all over. Cover the bowl tightly with plastic wrap and set aside in a warm, draft-free place until the dough has doubled in bulk, about 1½ hours.
4. Punch down the dough, then turn it out onto a clean, dry work surface. Divide it into 5 even balls for a small batch, 6 balls for a medium batch, or 8 balls for a large one.
5. For a small batch, lightly oil the inside of a 6-inch round cake pan and set the balls around its perimeter, separating them as much as possible.
6. For a medium batch, lightly oil the inside of a 7-inch round cake pan and set the balls in it with one ball at its center, separating them as much as possible.
7. For a large batch, lightly oil the inside of an 8-inch round cake pan and set the balls in it with one at the center, separating them as much as possible.
8. Cover with plastic wrap and set aside to rise for 30 minutes.
9. Preheat the toaster oven to 350°F.
10. Uncover the pan and brush the rolls with a little melted butter, perhaps ½ teaspoon per roll. When the machine is at temperature, set the cake pan in the air fryer oven. Air-fry undisturbed for 14 minutes, or until the rolls have risen and browned.
11. Using kitchen tongs and a nonstick-safe spatula, two hot pads, or silicone baking mitts, transfer the cake pan from the air fryer oven to a wire rack. Cool the rolls in the pan for a minute or two. Turn the rolls out onto a wire rack, set them top side up again, and cool for at least another couple of minutes before serving warm.

Hasty Home Fries

Servings: 4
Cooking Time: 20 Minutes
Ingredients:
- 2 medium baking potatoes, scrubbed and finely chopped
- ¼ cup onions, finely chopped
- 1 teaspoon hot sauce
- Salt and freshly ground black pepper

Directions:
1. Combine all the ingredients in a bowl. Transfer the mixture to an oiled or nonstick 8½ × 8½ × 2-inch square baking (cake) pan, adjusting the seasonings to taste.

2. BROIL for 10 minutes, then turn with tongs and broil again for 10 minutes, or until browned and crisped to your preference.

Grits Casserole

Servings: 4
Cooking Time: 30 Minutes
Ingredients:
- 10 fresh asparagus spears, cut into 1-inch pieces
- 2 cups cooked grits, cooled to room temperature
- 1 egg, beaten
- 2 teaspoons Worcestershire sauce
- ½ teaspoon garlic powder
- ¼ teaspoon salt
- 2 slices provolone cheese (about 1½ ounces)
- oil for misting or cooking spray

Directions:
1. Mist asparagus spears with oil and air-fry at 390°F for 5 minutes, until crisp-tender.
2. In a medium bowl, mix together the grits, egg, Worcestershire, garlic powder, and salt.
3. Spoon half of grits mixture into air fryer oven baking pan and top with asparagus.
4. Tear cheese slices into pieces and layer evenly on top of asparagus.
5. Top with remaining grits.
6. Bake at 360°F for 25 minutes. The casserole will rise a little as it cooks. When done, the top will have browned lightly with just a hint of crispiness.

Ranch Potatoes

Servings: 2
Cooking Time: 50 Minutes
Ingredients:
- 2 medium russet potatoes, scrubbed and cut lengthwise into ¼-inch strips
- 1 medium onion, chopped
- 2 tablespoons vegetable oil
- 2 tablespoons barbecue sauce
- ¼ teaspoon hot sauce
- Salt and freshly ground black pepper

Directions:
1. Preheat the toaster oven to 400° F.
2. Combine all the ingredients in a medium bowl, mixing well and adjusting the seasonings to taste.
3. Place equal portions of the potatoes on two 12 × 12-inch squares of heavy-duty aluminum foil. Fold up the edges of the foil to form a sealed packet and place on the oven rack.

4. BAKE for 40 minutes, or until the potatoes are tender. Carefully open the packet and fold back the foil.
5. BROIL 10 minutes, or until the potatoes are browned.

Crispy Herbed Potatoes

Servings: 6
Cooking Time: 20 Minutes
Ingredients:
- 3 medium baking potatoes, washed and cubed
- ½ teaspoon dried thyme
- 1 teaspoon minced dried rosemary
- ½ teaspoon garlic powder
- 1 teaspoon sea salt
- ½ teaspoon black pepper
- 2 tablespoons extra-virgin olive oil
- ¼ cup chopped parsley

Directions:
1. Preheat the toaster oven to 390°F.
2. Pat the potatoes dry. In a large bowl, mix together the cubed potatoes, thyme, rosemary, garlic powder, sea salt, and pepper. Drizzle and toss with olive oil.
3. Pour the herbed potatoes into the air fryer oven. Air-fry for 20 minutes, stirring every 5 minutes.
4. Toss the cooked potatoes with chopped parsley and serve immediately.
5. VARY IT! Potatoes are versatile — add any spice or seasoning mixture you prefer and create your own favorite side dish.

Blistered Tomatoes

Servings: 20
Cooking Time: 15 Minutes
Ingredients:
- 1½ pounds Cherry or grape tomatoes
- Olive oil spray
- 1½ teaspoons Balsamic vinegar
- ¼ teaspoon Table salt
- ¼ teaspoon Ground black pepper

Directions:
1. Put the pan in a drawer-style air fryer oven, or a baking tray in the lower third of a toaster oven–style air fryer oven. Place a 6-inch round cake pan in the pan or on the tray for a small batch, a 7-inch round cake pan for a medium batch, or an 8-inch round cake pan for a large one. Heat the air fryer oven to 400°F with the pan in the air fryer oven. When the machine is at temperature, keep heating the pan for 5 minutes more.

2. Place the tomatoes in a large bowl, coat them with the olive oil spray, toss gently, then spritz a couple of times more, tossing after each spritz, until the tomatoes are glistening.
3. Pour the tomatoes into the cake pan and air-fry undisturbed for 10 minutes, or until they split and begin to brown.
4. Use kitchen tongs and a nonstick-safe spatula, or silicone baking mitts, to remove the cake pan from the air fryer oven. Toss the hot tomatoes with the vinegar, salt, and pepper. Cool in the pan for a few minutes before serving.

Green Beans

Servings: 4
Cooking Time: 12 Minutes
Ingredients:
- 1 pound fresh green beans
- 2 tablespoons Italian salad dressing
- salt and pepper

Directions:
1. Wash beans and snap off stem ends.
2. In a large bowl, toss beans with Italian dressing.
3. Air-fry at 330°F for 5 minutes. Stir and cook 5 minutes longer. If needed, continue cooking for 2 minutes, until as tender as you like. Beans should shrivel slightly and brown in places.
4. Sprinkle with salt and pepper to taste.

Crispy Noodle Salad

Servings: 3
Cooking Time: 22 Minutes
Ingredients:
- 6 ounces Fresh Chinese-style stir-fry or lo mein wheat noodles
- 1½ tablespoons Cornstarch
- ¾ cup Chopped stemmed and cored red bell pepper
- 2 Medium scallion(s), trimmed and thinly sliced
- 2 teaspoons Sambal oelek or other pulpy hot red pepper sauce
- 2 teaspoons Thai sweet chili sauce or red ketchup-like chili sauce, such as Heinz
- 2 teaspoons Regular or low-sodium soy sauce or tamari sauce
- 2 teaspoons Unseasoned rice vinegar
- 1 tablespoon White or black sesame seeds

Directions:
1. Bring a large saucepan of water to a boil over high heat. Add the noodles and boil for 2 minutes. Drain in a colander set in the sink. Rinse several times with cold water, shaking the colander to drain the noodles very well. Spread the noodles out on a large cutting board and air-dry for 10 minutes.
2. Preheat the toaster oven to 400°F.
3. Toss the noodles in a bowl with the cornstarch until well coated. Spread them out across the entire air fryer oven (although they will be touching and overlapping a bit). Air-fry for 6 minutes, then turn the solid mass of noodles over as one piece. If it cracks in half or smaller pieces, just fit these back together after turning. Continue air-frying for 6 minutes, or until golden brown and crisp.
4. As the noodles cook, stir the bell pepper, scallion(s), sambal oelek, red chili sauce, soy sauce, vinegar, and sesame seeds in a serving bowl until well combined.
5. Turn the air fryer oven of noodles out onto a cutting board and cool for a minute or two. Break the mass of noodles into individual noodles and/or small chunks and add to the dressing in the serving bowl. Toss well to serve.

Perfect Asparagus

Servings: 3
Cooking Time: 10 Minutes
Ingredients:
- 1 pound Very thin asparagus spears
- 2 tablespoons Olive oil
- 1 teaspoon Coarse sea salt or kosher salt
- ¾ teaspoon Finely grated lemon zest

Directions:
1. Preheat the toaster oven to 400°F.
2. Trim just enough off the bottom of the asparagus spears so they'll fit in the air fryer oven. Put the spears on a large plate and drizzle them with some of the olive oil. Turn them over and drizzle more olive oil, working to get all the spears coated.
3. When the machine is at temperature, place the spears in one direction in the air fryer oven. They may be touching. Air-fry for 10 minutes, tossing and rearranging the spears twice, until tender.
4. Dump the contents of the air fryer oven on a serving platter. Spread out the spears. Sprinkle them with the salt and lemon zest while still warm. Serve at once.

Florentine Stuffed Tomatoes

Servings: 12
Cooking Time: 2 Minutes
Ingredients:
- 1 cup frozen spinach, thawed and squeezed dry
- ¼ cup toasted pine nuts
- ¼ cup grated mozzarella cheese
- ½ cup crumbled feta cheese
- ½ cup coarse fresh breadcrumbs
- 1 tablespoon olive oil
- salt and freshly ground black pepper
- 2 to 3 beefsteak tomatoes, halved horizontally and insides scooped out

Directions:
1. Combine the spinach, pine nuts, mozzarella and feta cheeses, breadcrumbs, olive oil, salt and freshly ground black pepper in a bowl. Spoon the mixture into the tomato halves. You should have enough filling for 2 to 3 tomatoes, depending on how big they are.
2. Preheat the toaster oven to 350°F.
3. Place three or four tomato halves (depending on whether you're using 2 or 3 tomatoes and how big they are) into the air fryer oven and air-fry for 12 minutes. The tomatoes should be soft but still manageable and the tops should be lightly browned. Repeat with second batch if necessary.
4. Let the tomatoes cool for just a minute or two before serving.

Tandoori Cauliflower

Servings: 4
Cooking Time: 10 Minutes
Ingredients:
- ½ cup Plain full-fat yogurt (not Greek yogurt)
- 1½ teaspoons Yellow curry powder, purchased or homemade
- 1½ teaspoons Lemon juice
- ¾ teaspoon Table salt (optional)
- 4½ cups (about 1 pound 2 ounces) 2-inch cauliflower florets

Directions:
1. Preheat the toaster oven to 400°F.
2. Whisk the yogurt, curry powder, lemon juice, and salt (if using) in a large bowl until uniform. Add the florets and stir gently to coat the florets well and evenly. Even better, use your clean, dry hands to get the yogurt mixture down into all the nooks of the florets.
3. When the machine is at temperature, transfer the florets to the air fryer oven, spreading them gently into as close to one layer as you can. Air-fry for 10 minutes, tossing and rearranging the florets twice so that any covered or touching parts are exposed to the air currents, until lightly browned and tender if still a bit crunchy.
4. Pour the contents of the air fryer oven onto a wire rack. Cool for at least 5 minutes before serving, or serve at room temperature.

Fried Cauliflower with Parmesan Lemon Dressing

Servings: 2
Cooking Time: 12 Minutes
Ingredients:
- 4 cups cauliflower florets (about half a large head)
- 1 tablespoon olive oil
- salt and freshly ground black pepper
- 1 teaspoon finely chopped lemon zest
- 1 tablespoon fresh lemon juice (about half a lemon)
- ¼ cup grated Parmigiano-Reggiano cheese
- 4 tablespoons extra virgin olive oil
- ¼ teaspoon salt
- lots of freshly ground black pepper
- 1 tablespoon chopped fresh parsley

Directions:
1. Preheat the toaster oven to 400°F.
2. Toss the cauliflower florets with the olive oil, salt and freshly ground black pepper. Air-fry for 12 minutes.
3. While the cauliflower is frying, make the dressing. Combine the lemon zest, lemon juice, Parmigiano-Reggiano cheese and olive oil in a small bowl. Season with salt and lots of freshly ground black pepper. Stir in the parsley.
4. Turn the fried cauliflower out onto a serving platter and drizzle the dressing over the top.

Roasted Brussels Sprouts With Bacon

Servings: 20
Cooking Time: 4 Minutes
Ingredients:
- 4 slices thick-cut bacon, chopped (about ¼ pound)
- 1 pound Brussels sprouts, halved (or quartered if large)
- freshly ground black pepper

Directions:
1. Preheat the toaster oven to 380°F.
2. Air-fry the bacon for 5 minutes.

3. Add the Brussels sprouts to the air fryer oven and drizzle a little bacon fat from the pan into the air fryer oven. Toss the sprouts to coat with the bacon fat. Air-fry for an additional 15 minutes, or until the Brussels sprouts are tender to a knifepoint.
4. Season with freshly ground black pepper.

Onions

Servings: 4
Cooking Time: 18 Minutes
Ingredients:
- 2 yellow onions (Vidalia or 1015 recommended)
- salt and pepper
- ¼ teaspoon ground thyme
- ¼ teaspoon smoked paprika
- 2 teaspoons olive oil
- 1 ounce Gruyère cheese, grated

Directions:
1. Peel onions and halve lengthwise (vertically).
2. Sprinkle cut sides of onions with salt, pepper, thyme, and paprika.
3. Place each onion half, cut-surface up, on a large square of aluminum foil. Pull sides of foil up to cup around onion. Drizzle cut surface of onions with oil.
4. Crimp foil at top to seal closed.
5. Place wrapped onions in air fryer oven and air-fry at 390°F for 18 minutes. When done, onions should be soft enough to pierce with fork but still slightly firm.
6. Open foil just enough to sprinkle each onion with grated cheese.
7. Air-fry for 30 seconds to 1 minute to melt cheese.

Salt And Pepper Baked Potatoes

Servings: 40
Cooking Time: 4 Minutes
Ingredients:
- 1 to 2 tablespoons olive oil
- 4 medium russet potatoes (about 9 to 10 ounces each)
- salt and coarsely ground black pepper
- butter, sour cream, chopped fresh chives, scallions or bacon bits (optional)

Directions:
1. Preheat the toaster oven to 400°F.
2. Rub the olive oil all over the potatoes and season them generously with salt and coarsely ground black pepper. Pierce all sides of the potatoes several times with the tines of a fork.
3. Air-fry for 40 minutes, turning the potatoes over halfway through the cooking time.
4. Serve the potatoes, split open with butter, sour cream, fresh chives, scallions or bacon bits.

Fingerling Potatoes

Servings: 4
Cooking Time: 15 Minutes
Ingredients:
- 1 pound fingerling potatoes
- 1 tablespoon light olive oil
- ½ teaspoon dried parsley
- ½ teaspoon lemon juice
- coarsely ground sea salt

Directions:
1. Cut potatoes in half lengthwise.
2. In a large bowl, combine potatoes, oil, parsley, and lemon juice. Stir well to coat potatoes.
3. Place potatoes in air fryer oven and air-fry at 360°F for 15 minutes or until lightly browned and tender inside.
4. Sprinkle with sea salt before serving.

Asparagus And Cherry Tomato Quiche

Servings: 4
Cooking Time: 50 Minutes
Ingredients:
- 6 asparagus spears, woody ends removed, cut into 1-inch pieces
- 1 premade unbaked pie crust
- 5 large eggs
- ½ cup half-and-half
- ¾ cup shredded Swiss cheese, divided
- Sea salt, for seasoning
- Freshly ground black pepper, for seasoning
- 10 cherry tomatoes, quartered
- 1 scallion, both white and green parts, finely chopped

Directions:
1. Place the rack in position 1 and preheat oven to 350°F on BAKE for 5 minutes.
2. Place a small saucepan three-quarters filled with water on high heat and bring to a boil. Blanch the asparagus until bright green, about 1 minute. Drain and set aside.
3. Line an 8-inch-round pie dish with the pie crust, then trim and flute the edges.
4. In a small bowl, beat the eggs, half-and-half, and ½ cup of the cheese until well blended; season with salt and pepper.

5. Arrange the asparagus, tomatoes, and scallion in the pie crust. Pour in the egg mixture and top with the remaining ¼ cup of cheese.
6. Bake for 45 to 50 minutes until the quiche is puffed and lightly browned, and a knife inserted in the center comes out clean.
7. Serve warm or cold.

Mushrooms

Servings: 4
Cooking Time: 12 Minutes
Ingredients:
- 8 ounces whole white button mushrooms
- ½ teaspoon salt
- ⅛ teaspoon pepper
- ¼ teaspoon garlic powder
- ¼ teaspoon onion powder
- 5 tablespoons potato starch
- 1 egg, beaten
- ¾ cup panko breadcrumbs
- oil for misting or cooking spray

Directions:
1. Place mushrooms in a large bowl. Add the salt, pepper, garlic and onion powders, and stir well to distribute seasonings.
2. Add potato starch to mushrooms and toss in bowl until well coated.
3. Dip mushrooms in beaten egg, roll in panko crumbs, and mist with oil or cooking spray.
4. Place mushrooms in air fryer oven. You can cook them all at once, and it's okay if a few are stacked.
5. Air-fry at 390°F for 5 minutes. Rotate, then continue cooking for 7 more minutes, until golden brown and crispy.

Rolled Chinese (napa) Cabbage With Chickpea Filling

Servings: 4
Cooking Time: 46 Minutes
Ingredients:
- 6 Chinese cabbage leaves, approximately 7 inches long
- Filling:
- 2 tablespoons low-fat ricotta cheese or Yogurt Cheese Spread
- 1 cup canned chickpeas (garbanzos), drained and mashed
- 1 teaspoon lemon juice
- Salt and butcher's pepper to taste
- 2 tablespoons olive oil for brushing
- 2 tablespoons chopped almonds

Directions:
1. Layer an 8½ × 8½ × 2-inch square baking (cake) pan with the cabbage leaves and add enough water to barely cover them.
2. BROIL 5 minutes, turn the leaves with tongs, and broil another 5 minutes, or until the leaves are partially cooked and just pliable. Spread the leaves on paper towels to drain and cool.
3. Mix the filling ingredients together in a medium bowl and adjust the seasonings to taste. Place equal portions of filling 2 inches from the stem end (base of the leaf) and roll up the leaf, enclosing the filling. Place each roll with the leaf edge down in an oiled or 8½ × 8½ × 2-inch square baking (cake) pan. Sprinkle with the almonds. Cover the pan with aluminum foil.
4. BAKE at 400° F. for 30 minutes, or until the rolls are tender. Remove the cover.
5. BROIL 6 minutes, or until the almonds and cabbage leaves are lightly browned.

Stuffed Onions

Servings: 6
Cooking Time: 27 Minutes
Ingredients:
- 6 Small 3½- to 4-ounce yellow or white onions
- Olive oil spray
- 6 ounces Bulk sweet Italian sausage meat (gluten-free, if a concern)
- 9 Cherry tomatoes, chopped
- 3 tablespoons Seasoned Italian-style dried bread crumbs (gluten-free, if a concern)
- 3 tablespoons (about ½ ounce) Finely grated Parmesan cheese

Directions:
1. Preheat the toaster oven to 325°F (or 330°F, if that's the closest setting).
2. Cut just enough off the root ends of the onions so they will stand up on a cutting board when this end is turned down. Carefully peel off just the brown, papery skin. Now cut the top quarter off each and place the onion back on the cutting board with this end facing up. Use a flatware spoon (preferably a serrated grapefruit spoon) or a melon baller to scoop out the "insides" (interior layers) of the onion, leaving enough of the bottom and side walls so that the onion does not collapse. Depending on the thickness of the layers in the onion, this may be one or two of those layers—or even three, if they're very thin.

3. Coat the insides and outsides of the onions with olive oil spray. Set the onion "shells" in the air fryer oven and air-fry for 15 minutes.

4. Meanwhile, make the filling. Set a medium skillet over medium heat for a couple of minutes, then crumble in the sausage meat. Cook, stirring often, until browned, about 4 minutes. Transfer the contents of the skillet to a medium bowl (leave the fat behind in the skillet or add it to the bowl, depending on your cross-trainer regimen). Stir in the tomatoes, bread crumbs, and cheese until well combined.

5. When the onions are ready, use a nonstick-safe spatula to gently transfer them to a cutting board. Increase the air fryer oven's temperature to 350°F.

6. Pack the sausage mixture into the onion shells, gently compacting the filling and mounding it up at the top.

7. When the machine is at temperature, set the onions stuffing side up in the air fryer oven with at least ¼ inch between them. Air-fry for 12 minutes, or until lightly browned and sizzling hot.

8. Use a nonstick-safe spatula, and perhaps a flatware fork for balance, to transfer the onions to a cutting board or serving platter. Cool for 5 minutes before serving.

Panzanella Salad With Crispy Croutons

Servings: 4
Cooking Time: 3 Minutes
Ingredients:
- ½ French baguette, sliced in half lengthwise
- 2 large cloves garlic
- 2 large ripe tomatoes, divided
- 2 small Persian cucumbers, quartered and diced
- ¼ cup Kalamata olives
- 1 tablespoon chopped, fresh oregano or 1 teaspoon dried oregano
- ¼ cup chopped fresh basil
- ¼ cup chopped fresh parsley
- ½ cup sliced red onion
- 2 tablespoons red wine vinegar
- ¼ cup extra-virgin olive oil
- Salt and pepper, to taste

Directions:
1. Preheat the toaster oven to 380°F.
2. Place the baguette into the air fryer oven and toast for 3 to 5 minutes or until lightly golden brown.
3. Remove the bread from air fryer oven and immediately rub 1 raw garlic clove firmly onto the inside portion of each piece of bread, scraping the garlic onto the bread.
4. Slice 1 of the tomatoes in half and rub the cut edge of one half of the tomato onto the toasted bread. Season the rubbed bread with sea salt to taste.
5. Cut the bread into cubes and place in a large bowl. Cube the remaining 1½ tomatoes and add to the bowl. Add the cucumbers, olives, oregano, basil, parsley, and onion; stir to mix. Drizzle the red wine vinegar into the bowl, and stir. Drizzle the olive oil over the top, stir, and adjust the seasonings with salt and pepper.
6. Serve immediately or allow to sit at room temperature up to 1 hour before serving.

Cauliflower

Servings: 4
Cooking Time: 6 Minutes
Ingredients:
- ½ cup water
- 1 10-ounce package frozen cauliflower (florets)
- 1 teaspoon lemon pepper seasoning

Directions:
1. Pour the water into air fryer oven.
2. Pour the frozen cauliflower into the air fryer oven and sprinkle with lemon pepper seasoning.
3. Air-fry at 390°F for approximately 6 minutes.

Parmesan Asparagus

Servings: 2
Cooking Time: 5 Minutes
Ingredients:
- 1 bunch asparagus, stems trimmed
- 1 teaspoon olive oil
- salt and freshly ground black pepper
- ¼ cup coarsely grated Parmesan cheese
- ½ lemon

Directions:
1. Preheat the toaster oven to 400°F.
2. Toss the asparagus with the oil and season with salt and freshly ground black pepper.
3. Transfer the asparagus to the air fryer oven and air-fry at 400°F for 5 minutes, turn the asparagus once or twice during the cooking process.
4. When the asparagus is cooked to your liking, sprinkle the asparagus generously with the Parmesan cheese and close the air fryer oven again. Let the asparagus sit for 1 minute in the turned-off air fryer oven. Then, remove the asparagus, transfer it to a serving dish and finish with a grind of black pepper and a squeeze of lemon juice.

Sesame Carrots And Sugar Snap Peas

Servings: 16
Cooking Time: 4 Minutes
Ingredients:
- 1 pound carrots, peeled sliced on the bias (½-inch slices)
- 1 teaspoon olive oil
- salt and freshly ground black pepper
- ⅓ cup honey
- 1 tablespoon sesame oil
- 1 tablespoon soy sauce
- ½ teaspoon minced fresh ginger
- 4 ounces sugar snap peas (about 1 cup)
- 1½ teaspoons sesame seeds

Directions:
1. Preheat the toaster oven to 360°F.
2. Toss the carrots with the olive oil, season with salt and pepper and air-fry for 10 minutes.
3. Combine the honey, sesame oil, soy sauce and minced ginger in a large bowl. Add the sugar snap peas and the air-fried carrots to the honey mixture, toss to coat and return everything to the air fryer oven.
4. Turn up the temperature to 400°F and air-fry for an additional 6 minutes.
5. Transfer the carrots and sugar snap peas to a serving bowl. Pour the sauce from the bottom of the cooker over the vegetables and sprinkle sesame seeds over top. Serve immediately.

Zucchini Boats With Ham And Cheese

Servings: 4
Cooking Time: 12 Minutes
Ingredients:
- 2 6-inch-long zucchini
- 2 ounces Thinly sliced deli ham, any rind removed, meat roughly chopped
- 4 Dry-packed sun-dried tomatoes, chopped
- ⅓ cup Purchased pesto
- ¼ cup Packaged mini croutons
- ¼ cup (about 1 ounce) Shredded semi-firm mozzarella cheese

Directions:
1. Preheat the toaster oven to 375°F.
2. Split the zucchini in half lengthwise and use a flatware spoon or a serrated grapefruit spoon to scoop out the insides of the halves, leaving at least a ¼-inch border all around the zucchini half. (You can save the scooped out insides to add to soups and stews—or even freeze it for a much later use.)
3. Mix the ham, sun-dried tomatoes, pesto, croutons, and half the cheese in a bowl until well combined. Pack this mixture into the zucchini "shells." Top them with the remaining cheese.
4. Set them stuffing side up in the air fryer oven without touching (even a fraction of an inch between them is enough room). Air-fry undisturbed for 12 minutes, or until softened and browned, with the cheese melted on top.
5. Use a nonstick-safe spatula to transfer the zucchini boats stuffing side up on a wire rack. Cool for 5 or 10 minutes before serving.

Desserts

Coconut Cake

Servings: 6
Cooking Time: 25 Minutes
Ingredients:
- 2 cups unbleached flour
- 2 teaspoons baking powder
- 1 cup skim or low-fat soy milk
- 2 tablespoons vegetable oil
- 3 1 teaspoon vanilla extract
- 1 egg, beaten
- ¾ cup sugar
- Salt to taste
- Creamy Frosting (recipe follows)

Directions:
1. Preheat the toaster oven to 350° F.
2. Combine all the ingredients in a large bowl, mixing well.
3. Pour the cake batter into an oiled or nonstick 8½ × 8½ × 2-inch square baking (cake) pan.
4. BAKE for 25 minutes, or until a toothpick inserted in the center comes out clean. Ice with Creamy Frosting and sprinkle with coconut.

Cheesecake Wontons

Servings: 6
Cooking Time: 16 Minutes
Ingredients:
- ¼ cup Regular or low-fat cream cheese (not fat-free)
- 2 tablespoons Granulated white sugar
- 1½ tablespoons Egg yolk
- ¼ teaspoon Vanilla extract
- ⅛ teaspoon Table salt
- 1½ tablespoons All-purpose flour
- 16 Wonton wrappers (vegetarian, if a concern)
- Vegetable oil spray

Directions:
1. Preheat the toaster oven to 400°F.
2. Using a flatware fork, mash the cream cheese, sugar, egg yolk, and vanilla in a small bowl until smooth. Add the salt and flour and continue mashing until evenly combined.
3. Set a wonton wrapper on a clean, dry work surface so that one corner faces you (so that it looks like a diamond on your work surface). Set 1 teaspoon of the cream cheese mixture in the middle of the wrapper but just above a horizontal line that would divide the wrapper in half. Dip your clean finger in water and run it along the edges of the wrapper. Fold the corner closest to you up and over the filling, lining it up with the corner farthest from you, thereby making a stuffed triangle. Press gently to seal. Wet the two triangle tips nearest you, then fold them up and together over the filling. Gently press together to seal and fuse. Set aside and continue making more stuffed wontons, 11 more for the small batch, 15 more for the medium batch, or 23 more for the large one.
4. Lightly coat the stuffed wrappers on all sides with vegetable oil spray. Set them with the fused corners up in the air fryer oven with as much air space between them as possible. Air-fry undisturbed for 6 minutes, or until golden brown and crisp.
5. Gently dump the contents of the air fryer oven onto a wire rack. Cool for at least 5 minutes before serving.

Buttermilk Confetti Cake

Servings: 10-12
Cooking Time: 25 Minutes
Ingredients:
- 1 1/2 cups all purpose flour
- 1/2 teaspoon baking soda
- 1/4 teaspoon salt
- 1/2 cup butter, softened
- 1 cup sugar
- 1 teaspoon vanilla extract
- 2 large eggs
- 3/4 cup buttermilk
- 1/4 cup multi-colored sprinkle
- Cream Cheese Frosting
- Multi-colored sprinkles

Directions:
1. Preheat the toaster oven to 350°F. Grease two 8-inch cake pans and line with parchment paper.
2. Stir flour, baking soda and salt in small bowl. Set mixture aside.
3. Beat butter, sugar and vanilla extract on HIGH in large bowl until blended. Add eggs, one at a time, until well blended.
4. Alternately add flour mixture and buttermilk until combined. Stir in 1/4 cup sprinkles.
5. Divide batter evenly between prepared pans. Place one pan on bottom rack and one pan on top rack, rotate halfway through baking.

6. Bake 20 to 25 minutes or until a toothpick inserted in center of cakes comes out clean. Cool 10 minutes on wire rack.
7. Remove cakes from pans and cool completely on wire racks. Frost with Cream Cheese Frosting and top with sprinkles.

Lemon Torte

Servings: 6
Cooking Time: 16 Minutes
Ingredients:
- First mixture:
- ¼ cup margarine, at room temperature
- ½ teaspoon grated lemon zest
- 3 egg yolks
- ¼ cup sugar
- ⅓ cup unbleached flour
- 3 tablespoons cornstarch
- Second mixture:
- 3 egg whites
- 2 tablespoons sugar
- Cream Cheese Frosting (recipe follows)

Directions:
1. Beat together the first mixture ingredients in a medium bowl with an electric mixer until the mixture is smooth. Set aside. Clean the electric mixer beaters.
2. Beat the second mixture together: Beat the egg whites into soft peaks in a medium bowl, gradually adding the sugar, and continue beating until the peaks are stiff. Fold the first mixture into the second mixture to make the torte batter.
3. Pour ½ cup torte batter into a small oiled or nonstick 3½ × 7½ × 2¼-inch loaf pan.
4. BROIL for 1 or 2 minutes, or until lightly browned. Remove from the oven.
5. Pour and spread evenly another ½ cup batter on top of the first layer. Broil again for 1 or 2 minutes, or until lightly browned. Repeat the process until all the batter is used up. When cool, run a knife around the sides to loosen and invert onto a plate. Chill. Frost with Cream Cheese Frosting and serve chilled.

Bourbon Bread Pudding

Servings: 2
Cooking Time: 120 Minutes
Ingredients:
- 6 ounces baguette, torn into 1-inch pieces (4 cups)
- ¼ cup raisins
- 2 tablespoons bourbon
- ¾ cup heavy cream
- ⅓ cup packed (2⅓ ounces) light brown sugar
- ¼ cup whole milk
- 2 large egg yolks
- 1 teaspoon vanilla extract
- ½ teaspoon ground cinnamon, divided
- ⅛ teaspoon table salt
- Pinch ground nutmeg
- 2 tablespoons unsalted butter, cut into ¼-inch pieces
- 1 tablespoon granulated sugar

Directions:
1. Adjust toaster oven rack to middle position and preheat the toaster oven to 375 degrees. Spread bread in single layer on small rimmed baking sheet and bake until golden brown and crisp, 10 to 20 minutes, tossing halfway through baking. Let bread cool completely.
2. Meanwhile, microwave raisins and bourbon in covered bowl until bubbling, 30 to 60 seconds. Let sit until softened, about 15 minutes.
3. Whisk cream, brown sugar, milk, egg yolks, vanilla, ¼ teaspoon cinnamon, salt, and nutmeg together in large bowl. Add bread and raisin mixture and toss until evenly coated. Let mixture sit, tossing occasionally, until bread begins to absorb custard and is softened, about 20 minutes.
4. Grease two 12-ounce ramekins. Divide bread mixture evenly between prepared ramekins and sprinkle with butter, granulated sugar, and remaining ¼ teaspoon cinnamon. Cover each ramekin with aluminum foil, place on small rimmed baking sheet, and bake for 30 minutes.
5. Remove foil from bread puddings and continue to bake until tops are crisp and golden brown, 10 to 15 minutes. Let bread puddings cool for 15 minutes before serving.

Almond-roasted Pears

Servings: 4
Cooking Time: 15 Minutes
Ingredients:
- Yogurt Topping
- 1 container vanilla Greek yogurt (5–6 ounces)
- ¼ teaspoon almond flavoring
- 2 whole pears
- ¼ cup crushed Biscoff cookies (approx. 4 cookies)
- 1 tablespoon sliced almonds
- 1 tablespoon butter

Directions:
1. Stir almond flavoring into yogurt and set aside while preparing pears.
2. Halve each pear and spoon out the core.
3. Place pear halves in air fryer oven.

4. Stir together the cookie crumbs and almonds. Place a quarter of this mixture into the hollow of each pear half.
5. Cut butter into 4 pieces and place one piece on top of crumb mixture in each pear.
6. Preheat the toaster oven to 400°F and air-fry for 15 minutes or until pears have cooked through but are still slightly firm.
7. Serve pears warm with a dollop of yogurt topping.

Goat Cheese–stuffed Nectarines

Servings: 4
Cooking Time: 10 Minutes
Ingredients:
- 4 ripe nectarines, halved and pitted
- 1 tablespoon olive oil
- 1 cup soft goat cheese, room temperature
- 1 tablespoon maple syrup
- ¼ teaspoon vanilla extract
- ¼ teaspoon ground cinnamon
- 2 tablespoons pecans, chopped

Directions:
1. Preheat the toaster oven to 350°F on AIR FRY for 5 minutes.
2. Place the air-fryer basket in the baking tray and place the nectarines in the basket, hollow-side up. Brush the tops and hollow of the fruit with the olive oil.
3. In position 2, air fry for 5 minutes to soften and lightly brown the fruit.
4. While the fruit is air frying, in a small bowl, stir the goat cheese, maple syrup, vanilla, and cinnamon until well blended.
5. Take the fruit out and evenly divide the cheese filling between the halves. Air fry for 5 minutes until the filling is heated through and a little melted.
6. Serve topped with pecans.

Individual Peach Crisps

Servings: 2
Cooking Time: 60 Minutes
Ingredients:
- 2 tablespoons granulated sugar, divided
- 1 teaspoon lemon juice
- ¼ teaspoon cornstarch
- ⅛ teaspoon table salt, divided
- 1 pound frozen sliced peaches, thawed
- ⅓ cup whole almonds or pecans, chopped fine
- ¼ cup (1¼ ounces) all-purpose flour
- 2 tablespoons packed light brown sugar
- ⅛ teaspoon ground cinnamon
- Pinch ground nutmeg
- 3 tablespoons unsalted butter, melted and cooled

Directions:
1. Adjust toaster oven rack to lowest position and preheat the toaster oven to 425 degrees. Combine 1 tablespoon granulated sugar, lemon juice, cornstarch, and pinch salt in medium bowl. Gently toss peaches with sugar mixture and divide evenly between two 12-ounce ramekins.
2. Combine almonds, flour, brown sugar, cinnamon, nutmeg, remaining pinch salt, and remaining 1 tablespoon granulated sugar in now-empty bowl. Drizzle with melted butter and toss with fork until evenly moistened and mixture forms large chunks with some pea-size pieces throughout. Sprinkle topping evenly over peaches, breaking up any large chunks.
3. Place ramekins on aluminum foil–lined small rimmed baking sheet and bake until filling is bubbling around edges and topping is deep golden brown, 25 to 30 minutes, rotating sheet halfway through baking. Let crisps cool on wire rack for 15 minutes before serving.

Coconut Rice Cake

Servings: 8
Cooking Time: 30 Minutes
Ingredients:
- 1 cup all-natural coconut water
- 1 cup unsweetened coconut milk
- 1 teaspoon almond extract
- ¼ teaspoon salt
- 4 tablespoons honey
- cooking spray
- ¾ cup raw jasmine rice
- 2 cups sliced or cubed fruit

Directions:
1. In a medium bowl, mix together the coconut water, coconut milk, almond extract, salt, and honey.
2. Spray air fryer oven baking pan with cooking spray and add the rice.
3. Pour liquid mixture over rice.
4. Preheat the toaster oven to 360°F and air-fry for 15 minutes. Stir and air-fry for 15 minutes longer or until rice grains are tender.
5. Allow cake to cool slightly. Run a dull knife around edge of cake, inside the pan. Turn the cake out onto a platter and garnish with fruit.

Chewy Coconut Cake

Servings: 6
Cooking Time: 22 Minutes
Ingredients:
- ¾ cup plus 2½ tablespoons All-purpose flour
- ¾ teaspoon Baking powder
- ⅛ teaspoon Table salt
- 7½ tablespoons (1 stick minus ½ tablespoon) Butter, at room temperature
- ⅓ cup plus 1 tablespoon Granulated white sugar
- 5 tablespoons Packed light brown sugar
- 5 tablespoons Pasteurized egg substitute, such as Egg Beaters
- 2 teaspoons Vanilla extract
- ½ cup Unsweetened shredded coconut
- Baking spray

Directions:
1. Preheat the toaster oven to 325°F.
2. Mix the flour, baking powder, and salt in a small bowl until well combined.
3. Using an electric hand mixer at medium speed, beat the butter, granulated white sugar, and brown sugar in a medium bowl until creamy and smooth, about 3 minutes, occasionally scraping down the inside of the bowl. Beat in the egg substitute or egg and vanilla until smooth.
4. Scrape down and remove the beaters. Fold in the flour mixture with a rubber spatula just until all the flour is moistened. Fold in the coconut until the mixture is a uniform color.
5. Use the baking spray to generously coat the inside of a 6-inch round cake pan for a small batch, a 7-inch round cake pan for a medium batch, or an 8-inch round cake pan for a large batch. Scrape and spread the batter into the pan, smoothing the batter out to an even layer.
6. Set the pan in the toaster oven and air-fry for 18 minutes for a 6-inch layer, 20 minutes for a 7-inch layer, or 22 minutes for an 8-inch layer, or until the cake is well browned and set even if there's a little soft give right at the center. Start checking it at the 16-minute mark to know where you are.
7. Use hot pads or silicone baking mitts to transfer the cake pan to a wire rack. Cool for at least 1 hour or up to 4 hours. Use a nonstick-safe knife to slice the cake into wedges right in the pan, lifting them out one by one.

Midnight Nutella® Banana Sandwich

Servings: 2
Cooking Time: 8 Minutes
Ingredients:
- butter, softened
- 4 slices white bread
- ¼ cup chocolate hazelnut spread (Nutella®)
- 1 banana

Directions:
1. Preheat the toaster oven to 370°F.
2. Spread the softened butter on one side of all the slices of bread and place the slices buttered side down on the counter. Spread the chocolate hazelnut spread on the other side of the bread slices. Cut the banana in half and then slice each half into three slices lengthwise. Place the banana slices on two slices of bread and top with the remaining slices of bread (buttered side up) to make two sandwiches. Cut the sandwiches in half (triangles or rectangles) – this will help them all fit in the air fryer oven at once. Transfer the sandwiches to the air fryer oven.
3. Air-fry at 370°F for 5 minutes. Flip the sandwiches over and air-fry for another 2 to 3 minutes, or until the top bread slices are nicely browned. Pour yourself a glass of milk or a midnight nightcap while the sandwiches cool slightly and enjoy!

Blueberry Clafoutis

Servings: 6
Cooking Time: 35 Minutes
Ingredients:
- 2 tablespoons salted butter, melted, plus extra for greasing the baking dish
- ½ cup all-purpose flour, plus extra for dusting the baking dish
- 2 cups fresh blueberries
- 1 cup whole milk
- 3 large eggs
- ½ cup granulated sugar
- ¼ cup light brown sugar
- 2 teaspoons vanilla extract

Directions:
1. Place the rack in position 1 and preheat the toaster oven to 350°F on BAKE for 5 minutes.
2. Lightly grease and flour a 9-inch-square baking dish.
3. Spread the blueberries in the bottom of the baking dish.
4. In a large bowl, whisk the milk, eggs, sugar, brown sugar, butter, and vanilla until smooth.
5. Add the flour and whisk to combine.
6. Pour the batter into the baking dish and bake for 35 minutes or until light brown and a toothpick inserted into the

center comes out clean. If the top starts to get too brown, cover the dish lightly with foil.
7. Cool for 10 minutes and serve.

Keto Cheesecake Cups

Servings: 6
Cooking Time: 10 Minutes
Ingredients:
- 8 ounces cream cheese
- ¼ cup plain whole-milk Greek yogurt
- 1 large egg
- 1 teaspoon pure vanilla extract
- 3 tablespoons monk fruit sweetener
- ¼ teaspoon salt
- ½ cup walnuts, roughly chopped

Directions:
1. Preheat the toaster oven to 315°F.
2. In a large bowl, use a hand mixer to beat the cream cheese together with the yogurt, egg, vanilla, sweetener, and salt. When combined, fold in the chopped walnuts.
3. Set 6 silicone muffin liners inside an air-fryer-safe pan.
4. Evenly fill the cupcake liners with cheesecake batter.
5. Carefully place the pan into the air fryer oven and air-fry for about 10 minutes, or until the tops are lightly browned and firm.
6. Carefully remove the pan when done and place in the refrigerator for 3 hours to firm up before serving.

Glazed Apple Crostata

Servings: 6
Cooking Time: 35 Minutes
Ingredients:
- PASTRY
- 1 ¼ cups all-purpose flour
- 3 tablespoons granulated sugar
- ¼ teaspoon table salt
- ½ cup unsalted butter, cut into 1-inch pieces
- 2 ½ to 3 ½ tablespoons ice water
- FILLING
- ¼ cup granulated sugar
- 3 tablespoons all-purpose flour
- ½ teaspoon ground cinnamon
- ¼ teaspoon ground nutmeg
- Dash table salt
- 3 large Granny Smith apples, peeled, cored, and thinly sliced
- 1 tablespoon unsalted butter, cut into small pieces
- 1 large egg
- Coarse white sugar
- GLAZE
- ¼ cup apricot preserves or apple jelly

Directions:
1. Place the flour, sugar, and salt in the work bowl of a food processor. Pulse to combine. Add the butter and pulse until it forms coarse crumbs. With the motor running, drizzle in enough cold water that the mixture comes together and forms a dough. Shape the dough into a disk, wrap in plastic wrap, and refrigerate for at least 1 hour or until chilled.
2. Make the filling: Stir the sugar, flour, cinnamon, nutmeg, and salt in a large bowl. Add the apples and stir to coat; set aside.
3. Preheat the toaster oven to 400°F. Line a 12-inch pizza pan or 12 x 12-inch baking pan with parchment paper.
4. Roll the pastry into a 12-inch circle on a lightly floured board. Gently fold the dough into quarters and transfer to the prepared pan. Unfold the dough. Pile the filling in the center of the pastry, leaving a 1- to 2-inch border around the edges. Dot the apples with the butter. Fold the edges of the crust up around the outer edge of the apples. Whisk the egg in a small bowl, then brush the edges of the crust with the egg. Sprinkle the crust with coarse sugar.
5. Bake for 30 to 35 minutes or until golden brown and the apples are tender.
6. Set on a wire rack. For the glaze, microwave the preserves in a small, microwave-safe glass bowl on High (100 percent) power for 30 seconds or until melted. Pour the preserves through a fine mesh strainer. Brush the warm preserves over the apples (but not over the crust). Serve warm.

Peanut Butter Cup Doughnut Holes

Servings: 24
Cooking Time: 4 Minutes
Ingredients:
- 1 ½ cups bread flour
- 1 teaspoon active dry yeast
- 1 tablespoon sugar
- ¼ teaspoon salt
- ½ cup warm milk
- ½ teaspoon vanilla extract
- 2 egg yolks
- 2 tablespoons melted butter
- 24 miniature peanut butter cups, plus a few more for garnish
- vegetable oil, in a spray bottle
- Doughnut Topping
- 1 cup chocolate chips

- 2 tablespoons milk

Directions:
1. Combine the flour, yeast, sugar and salt in a bowl. Add the milk, vanilla, egg yolks and butter. Mix well until the dough starts to come together. Transfer the dough to a floured surface and knead by hand for 2 minutes. Shape the dough into a ball and transfer it to a large oiled bowl. Cover the bowl with a towel and let the dough rise in a warm place for 1 to 1½ hours, until the dough has doubled in size.
2. When the dough has risen, punch it down and roll it into a 24-inch long log. Cut the dough into 24 pieces. Push a peanut butter cup into the center of each piece of dough, pinch the dough shut and roll it into a ball. Place the dough balls on a cookie sheet and let them rise in a warm place for 30 minutes.
3. Preheat the toaster oven to 400°F.
4. Spray or brush the dough balls lightly with vegetable oil. Air-fry eight at a time, at 400°F for 4 minutes, turning them over halfway through the cooking process.
5. While the doughnuts are air frying, prepare the topping. Place the chocolate chips and milk in a microwave safe bowl. Microwave on high for 1 minute. Stir and microwave for an additional 30 seconds if necessary to get all the chips to melt. Stir until the chips are melted and smooth.
6. Dip the top half of the doughnut holes into the melted chocolate. Place them on a rack to set up for just a few minutes and watch them disappear.

Chocolate Caramel Pecan Cupcakes

Servings: 6
Cooking Time: 20 Minutes

Ingredients:
- 6 tablespoons all-purpose flour
- 6 tablespoons unsweetened cocoa powder
- ¼ teaspoon baking soda
- ¼ teaspoon baking powder
- ⅛ teaspoon table salt
- 6 tablespoons unsalted butter, softened
- ½ cup granulated sugar
- 1 large egg
- ½ teaspoon pure vanilla extract
- ½ cup sour cream
- BUTTERCREAM FROSTING
- ¼ cup unsalted butter, softened
- 1 ¾ cups confectioners' sugar
- 2 to 3 tablespoons half-and-half or milk
- 1 teaspoon pure vanilla extract
- Caramel ice cream topping
- ¼ cup caramelized chopped pecans

Directions:
1. Preheat the toaster oven to 350°F. Line a 6-cup muffin pan with cupcake papers.
2. Whisk the flour, cocoa, baking soda, baking powder, and salt in a small bowl; set aside.
3. Beat the butter and granulated sugar in a large bowl with a handheld mixer at medium-high speed for 2 minutes, or until the mixture is light and creamy. Beat in the egg well. Beat in the vanilla.
4. On low speed, beat in the flour mixture in thirds, alternating with the sour cream, beginning and ending with the flour mixture. The batter will be thick.
5. Spoon the batter evenly into the prepared cupcake cups, filling each about three-quarters full. Bake for 18 to 20 minutes, or until a wooden pick inserted into the center comes out clean. Place on a wire rack and let cool completely.
6. Meanwhile, make the frosting: Beat the butter in a large bowl using a handheld mixer on medium-high speed until creamy. Gradually beat in the confectioners' sugar. Beat in 2 tablespoons of half-and-half and the vanilla. Beat in the remaining tablespoon of half-and-half, as needed, until the frosting is of desired consistency.
7. Frost each cooled cupcake. Drizzle the caramel topping in thin, decorative stripes over the frosting. Top with the caramelized pecans.

Fried Snickers Bars

Servings: 8
Cooking Time: 4 Minutes

Ingredients:
- ⅓ cup All-purpose flour
- 1 Large egg white(s), beaten until foamy
- 1½ cups (6 ounces) Vanilla wafer cookie crumbs
- 8 Fun-size (0.6-ounce/17-gram) Snickers bars, frozen
- Vegetable oil spray

Directions:
1. Preheat the toaster oven to 400°F.
2. Set up and fill three shallow soup plates or small pie plates on your counter: one for the flour, one for the beaten egg white(s), and one for the cookie crumbs.
3. Unwrap the frozen candy bars. Dip one in the flour, turning it to coat on all sides. Gently stir any excess, then set it in the beaten egg white(s). Turn it to coat all sides, even the ends, then let any excess egg white slip back into the rest. Set the candy bar in the cookie crumbs. Turn to coat on all sides, even the ends. Dip the candy bar back in the egg white(s) a second time, then into the cookie crumbs a second time, making sure you have an even coating all around. Coat

the covered candy bar all over with vegetable oil spray. Set aside so you can dip and coat the remaining candy bars.
4. Set the coated candy bars in the pan with as much air space between them as possible. Air-fry undisturbed for 4 minutes, or until golden brown.
5. Remove the pan from the machine and let the candy bars cool in the pan for 10 minutes. Use a nonstick-safe spatula to transfer them to a wire rack and cool for 5 minutes more before chowing down.

Baked Apple

Servings: 4
Cooking Time: 20 Minutes
Ingredients:
- 3 small Honey Crisp or other baking apples
- 3 tablespoons maple syrup
- 3 tablespoons chopped pecans
- 1 tablespoon firm butter, cut into 6 pieces

Directions:
1. Put ½ cup water in the drawer of the air fryer oven.
2. Wash apples well and dry them.
3. Split apples in half. Remove core and a little of the flesh to make a cavity for the pecans.
4. Place apple halves in air fryer oven, cut side up.
5. Spoon 1½ teaspoons pecans into each cavity.
6. Spoon ½ tablespoon maple syrup over pecans in each apple.
7. Top each apple with ½ teaspoon butter.
8. Preheat the toaster oven to 360°F and air-fry for 20 minutes, until apples are tender.

Coconut Drop Cookies

Servings: 4
Cooking Time: 12 Minutes
Ingredients:
- 1 14-ounce package shredded and sweetened coconut
- 2 eggs
- 1 tablespoon margarine
- ¾ cup unbleached flour
- 1 teaspoon baking powder
- Salt to taste

Directions:
1. Preheat the toaster oven to 250° F.
2. Combine all the ingredients in a medium bowl, mixing well. Drop in small portions with a teaspoon onto an oiled or nonstick 6½ × 10-inch baking sheet or an oiled or nonstick 8½ × 8½ × 2-inch square baking (cake) pan.
3. BAKE for 10 minutes, or until golden brown.

Make-ahead Chocolate Chip Cookies

Servings: 12
Cooking Time: 45 Minutes
Ingredients:
- 2⅛ cups (10⅔ ounces) all-purpose flour
- ½ teaspoon baking soda
- ½ teaspoon table salt
- 1 cup packed (7 ounces) light brown sugar
- ½ cup (3½ ounces)granulated sugar
- 12 tablespoons unsalted butter, melted and cooled
- 1 large egg plus 1 large yolk
- 2 teaspoons vanilla extract
- 1 cup (6 ounces) semisweet chocolate chips

Directions:
1. Adjust toaster oven rack to middle position and preheat the toaster oven to 350 degrees. Line large and small rimmed baking sheets with parchment paper. Whisk flour, baking soda, and salt together in bowl.
2. Whisk brown sugar and granulated sugar together in medium bowl. Whisk in melted butter until combined. Whisk in egg and yolk and vanilla until smooth. Gently stir in flour mixture with rubber spatula until soft dough forms. Fold in chocolate chips.
3. Working with 2 tablespoons dough at a time, roll into balls. Space desired number of dough balls at least 1½ inches apart on prepared small sheet; space remaining dough balls evenly on prepared large sheet. Using bottom of greased dry measuring cup, press each ball until 2 inches in diameter.
4. Bake small sheet of cookies until edges are just beginning to brown and centers are soft and puffy, 10 to 15 minutes. Let cookies cool slightly on sheet. Serve warm or at room temperature.
5. Freeze remaining large sheet of cookies until firm, about 1 hour. Transfer cookies to 1-gallon zipper-lock bag and freeze for up to 1 month. Bake frozen cookies as directed; do not thaw.

Mississippi Mud Brownies

Servings: 16
Cooking Time: 34 Minutes
Ingredients:
- Nonstick cooking spray
- 3 tablespoons unsweetened cocoa powder
- ¼ cup canola or vegetable oil
- ¼ cup unsalted butter, softened
- 1 cup granulated sugar
- 2 large eggs

- 1 teaspoon pure vanilla extract
- ¾ cup all-purpose flour
- ½ teaspoon table salt
- ½ cup pecan pieces, toasted
- 2 cups mini marshmallows
- FROSTING
- ¼ cup unsalted butter, melted
- 3 tablespoons unsweetened cocoa powder
- ½ teaspoon pure vanilla extract
- 2 cups confectioners' sugar
- 2 to 3 tablespoons whole milk

Directions:
1. Preheat the toaster oven to 350°F. Spray an 8-inch square baking pan with nonstick cooking spray.
2. Beat the cocoa and oil in a large bowl with a handheld mixer at medium speed. Add the butter and mix until smooth. Beat in the granulated sugar. Add the eggs, one at a time, mixing after each addition. Add the vanilla and mix. On low speed, blend in the flour and salt. Stir in the pecans.
3. Pour the batter into the prepared pan. Bake for 28 to 32 minutes, or until a wooden pick inserted into the center comes out clean.
4. Remove the brownies from the oven and sprinkle the marshmallows over the top. Return to the oven and bake for about 2 minutes or until the marshmallows are puffed. Place on a wire rack and let cool completely.
5. Meanwhile, make the frosting: Combine the butter, cocoa, vanilla, confectioners' sugar, and 2 tablespoons milk in a large bowl. Beat until smooth. If needed for the desired consistency, add additional milk. Frost the cooled brownies.

Raspberry Hand Pies

Servings: 6
Cooking Time: 20 Minutes
Ingredients:
- 2 cups fresh raspberries
- ¼ cup granulated sugar, plus extra for topping
- 1 tablespoon cornstarch
- 1 tablespoon freshly squeezed lemon juice
- 2 store-bought unbaked pie crusts
- 1 large egg
- 1 tablespoon water
- Oil spray (hand-pumped)

Directions:
1. Preheat the toaster oven to 350°F on AIR FRY for 5 minutes.
2. Place the air-fryer basket in the baking tray.
3. In a medium bowl, stir the raspberries, sugar, cornstarch, and lemon juice until well mixed.
4. Lay the pie crusts on a clean work surface and cut out 6 (6-inch) circles.
5. Evenly divide the raspberry mixture among the circles, placing it in the center.
6. In a small bowl, beat together the egg and water with a fork. Use the egg wash to lightly moisten the edges of the circles, then fold them over to create a half-moon shape. Use a fork to crimp around the rounded part of the pies to seal.
7. Lightly spray the pies with the oil and sprinkle with sugar. Cut 2 to 3 small slits in each pie and place three pies in the basket.
8. In position 2, air fry for 10 minutes until golden brown. Repeat with the remaining pies.
9. Cool the pies and serve.

Easy Churros

Servings: 12
Cooking Time: 10 Minutes
Ingredients:
- ½ cup Water
- 4 tablespoons (¼ cup/½ stick) Butter
- ¼ teaspoon Table salt
- ½ cup All-purpose flour
- 2 Large egg(s)
- ¼ cup Granulated white sugar
- 2 teaspoons Ground cinnamon

Directions:
1. Bring the water, butter, and salt to a boil in a small saucepan set over high heat, stirring occasionally.
2. When the butter has fully melted, reduce the heat to medium and stir in the flour to form a dough. Continue cooking, stirring constantly, to dry out the dough until it coats the bottom and sides of the pan with a film, even a crust. Remove the pan from the heat, scrape the dough into a bowl, and cool for 15 minutes.
3. Using an electric hand mixer at medium speed, beat in the egg, or eggs one at a time, until the dough is smooth and firm enough to hold its shape.
4. Mix the sugar and cinnamon in a small bowl. Scoop up 1 tablespoon of the dough and roll it in the sugar mixture to form a small, coated tube about ½ inch in diameter and 2 inches long. Set it aside and make 5 more tubes for the small batch or 11 more for the large one.
5. Set the tubes on a plate and freeze for 20 minutes. Meanwhile, preheat the toaster oven to 375°F.
6. Set 3 frozen tubes in the air fryer oven for a small batch or 6 for a large one with as much air space between them as possible. Air-fry undisturbed for 10 minutes, or until puffed, brown, and set.

7. Use kitchen tongs to transfer the churros to a wire rack to cool for at least 5 minutes. Meanwhile, air-fry and cool the second batch of churros in the same way.

Heritage Chocolate Chip Cookies

Servings: 16-18
Cooking Time: 12 Minutes
Ingredients:
- 1 1/2 cups all-purpose flour
- 1 teaspoon baking powder
- 1/2 teaspoon salt
- 1 large egg, unbeaten
- 1/2 cup shortening
- 1/2 cup packed dark brown sugar
- 1/4 cup granulated sugar
- 2 teaspoons vanilla extract
- 1 tablespoon milk
- 1 cup chocolate chips

Directions:
1. Preheat the toaster oven to 375ºF.
2. Place all ingredients except chocolate chips in large mixer bowl. With electric mixer on low speed, beat until ingredients are mixed. Gradually increase speed to medium and beat 3 minutes, stopping to scrape bowl as needed.
3. Add chocolate chips and beat on low until blended.
4. Line cookie sheets with parchment paper. Using a small scoop, place 12 scoops of cookie dough about 1-inch apart on parchment.
5. Bake 10 to 12 minutes or until cookies are browned. Slide parchment with baked cookies onto rack to cool. Repeat with remaining dough.

Carrot Cake

Servings: 6
Cooking Time: 30 Minutes
Ingredients:
- FOR THE CAKE
- ½ cup canola oil, plus extra for greasing the baking dish
- 1 cup all-purpose flour, plus extra for dusting the baking dish
- 1 cup granulated sugar
- 1 teaspoon baking powder
- ½ teaspoon sea salt
- 2 teaspoons pumpkin pie spice
- 2 large eggs
- 1 cup carrot, finely shredded
- ½ cup dried apricot, chopped
- FOR THE ICING
- 4 ounces cream cheese, room temperature
- ¼ cup salted butter, room temperature
- 1 teaspoon vanilla extract
- 2 cups confectioners' sugar

Directions:
1. To make the cake
2. Place the rack in position 1 and preheat the oven to 325°F on BAKE for 5 minutes.
3. Lightly grease an 8-inch-square baking dish with oil and dust with flour.
4. Place the rack in position 1.
5. In a large bowl, stir the flour, sugar, baking powder, salt, and pumpkin pie spice.
6. Make a well in the center and add the oil and eggs, stirring until just combined. Add the carrot and apricot and stir until well mixed.
7. Transfer the batter to the baking dish and bake for about 30 minutes until golden brown and a toothpick inserted in the center comes out clean.
8. Remove the cake from the oven and cool completely in the baking dish.
9. To make the icing
10. When the cake is cool, whisk the cream cheese, butter, and vanilla until very smooth and blended. Add the confectioners' sugar and whisk until creamy and thick, about 2 minutes.
11. Ice the cake and serve.

Baked Custard

Servings: 2
Cooking Time: 45 Minutes
Ingredients:
- 2 eggs
- ¼ cup sugar
- 1 cup low-fat evaporated milk
- ½ teaspoon vanilla extract
- Pinch of grated nutmeg
- Fat-free half-and-half

Directions:
1. Preheat the toaster oven to 350° F.
2. Beat together the eggs, sugar, milk, vanilla, and nutmeg in a small bowl with an electric mixer at medium speed. Pour equal portions of the custard mixture into 2 oiled 1-cup-size ovenproof dishes.
3. BAKE for 45 minutes, or until a toothpick inserted in the center comes out clean. Serve drizzled with warm fat-free half-and-half.

Donut Holes

Servings: 13
Cooking Time: 12 Minutes
Ingredients:
- 6 tablespoons Granulated white sugar
- 1½ tablespoons Butter, melted and cooled
- 2 tablespoons (or 1 small egg, well beaten) Pasteurized egg substitute, such as Egg Beaters
- 6 tablespoons Regular or low-fat sour cream (not fat-free)
- ¾ teaspoon Vanilla extract
- 1⅔ cups All-purpose flour
- ¾ teaspoon Baking powder
- ¼ teaspoon Table salt
- Vegetable oil spray

Directions:
1. Preheat the toaster oven to 350°F.
2. Whisk the sugar and melted butter in a medium bowl until well combined. Whisk in the egg substitute or egg, then the sour cream and vanilla until smooth. Remove the whisk and stir in the flour, baking powder, and salt with a wooden spoon just until a soft dough forms.
3. Use 2 tablespoons of this dough to create a ball between your clean palms. Set it aside and continue making balls: 8 more for the small batch, 12 more for the medium batch, or 17 more for the large one.
4. Coat the balls in the vegetable oil spray, then set them in the air fryer oven with as much air space between them as possible. Even a fraction of an inch will be enough, but they should not touch. Air-fry undisturbed for 12 minutes, or until browned and cooked through. A toothpick inserted into the center of a ball should come out clean.
5. Pour the contents of the air fryer oven onto a wire rack. Cool for at least 5 minutes before serving.

Chocolate And Vanilla Swirled Pudding

Servings: 4
Cooking Time: 25 Minutes
Ingredients:
- 1 square semisweet chocolate
- 1½ cups fat-free half-and-half
- 1 tablespoon sugar
- 2 egg yolks
- ½ teaspoon vanilla extract
- Fat-free whipped topping

Directions:
1. Melt the chocolate in an oiled or nonstick 8½ × 8½ × 2-inch square baking (cake) pan under the broiler for approximately 5 minutes, removing the pan from the oven before the chocolate is completely melted. Stir until melted and smooth. Set aside.
2. Whisk together the half-and-half, sugar, egg yolks, and vanilla in a medium bowl. Divide into two portions and add the melted chocolate to one, stirring to blend well.
3. Fill four 1-cup-size ovenproof dishes with equal portions of the vanilla mixture, then top with equal portions of the chocolate mixture. With a skewer or toothpick, stir the pudding in little circles to create a swirling pattern of light and dark.
4. BAKE at 350° F. for 25 minutes, or until the pudding is firm. Chill before serving. Top with fat-free whipped topping.

Peanut Butter S'mores

Servings: 10
Cooking Time: 1 Minutes
Ingredients:
- 10 Graham crackers (full, double-square cookies as they come out of the package)
- 5 tablespoons Natural-style creamy or crunchy peanut butter
- ½ cup Milk chocolate chips
- 10 Standard-size marshmallows (not minis and not jumbo campfire ones)

Directions:
1. Preheat the toaster oven to 350°F.
2. Break the graham crackers in half widthwise at the marked place, so the rectangle is now in two squares. Set half of the squares flat side up on your work surface. Spread each with about 1½ teaspoons peanut butter, then set 10 to 12 chocolate chips point side up into the peanut butter on each, pressing gently so the chips stick.
3. Flatten a marshmallow between your clean, dry hands and set it atop the chips. Do the same with the remaining marshmallows on the other coated graham crackers. Do not set the other half of the graham crackers on top of these coated graham crackers.
4. When the machine is at temperature, set the treats graham cracker side down in a single layer in the air fryer oven. They may touch, but even a fraction of an inch between them will provide better air flow. Air-fry undisturbed for 45 seconds.
5. Use a nonstick-safe spatula to transfer the topped graham crackers to a wire rack. Set the other graham cracker squares flat side down over the marshmallows. Cool for a couple of minutes before serving.

Orange Strawberry Flan

Servings: 4
Cooking Time: 45 Minutes
Ingredients:
- ¼ cup sugar
- ½ cup concentrated orange juice
- 1 12-ounce can low-fat evaporated milk
- 3 egg yolks
- 1 cup frozen strawberries, thawed and sliced, or 1 cup fresh strawberries, washed, stemmed, and sliced
- 4 fresh mint sprigs

Directions:
1. Preheat the toaster oven to 375° F.
2. Place the sugar in a baking pan and broil for 4 minutes, or until the sugar melts. Remove from the oven, stir briefly, and pour equal portions of the caramelized sugar into four 1-cup-size ovenproof dishes. Set aside.
3. Blend the orange juice, evaporated milk, and egg yolks in a food processor or blender until smooth. Transfer the mixture to a medium bowl and fold in the sliced strawberries. Pour the mixture in equal portions into the four dishes.
4. BAKE for 45 minutes, or until a knife inserted in the center comes out clean. Chill for several hours. The flan may be loosened by running a knife around the edge and inverted on individual plates or served in the dishes. Garnish with fresh mint sprigs.

Strawberry Blueberry Cobbler

Servings: 6
Cooking Time: 30 Minutes
Ingredients:
- Berry filling:
- 1 10-ounce package frozen blueberries, thawed, or 1½ cups fresh blueberries
- 1 10-ounce package frozen strawberries, thawed, or 1½ cups fresh strawberries
- ½ cup strawberry preserves
- ¼ cup unbleached flour
- 1 teaspoon lemon juice
- Topping:
- ¼ cup unbleached flour
- 2 tablespoons margarine
- 1 tablespoon fat-free half-and-half
- ½ teaspoon baking powder
- 1 tablespoon sugar

Directions:
1. Preheat the toaster oven to 400° F.
2. Combine the berry filling ingredients in a large bowl, mixing well. Transfer to an oiled or nonstick 8½ × 8½ × 2-inch square baking (cake) pan. Set aside.
3. Combine the topping ingredients in a small bowl, blending with a fork until the mixture is crumbly. Sprinkle the mixture evenly over the berries.
4. BAKE for 30 minutes, or until the top is lightly browned.

Vegan Swedish Cinnamon Rolls (kanelbullar)

Servings: 8
Cooking Time: 18 Minutes
Ingredients:
- Dough
- 1 cup unsweetened almond milk, slightly warm (100°-110°F)
- ¼ cup vegan butter, melted
- 2 tablespoon organic sugar
- 1 teaspoon instant dry yeast
- ½ teaspoon kosher salt
- 2¾ cups all-purpose flour, divided
- Filling
- 6 tablespoons vegan butter, room temperature
- 6 tablespoons organic dark brown sugar
- 1 tablespoon ground cinnamon
- Egg Wash
- 2 tablespoons unsweetened almond milk
- 1 teaspoon agave nectar
- Glaze
- 2 tablespoons unsweetened almond milk
- ½ cup powdered sugar
- ¼ teaspoon vanilla extract
- Swedish pearl sugar, for sprinkling

Directions:
1. Whisk together the almond milk, melted butter, and sugar from the dough ingredients in a large mixing bowl.
2. Sprinkle the yeast into the milk mixture and allow it to bloom for 5 minutes.
3. Add kosher salt and 2¼-cups of flour into the milk and yeast mixture, then mix until well combined.
4. Cover the bowl with a towel or plastic wrap and set in a warm place to rise for 1 hour, or until it doubles in size.
5. Uncover and knead ½-cup all purpose flour into the risen dough. Continue kneading until it just loses its stickiness. You may need to add additional flour.
6. Roll the dough out into a large rectangle, about ½-inch thick. Fix the corners to make sure they are sharp and even.

7. Spread the softened vegan butter from the filling ingredients over the dough and sprinkle evenly with brown sugar and cinnamon.
8. Roll up the dough, forming a log, and pinch the seam closed. Place seam-side down. Trim off any unevenness on either end.
9. Cut the log in half, then divide each half into 8 evenly sized pieces, about 1½-inches thick each.
10. Line the food tray with parchment paper, then place the cinnamon rolls on the tray.
11. Cover with plastic wrap and place in a warm place to rise for 30 minutes.
12. Preheat the toaster Oven to 375°F.
13. Whisk together egg wash ingredients and lightly brush the wash on the tops of the cinnamon rolls.
14. Insert the food tray with the cinnamon rolls at mid position in the preheated oven.
15. Select the Bake function, adjust time to 18 minutes, and press Start/Pause.
16. Remove when done.
17. Whisk together almond milk, powdered sugar, and vanilla extract from the glaze ingredients to make the icing, brush it all over the cinnamon rolls, then sprinkle the rolls with Swedish pearl sugar.
18. Cool before serving, or eat warm.

Blueberry Cookies

Servings: 4
Cooking Time: 12 Minutes
Ingredients:
- 1 egg
- 1 tablespoon margarine, at room temperature
- ⅓ cup sugar
- 1¼ cups unbleached flour
- Salt to taste
- 1 teaspoon baking powder
- 1 10-ounce package frozen blueberries, well drained, or
- 1½ cups fresh blueberries, rinsed and drained

Directions:
1. Preheat the toaster oven to 400° F.
2. Beat together the egg, margarine, and sugar in a medium bowl with an electric mixer until smooth. Add the flour, salt, and baking powder, mixing thoroughly. Gently stir in the blueberries just to blend. Do not overmix.
3. Drop by teaspoonfuls on an oiled or nonstick 6½ × 10-inch baking sheet or an oiled or nonstick 8½ × 8½ × 2-inch square baking (cake) pan.
4. BAKE for 12 minutes, or until the cookies are golden brown.

Black And Blue Clafoutis

Servings: 2
Cooking Time: 15 Minutes
Ingredients:
- 6-inch pie pan
- 3 large eggs
- ½ cup sugar
- 1 teaspoon vanilla extract
- 2 tablespoons butter, melted 1 cup milk
- ½ cup all-purpose flour
- 1 cup blackberries
- 1 cup blueberries
- 2 tablespoons confectioners' sugar

Directions:
1. Preheat the toaster oven to 320°F.
2. Combine the eggs and sugar in a bowl and whisk vigorously until smooth, lighter in color and well combined. Add the vanilla extract, butter and milk and whisk together well. Add the flour and whisk just until no lumps or streaks of white remain.
3. Scatter half the blueberries and blackberries in a greased (6-inch) pie pan or cake pan. Pour half of the batter (about 1¼ cups) on top of the berries and transfer the tart pan to the air fryer oven. You can use an aluminum foil sling to help with this by taking a long piece of aluminum foil, folding it in half lengthwise twice until it is roughly 26-inches by 3-inches. Place this under the pie dish and hold the ends of the foil to move the pie dish in and out of the air fryer oven. Tuck the ends of the foil beside the pie dish while it cooks in the air fryer oven.
4. Air-fry at 320°F for 15 minutes or until the clafoutis has puffed up and is still a little jiggly in the center. Remove the clafoutis from the air fryer oven, invert it onto a plate and let it cool while you bake the second batch. Serve the clafoutis warm, dusted with confectioners' sugar on top.

Heavenly Chocolate Cupcakes

Servings: 6
Cooking Time: 30 Minutes
Ingredients:
- 2 squares semisweet chocolate
- 2 tablespoons margarine
- 1 cup unbleached flour
- 2 teaspoons baking powder
- Salt to taste
- ¾ cup brown sugar
- ½ cup skim milk
- 1 egg, beaten

- ½ cup chopped pecans
- ½ teaspoon vanilla extract

Directions:
1. Melt the chocolate and margarine in an oiled or nonstick 8½ × 8½ × 2-inch square baking (cake) pan under the broiler for 5 minutes, or until about half melted. Remove from the oven and stir until completely melted and blended.
2. Combine the flour, baking powder, salt, and sugar in a medium bowl, mixing well. Add the melted chocolate/margarine mixture, then the milk and egg. Stir to blend well, then stir in the pecans and vanilla. Fill paper baking cups or well-oiled tins in a 6-muffin pan three-quarters full with batter.
3. BAKE at 350° F. for 25 minutes, or until a toothpick inserted in the center comes out clean.

Cinnamon Sugar Rolls

Servings: 8
Cooking Time: 10 Minutes

Ingredients:
- ½ cup margarine
- Filling mixture:
- 1 tablespoon ground cinnamon
- ½ cup brown sugar
- ½ cup finely chopped walnuts
- 10 sheets phyllo pastry, thawed

Directions:
1. BROIL the margarine in an oiled or nonstick 8½ × 8½ × 2-inch square baking (cake) pan for 3 minutes, or until almost melted. Remove from the oven and stir until melted (the pan will be hot and the margarine will continue to melt). Set aside.
2. Combine the filling mixture in a small bowl, mixing well.
3. Lay a sheet of phyllo pastry on a clean flat surface. Brush with the melted margarine, sprinkle with a heaping tablespoon of the filling mixture, and spread evenly to cover the sheet of pastry. Repeat the brushing and sprinkling procedure for each sheet, layering one on top of the other until all 10 sheets are done. Use up any remaining filling mixture on the last sheet. Starting at the 9-inch (long) edge, slowly roll all of the sheets up like a jelly roll. With a sharp knife, cut the roll into 1¼-inch slices. Place the slices on an oiled or nonstick baking sheet or baking pan.
4. BAKE at 350° F. for 10 minutes, or until golden brown.

Cheese Blintzes

Servings: 6
Cooking Time: 10 Minutes

Ingredients:
- 1½ 7½-ounce package(s) farmer cheese
- 3 tablespoons Regular or low-fat cream cheese (not fat-free)
- 3 tablespoons Granulated white sugar
- ¼ teaspoon Vanilla extract
- 6 Egg roll wrappers
- 3 tablespoons Butter, melted and cooled

Directions:
1. Preheat the toaster oven to 375°F.
2. Use a flatware fork to mash the farmer cheese, cream cheese, sugar, and vanilla in a small bowl until smooth.
3. Set one egg roll wrapper on a clean, dry work surface. Place ¼ cup of the filling at the edge closest to you, leaving a ½-inch gap before the edge of the wrapper. Dip your clean finger in water and wet the edges of the wrapper. Fold the perpendicular sides over the filling, then roll the wrapper closed with the filling inside. Set it aside seam side down and continue filling the remainder of the wrappers.
4. Brush the wrappers on all sides with the melted butter. Be generous. Set them seam side down in the air fryer oven with as much space between them as possible. Air-fry undisturbed for 10 minutes, or until lightly browned.
5. Use a nonstick-safe spatula to transfer the blintzes to a wire rack. Cool for at least 5 minutes or up to 20 minutes before serving.

Orange Almond Ricotta Cookies

Servings: 24
Cooking Time: 15 Minutes

Ingredients:
- Cookie Ingredients
- ½ stick unsalted butter, room temperature
- 1 cup sugar
- 1 large egg
- 1 cup ricotta cheese, drained
- 1½ tablespoons orange juice
- 1 orange, zested
- ¼ teaspoon almond extract
- 1¼ cups all purpose flour
- ½ teaspoon baking powder
- ½ teaspoon salt
- Glaze Ingredients
- 1 cup powdered sugar
- 1½ tablespoons orange juice
- ½ orange, zested

Directions:
1. Beat together the butter and sugar for 3 minutes or until light and fluffy.

2. Add the egg, ricotta, orange juice, orange zest, and almond extract and beat until well combined. Add the flour, baking powder, and salt, then fold gently to combine. Don't overmix.
3. Preheat the toaster Oven to 350°F.
4. Line the food tray with parchment paper, then divide the dough into 1½-tablespoon pieces and place on the tray.
5. Insert the tray at mid position in the preheated oven.
6. Select the Bake function, adjust time to 15 minutes, and press Start/Pause.
7. Remove when done and allow cookies to cool completely before glazing.
8. Make the glaze by stirring together the powdered sugar, orange juice, and zest until smooth. According to your preference, add more powdered sugar to make the glaze thicker, or more orange juice to make the glaze thinner.
9. Spoon about ½-teaspoon of the glaze on each cookie and spread gently. Allow the glaze to harden before serving

Sweet Potato Donut Holes

Servings: 18
Cooking Time: 4 Minutes
Ingredients:
- 1 cup flour
- ⅓ cup sugar
- ¼ teaspoon baking soda
- 1 teaspoon baking powder
- ⅛ teaspoon salt
- ½ cup cooked mashed purple sweet potatoes
- 1 egg, beaten
- 2 tablespoons butter, melted
- 1 teaspoon pure vanilla extract
- oil for misting or cooking spray

Directions:
1. Preheat the toaster oven to 390°F.
2. In a large bowl, stir together the flour, sugar, baking soda, baking powder, and salt.
3. In a separate bowl, combine the potatoes, egg, butter, and vanilla and mix well.
4. Add potato mixture to dry ingredients and stir into a soft dough.
5. Shape dough into 1½-inch balls. Mist lightly with oil or cooking spray.
6. Place 9 donut holes in air fryer oven, leaving a little space in between. Air-fry for 4 minutes, until done in center and lightly browned outside.
7. Repeat step 6 to cook remaining donut holes.

Sour Cream Pound Cake

Servings: 6
Cooking Time: 60 Minutes
Ingredients:
- ¾ cup unsalted butter, plus extra for greasing the baking pan
- 2½ cups all-purpose flour, sifted, plus extra for dusting the baking pan
- 1½ cups granulated sugar
- 4 large eggs
- 2 teaspoons pure vanilla extract
- ½ teaspoon baking soda
- ¾ cup sour cream

Directions:
1. Place the rack in position 1 and preheat the toaster oven to 350°F on BAKE for 5 minutes.
2. Lightly grease and dust a 9-by-5-inch loaf pan.
3. In a large bowl, cream the butter and sugar with an electric hand beater until very light and fluffy, about 4 minutes.
4. Beat in the eggs one at a time, scraping down the sides of the bowl after each addition.
5. Beat in the vanilla.
6. In a medium bowl, stir the flour and baking soda.
7. Fold the flour mixture and sour cream into the butter mixture, alternating two times each, until well combined.
8. Spoon the batter into the loaf pan and bake for 1 hour, or until a toothpick inserted in the center comes out clean.
9. Let cool completely in the pan and serve

INDEX

A
Air-fried Potato Salad 98
Albóndigas 46
Almond And Sun-dried Tomato Crusted Pork Chops 52
Almond Crab Cakes 87
Almond Granola With Dried Fruit 20
Almond-crusted Fish 96
Almond-roasted Pears 111
Asparagus And Cherry Tomato Quiche 106
Asparagus Ronald 98
Asparagus With Pistachio Dukkah 34

B
Bacon Corn Muffins 33
Bagel Melt 21
Baked Apple 116
Baked Custard 118
Baked Eggs And Bacon 19
Baked Stuffed Acorn Squash 102
Baked Tomato Casserole 82
Balsamic Sweet Potatoes 99
Banana Baked Oatmeal 25
Barbecue Chicken Nachos 41
Barbecued Broiled Pork Chops 55
Barbeque Ribs 56
Beef And Spinach Braciole 56
Beef-stuffed Bell Peppers 55
Beer-baked Pork Tenderloin 45
Beer-battered Cod 91
Berry Crisp 20
Best-dressed Trout 94
Better Fish Sticks 92
Better-than-chinese-take-out Pork Ribs 53
Black And Blue Clafoutis 121
Blackened Catfish 91
Blistered Green Beans 101
Blistered Tomatoes 103
Blueberry Clafoutis 113

Blueberry Cookies 121
Blueberry Lemon Muffins 28
Bourbon Bread Pudding 111
Brazilian Cheese Bread (pão De Queijo) 40
Bread Boat Eggs 25
Breakfast Banana Bread 29
Broiled Scallops 85
Buffalo Cauliflower 37
Buffalo Egg Rolls 61
Buttered Poppy Seed Bread 24
Buttermilk Confetti Cake 110
Buttery Rolls 102

C
Calf's Liver 46
Capered Crab Cakes 91
Caramelized Onion Dip 35
Carrot Cake 118
Cauliflower 108
Cheddar Cheese Biscuits 26
Cheese Blintzes 122
Cheesecake Wontons 110
Cheesy Chicken–stuffed Shells 80
Cheesy Potato Skins 99
Cherries Jubilee 29
Cherry Chipotle Bbq Chicken Wings 36
Chewy Coconut Cake 113
Chicken Breast With Chermoula Sauce 59
Chicken Cutlets With Broccoli Rabe And Roasted Peppers 63
Chicken Fajitas 59
Chicken Fried Steak 51
Chicken Hand Pies 61
Chicken In Mango Sauce 69
Chicken Noodle Soup 76
Chicken Potpie 63
Chicken Souvlaki Gyros 69

Chicken Thighs With Roasted Rosemary Root Vegetables 78

Chicken Wellington 67

Chicken-fried Steak With Gravy 71

Chipotle-glazed Meat Loaf 50

Chocolate And Vanilla Swirled Pudding 119

Chocolate Caramel Pecan Cupcakes 115

Chocolate Chip Banana Muffins 29

Cilantro-crusted Flank Steak 54

Cinnamon Apple Chips 41

Cinnamon Pita Chips 43

Cinnamon Rolls 30

Cinnamon Sugar Rolls 122

Classic Beef Stew 81

Classic Crab Cakes 85

Classic Potato Chips 40

Classic Tuna Casserole 83

Coconut Cake 110

Coconut Chicken With Apricot-ginger Sauce 64

Coconut Drop Cookies 116

Coconut Rice Cake 112

Coconut-shrimp Po' Boys 90

Connecticut Garden Chowder 79

Crab Cakes 89

Crab Chowder 78

Crab Rangoon Dip With Wonton Chips 42

Crab-stuffed Peppers 90

Creamy Bacon + Almond Crostini 27

Creamy Crab Dip 40

Creamy Parmesan Polenta 32

Creamy Scalloped Potatoes 34

Crispy Bacon 21

Crispy Chili Kale Chips 33

Crispy Curry Chicken Tenders 67

Crispy Herbed Potatoes 103

Crispy Noodle Salad 104

Crispy Smelts 92

Crispy Smoked Pork Chops 53

Crispy Sweet-and-sour Cod Fillets 95

Crunchy And Buttery Cod With Ritz® Cracker Crust 87

Crunchy Baked Chicken Tenders 74

Crunchy Clam Strips 96

Crunchy Fried Pork Loin Chops 57

D

Dijon Salmon With Green Beans Sheet Pan Supper 83

Donut Holes 119

E

Easy Churros 117

Easy Tex-mex Chimichangas 54

Egg-loaded Potato Skins 19

Empty-the-refrigerator Roasted Vegetables 100

F

Family Favorite Pizza 77

Favorite Baked Ziti 72

Fiesta Chicken Plate 71

Fingerling Potatoes 106

Fish Sticks For Kids 88

Fish Tacos With Jalapeño-lime Sauce 88

Florentine Stuffed Tomatoes 105

Flounder Fillets 94

Foiled Rosemary Chicken Breasts 62

French Onion Soup 73

French Toast 19

Fried Cauliflowerwith Parmesan Lemon Dressing 105

Fried Corn On The Cob 99

Fried Eggplant Slices 100

Fried Okra 98

Fried Scallops 97

Fried Snickers Bars 115

Fried Wontons 38

G

Garden Fresh Bruschetta 35

Gardener's Rice 75

Garlic Breadsticks 32

Garlic Parmesan Kale Chips 40

Garlic-cheese Biscuits 22

Ginger Miso Calamari 86

Glazed Apple Crostata 114

Glazed Meatloaf 49

Gluten-free Nutty Chicken Fingers 65

Goat Cheese–stuffed Nectarines 112

Good Stuff Bread 27

Green Beans 104

Green Onion Pancakes 24
Grilled Ham & Muenster Cheese On Raisin Bread 32
Grits Casserole 103
Guiltless Bacon 69

H

Halibut Tacos 90
Ham And Cheese Palmiers 43
Ham And Swiss Melts 24
Harissa Lemon Whole Chicken 66
Hashbrown Potatoes Lyonnaise 25
Hasty Home Fries 102
Healthy Southwest Stuffed Peppers 76
Heavenly Chocolate Cupcakes 121
Herbal Summer Casserole 74
Heritage Chocolate Chip Cookies 118
Hole In One 21
Home Fries 101
Homemade Pizza Sauce 81
Honey Bourbon–glazed Pork Chops With Sweet Potatoes + Apples 77
Honey Ham And Swiss Broiler 30
Hot Italian-style Sub 19
Hot Mexican Bean Dip 41
Hot Thighs 60

I

I Forgot To Thaw—garlic Capered Chicken Thighs 60
Indian Fry Bread Tacos 47
Individual Peach Crisps 112
Inspirational Personal Pizza 75
Italian Meatballs 51
Italian Roasted Chicken Thighs 58
Italian Sausage & Peppers 52
Italian Stuffed Zucchini Boats 74

J

Jerk Turkey Meatballs 64

K

Kashaburgers 73
Keto Cheesecake Cups 114
Kielbasa Sausage With Pierogies And Caramelized Onions 57

L

Lamb Burger With Feta And Olives 49
Lamb Curry 53
Lamb Koftas Meatballs 50
Lemon Blueberry Scones 21
Lemon Torte 111
Lemon-glazed Baby Carrots 101
Lentil And Carrot Soup 80
Light And Lovely Loaf 62
Light Trout Amandine 92
Lime-ginger Pork Tenderloin 54

M

Make-ahead Chocolate Chip Cookies 116
Maple Bacon 80
Maple-crusted Salmon 85
Mediterranean Egg Sandwich 29
Middle Eastern Roasted Chicken 82
Midnight Nutella® Banana Sandwich 113
Minted Lamb Chops 52
Miso-rubbed Salmon Fillets 86
Mississippi Mud Brownies 116
Morning Glory Muffins 22
Moroccan Cauliflower 101
Moroccan Couscous 75
Mushrooms 107
Mushroom-spinach Frittata With Feta 23
Mustard-herb Lamb Chops 57

N

Not-so-english Muffins 25

O

One-step Classic Goulash 83
Onions 106
Orange Almond Ricotta Cookies 122
Orange Strawberry Flan 120
Orange-glazed Roast Chicken 59
Oven-baked Couscous 79
Oven-baked Rice 79
Oven-crisped Chicken 67

P

Panzanella Salad With Crispy Croutons 108
Parmesan Artichoke Pizza 77
Parmesan Asparagus 108

Parmesan Crusted Chicken Cordon Bleu 66

Parmesan Crusted Tilapia 75

Pea Soup 73

Peanut Butter Cup Doughnut Holes 114

Peanut Butter S'mores 119

Pecan Parmesan Cauliflower 101

Pecan Turkey Cutlets 58

Pecan-crusted Tilapia 87

Perfect Asparagus 104

Pesto Pizza 76

Pesto-crusted Chicken 63

Philly Chicken Cheesesteak Stromboli 70

Pickle Brined Fried Chicken 62

Poblano Bake 68

Pork Cutlets With Almond-lemon Crust 44

Pork Pot Stickers With Yum Yum Sauce 36

Pork Taco Gorditas 47

Portable Omelet 23

Potato Samosas 33

Pretzel-coated Pork Tenderloin 44

Q

Quick Chicken For Filling 65

Quick Pan Pizza 72

R

Ranch Potatoes 103

Raspberry Hand Pies 117

Red Curry Flank Steak 51

Roasted Brussels Sprouts Au Gratin 39

Roasted Brussels Sprouts With Bacon 105

Roasted Game Hens With Vegetable Stuffing 58

Roasted Vegetable Frittata 26

Roasted Vegetable Gazpacho 82

Rolled Chinese (napa) Cabbage With Chickpea Filling 107

Romaine Wraps With Shrimp Filling 94

Rosemary Roasted Potatoes With Lemon 100

Rotisserie-style Chicken 65

Rumaki 38

S

Sage Butter Roasted Butternut Squash With Pepitas 31

Sage, Chicken + Mushroom Pasta Casserole 72

Salad Lentils 81

Salmon Burgers 27

Salt And Pepper Baked Potatoes 106

Savory Breakfast Bread Pudding 20

Savory Salsa Cheese Rounds 27

Savory Sausage Balls 37

Scalloped Corn Casserole 80

Sea Bass With Potato Scales And Caper Aïoli 95

Sea Scallops 95

Seasoned Boneless Pork Sirloin Chops 55

Sesame Carrots And Sugar Snap Peas 109

Sesame Chicken Breasts 66

Sesame Orange Chicken 68

Sesame-crusted Tuna Steaks 93

Sheet Pan Chicken Nachos 36

Sheet Pan French Toast 23

Shrimp 89

Shrimp, Chorizo And Fingerling Potatoes 86

Simple Holiday Stuffing 39

Skewered Salsa Verde Shrimp 93

Skirt Steak Fajitas 45

Sloppy Joes 48

Slow Cooked Carnitas 50

Smoked Gouda Bacon Macaroni And Cheese 31

Smoked Salmon Puffs 37

Snapper With Capers And Olives 97

Soft Pretzels 28

Sour Cream Pound Cake 123

Spanish Pork Skewers 45

Spanish Rice 79

Spice-rubbed Split Game Hen 61

Spicy Fish Street Tacos With Sriracha Slaw 92

Spicy Flank Steak With Fresh Tomato-corn Salsa 44

Spicy Little Beef Birds 55

Steak Pinwheels With Pepper Slaw And Minneapolis Potato Salad 53

Steak With Herbed Butter 49

Sticky Soy Chicken Thighs 69

Strawberry Blueberry Cobbler 120

Strawberry Shortcake With Buttermilk Biscuits 22

Stuffed Baby Bella Caps 41

Stuffed Baked Red Snapper 94

Stuffed Onions 107

Sweet Chili Shrimp 89

Sweet Or Savory Baked Sweet Potatoes 42

Sweet Potato Casserole 31

Sweet Potato Donut Holes 123

Sweet Potato Fries With Sweet And Spicy Dipping Sauce 33

Sweet-and-sour Chicken 60

T

Tandoori Cauliflower 105

Tandoori Chicken 65

Teriyaki Chicken Drumsticks 70

Tex-mex Fish Tacos 88

Thick-crust Pepperoni Pizza 38

Tortilla-crusted Tilapia 96

Tuna Nuggets In Hoisin Sauce 85

Turkey Burger Sliders 43

Tuscan Toast 22

V

Vegan Swedish Cinnamon Rolls (kanelbullar) 120

Very Quick Pizza 82

Vietnamese Beef Lettuce Wraps 48

W

Warm And Salty Edamame 42

Wonton Cups 33

Y

Yeast Dough For Two Pizzas 84

Z

Zucchini Boats With Ham And Cheese 109

Zucchini Bread 30

Printed in Great Britain
by Amazon